D0305830

Out of the Woods but not Over the Hill

Gervase
PHINN

Out of the Woods but not Over the Hill

HODDER &
STOUGHTON

First published in Great Britain in 2010 by Hodder & Stoughton
An Hachette UK company

1

Copyright © Gervase Phinn 2010
Illustrations © Jim Kay

A CIP catalogue record for this title is available from the British Library.

ISBN 978 1 444 70538 6

Typeset in Bembo by Hewer Text UK Ltd, Edinburgh
Printed and bound by Clays Ltd, St Ives plc

Hodder & Stoughton policy is to use papers that are natural, renewable
and recyclable products and made from wood grown in sustainable
forests. The logging and manufacturing processes are expected to conform
to the environmental regulations of the country of origin.

Hodder & Stoughton Ltd
338 Euston Road
London NW1 3BH

www.hodder.co.uk

For my mother and father, Pat and Jimmy Phinn, who encouraged me to aim for the moon.

Contents

Introduction

When my son Richard and his fiancée were planning their wedding, they asked me if I would write a poem for this special occasion; something about love and families, a verse which was both touching and maybe a little sentimental. They would then have it framed as a reminder of the day they tied the knot.

Picture the scene: the happy couple sitting in the centre of the top table with the parents of the bride and groom, the two best men (my other sons, Matthew and Dominic) and the three pretty bridesmaids. Following the usual speeches, I was called upon to stand and declaim my poem, especially written for the occasion. And here it is:

When I am Old!
When I'm old and I'm wrinkly, I shall not live alone
In a pensioner's flat or an old people's home,
Or take an apartment on some distant shore.
I'll move in with my son and my daughter-in-law.

Out of the Woods but not Over the Hill

I'll return all the joy that my son gave to me
When he sat as a child on his dear father's knee.
He will welcome me willingly into his home
When I'm old and I'm wrinkly and all on my own.

I'll spill coffee on the carpet, leave marks on the wall,
I'll stagger home drunk and be sick in the hall.
I'll sing really loudly and slam every door,
When I live with my son and my daughter-in-law.

I'll rise from my bed in the late afternoon,
Throw the sheets on the floor and mess up my room.
I'll play ear-splitting music well into the night,
Go down for a snack and leave on every light.

I'll rest my old feet on the new leather chairs.
I'll drape dirty underwear all down the stairs,
I'll talk to my friends for hours on the phone
When I live with my son in his lovely new home.

I'll come in from the garden with mud on my shoes,
Flop on the settee for my afternoon snooze,
Expect that my tea will be ready by four
When I live with my son and my daughter-in-law.

I'll leave all the dishes piled up in the sink
And invite all my noisy friends round for a drink,
I'll grumble and mumble, I'll complain and I'll moan
When I'm old and I'm wrinkly and all on my own.

I'll watch television hour after hour,
I'll not flush the toilet or wash out the shower.
Oh, bliss, what a future for me is in store
When I move in with my son and my daughter-in-law.

A month after the wedding, my son and daughter-in-law moved to Bermuda!

Like many other 'oldies' who are approaching their three score years and ten, I am feeling my age. You know you are growing old, they say, when everything aches and what doesn't ache doesn't work, you sit in a rocking chair and can't make it work and you get wind playing cards. You know you are growing old when you have more hair in your ears than on your head, a dripping tap causes an uncontrollable urge and you look forward to a good night in. You help an old woman across the road and discover it's your wife, someone compliments you on your crocodile shoes and you tell them that you're in bare feet and your children look middle-aged. When I was approached by a bald, bent and wrinkled individual who informed me that I used to teach him, and another time when a small child in an infant school observed that, 'when I'm twenty-one, you'll probably be dead', I really did feel my age.

The thing about growing old is that you become increasingly nostalgic, remembering 'the good old days' and inflicting your memories on the younger generation:

> When I was a lad, I walked to school
> In pouring rain and freezing sleet,
> With satchel crammed with heavy books,
> I trekked for miles with aching feet . . .
> But I was happy!

> When I was a lad, I shared a bed
> In a room with bare boards on the floor.
> No central heating, double glazing,
> We didn't even have a door . . .
> But I was happy!

When I was a lad I had no toys,
Computers, TVs and the like.
You were thought to me a millionaire
If you owned a football or a bike . . .
But I was happy!

When I was a lad, food was scarce,
I licked the pattern off the plate.
We never saw an ice-cream cone,
A bag of sweets or a chocolate cake . . .
But I was happy!

When I was a lad, school was strict,
And teachers hit you with a cane
Just for speaking out in class.
I never opened my mouth again . . .
But I was happy!

I remember well that golden age,
The memories make me feel quite sad.
Why every day was a holiday,
In the good old days, when I was a lad.

More and more these days, I seem to be harking back to this 'golden age' when bobbies walked the beat, people stood up for the National Anthem in cinemas and 'gay' meant happy. There were no Chinese take-aways, fast food outlets or supermarkets, and milk was delivered in glass bottles. Cars had chokes, MOTs hadn't been invented and there were no computers, sound systems or mobile phones. The television, when it arrived in 1959, was housed in an ugly wooden cabinet, had an eight-inch screen and showed black and white programmes. There were no sex scenes, bad language or gratuitous violence on the screen, and the actors kissed with their lips closed.

When I was young, my father handed his wage packet over to my mother every Friday. He didn't have a credit card, rarely went out without wearing his trilby hat and never set foot on a golf course. We didn't go to an ice rink or a bowling alley or travel abroad, and we never 'ate out'. The family would sit down around the table at teatime. If we children didn't clean our plates, there was no dessert and, when we had finished, we had to ask 'to be excused'. I wore short trousers until I was eleven, always had 'short back and sides' at the barber's and walked to school in sensible shoes.

Of course, there are certain benefits to getting old: you receive a pension, a bus pass, a senior railcard and a winter fuel allowance. You can get into the cinema half price and people help you with your heavy case. But the great advantage of being a 'wrinkly' is that you can express your feelings and opinions freely and as forcefully as you like, for, as Dr David Olivier, an expert on ageing, concludes: 'age can bring people independence of thought. Older people are not afraid to be original.'

For my father's generation, being in your sixties was considered old and there was little more to look forward to than a leisurely walk to the pub, a game of dominoes and then back home for a snooze in your favourite arm chair. A woman in her sixties settled for a quiet, uneventful life; she dressed modestly, recalled wistfully her youthful good looks and resigned herself to looking after the home. Not any more. Today's oldies are not interested in growing old. They are more likely to spend their children's inheritance enjoying life rather than brooding about retirement and slowing down. They may be 'out of the woods' but they are certainly not 'over the hill'.

Considering myself just such an 'oldie with attitude', I have collected together a selection of my own reflections – social comment, autobiographical anecdotes, descriptions of the oddities of life, random observations and idiosyncratic musings – in which I look back over the years. In this book you will find me rattling on about childhood and schooldays, family life and the world of work, the English language and, of course, 'God's own country', Yorkshire. My aim is primarily to entertain and amuse. Perhaps, though, I might occasionally manage to stimulate an emotion and provoke a reaction. In any event, I hope they give you some pleasure.

'When I Was a Lad'

Growing Up

A Singular Sort of Town

Rotherham, the town where I was born and in which I grew up and went to school, has always had a bit of an image problem. It is viewed in the popular mind as a gloomy, depressing, industrial place, full of dust and dirt, of noisy steelworks and ugly pitheads. Comedians make fun of the town with jokes like 'Rotherham doesn't have a twin town – it has a suicide pact with Scunthorpe' or 'Rotherham's like Barnsley without the carpets'. The celebrity chef, Jamie Oliver, on his television programme about healthy eating, did the town no favours either and, on the screen, Rotherham lived up to its unattractive stereotype.

In educational circles, Rotherham is seen by some, who probably have never visited the town, as a deprived and impoverished part of Yorkshire, as unlike Harrogate as chalk is from cheese. I recall once a speaker at a conference remarking that teachers should pay particular attention to the most ill-favoured and vulnerable children. 'The Gervases of Eton will inevitably achieve, be successful and have the best of support and encouragement,' he told his audience, 'but it is the disadvantaged and underprivileged Jasons of Rotherham who are in most need of the teachers' attention.' I did point out to the speaker later that *I* was called Gervase and hailed from that particular town, and that not all children there are 'ill-favoured and vulnerable'. Growing up in Rotherham in the 1950s, I certainly didn't feel in any way 'disadvantaged and underprivileged'. In fact, I thought I was very lucky.

Rotherham is not as bad a place as it is sometimes painted. In the 1950s, the town was bustling and interesting, with a real Yorkshire gritty character to it – solid, uncompromising, unostentatious – a vibrant, friendly, hard-bitten part of 'God's own country', and there was nowhere in England where the inhabitants were warmer or more hospitable. I grew up surrounded by people with an unflagging generosity, a sharp humour and a shrewd insight into human nature which I learnt to love.

When I was young there were, of course, the smoky mornings, impenetrable smog and the unpleasant odour which sometimes emanated from the canal, but a bus ride out of the centre of the town, with its magnificent red sandstone medieval church and the rare Chapel-in-the-Bridge, took me in minutes into open countryside. In the school holidays and at weekends I would explore the area around the town, setting off in the morning on my bike, with a bottle of pop and a sandwich, and cycle into the country.

One of the favourite destinations on my weekend jaunts was Conisborough Castle, the great white stone Norman fortress set high on a mound between Rotherham and Doncaster. After I had read Sir Walker Scott's epic story *Ivanhoe,* I cycled out one bright Saturday morning to where the novel is set. I recall sitting on the perimeter wall, staring up at the imposing edifice and imagining knights in glittering armour, gallant Crusaders, dastardly villains, jousting and sieges, dark dungeons and great battles.

Another favourite spot was Roche Abbey. I would cycle out to Wickersley, famous for the grindstones used in the Sheffield cutlery trade, through the mining town of Maltby, eventually arriving at the crumbling remains of the magnificent Cistercian abbey. It was such a quiet, atmospheric place and I would sit amongst the crumbling stones in the sheltered valley and imagine the abbey in its heyday.

My mother, like my pals' parents, encouraged me to 'get out from under my feet' on Saturdays so she could do the cleaning and washing. There was no sitting inside watching the television or playing on the computer. We had to be out of the house and would not be expected back until it began to get dark. My parents never worried that I would be abducted or set upon and, unlike some overly anxious parents today, never thought there was a paedophile hiding behind every bush ready to pounce. It seemed to me a safe, warm environment in which to grow up. I had the freedom to play out all day in the street or at the park, something which is sadly denied to many children today. These days so many parents seem so obsessively concerned with giving their children long and happy childhoods, with keeping them safe from harm and injury, in need of constant protection, away from potential risks, that they underestimate their offsprings' abilities and resilience and deny them the great sense of freedom I had. The children of my generation were happy as crickets, unhindered by adult restraint.

A Boy Called Gervase

One has to admit that my parents had a sense of humour calling a child born in a redbrick semi in Rotherham, Gervase. In the

1950s when I was growing up, there were Jimmys and Terrys, Michaels and Ronalds, Martins and Kevins and one or two Alberts and Harolds but, to my knowledge, no Gervases. The first Gervase I came across was in Chaucer's *Canterbury Tales* – he was the blacksmith in the raunchiest of the stories. Now, of course, children are given the most unusual, not to say bizarre, names. Brooklyn and Romeo Beckham, Peaches Geldof and the other children of the rich and famous are not alone in their unusual appellations.

Over my years as a school inspector, I collected quite a list. I have met Barbie, Kristofer, Buzz, Curston, Randy, Mykell, Charleen, Kaylee, Scarlet, Egypt, Heyleigh, Jordana, Aztec, Blasé (pronounced Blaze), Gooey (spelt Guy), a child whose surname was Pipe and first name Duane and a child called Portia but spelt Porsche for, as the teacher explained to me with a wry smile, the girl's father had always wanted a Porsche car. I've come across Demi, Dayle, Shalott (pronounced Charlotte), Precious, Roxanne, Tiggy, Trixie, Terri, Cheyenne, Billi-Jo, Tammy-Lou, Princess, Duncan Biscuit and Eileen Dover, a boy named Gilly and a girl called Barney. In one school there were two sets of twins from the same family, aged ten and eleven respectively, named after great tragic heroines: Cleopatra and Cassandra, Desdemona and Dido. Then there were the brother and sister, Sam and Ella, whose names, when said at speed, sounded like food poisoning. I have met Hadrian Wall (with a father called Walter Wall), Victoria Plumb, Sunny Day, Holly Wood and Justin Finnerty. I have never met them, but was told by a teacher that she had had the pleasure of teaching a Teresa Green, an Annette Curtain and a Poppy Field.

A head teacher told me once that she taught three sisters called Paris Smout, Vienna Smout and Seville Smout, all, no doubt, conceived after three particularly memorable trips abroad. 'It is just as well,' she told me, 'that her parents didn't go on a weekend break to Brussels.'

In one infant school in Bradford, I came across a large girl with a plump face, frizzy hair in huge bunches and great wide eyes.

'What's your name?' I asked the child.

'Tequila,' she replied. 'I'm named after a drink.'

'Tequila Sunrise,' I murmured.

'No,' pouted the child. 'Tequila Braithwaite.'

Perhaps she had a brother called Bacardi in the Juniors.

I was told by the head teacher of a Catholic school that it was the practice in the Church for children to be named after saints, and he was at school with a boy called Innocent, a name adopted by a number of popes.

'I suppose it must have been difficult having to live up to the name Innocent,' I observed.

'It certainly was,' he replied, 'and something of a cross to bear. His second name was Bystander.'

'I cannot say that modern parents are very well acquainted with the Bible,' a vicar once told me. 'Gone are the fine biblical names like Hannah and Simon. Instead, parents want their offspring named after pop singers, film stars and footballers. I draw the line though when I get requests for Jezebel, Salome and Delilah,' he bemoaned. 'It's very difficult explaining to the parents who these women were and what line of work they were in. One child very nearly went through life with the exotic name of Onacardie. I asked the parents at the christening: "And what do you name this child?" The mother replied loudly, "Onacardie." I had just begun sprinkling the water over the baby's head and intoning: "I christen this child Onacardie," only to be quickly interrupted by the irate mother. "No, no, vicar!" she hissed. "On 'er cardy. The name's written on her cardigan. We want her to be called Siobhan."'

'I have a pet theory about first names,' another head teacher told me. 'Over the many years I have been in education, I have come to the conclusion that Shakespeare got it wrong when he said that "a rose by any other name would smell as sweet". I learned very early on that boys called Richard tend to be well-behaved, quiet children who work hard, Matthews are very polite and thoughtful, Dominics are little charmers, Damiens have far too much to say for themselves and Kevins are accident-prone. Penelopes tend to be lively and interested, Jennys tend to be sporty, Traceys too big for their boots and Elizabeths little darlings.'

'And what about the boy called Gervase?' I asked.

'I have never taught one,' she told me. Then she thought for a moment. 'However did you manage,' she asked, 'growing up in Rotherham, with a name like that?'

Famous Forebears

There's a television programme which investigates the family history of celebrities. It has revealed some amazing facts and fascinating characters. Some of the forebears were rich and illustrious, others dark and villainous, which surprised, horrified and sometimes moved to tears their celebrated descendents. When I was young, reading adventure stories and blessed with an over-developed imagination, I thought that I might one day discover I was descended from someone great and good and that I would inherit a grand fortune.

A friend of mine has been researching his family history and discovered that he had many a distinguished ancestor, including the first professor of mathematics at Cambridge University and friend of Prince Albert, a number of eminent vicars of Dent and possibly General John Lambert of Calton Hall, Kirkby Malham, architect of the Cromwellian Protectorate. On a recent literary-themed cruise, a fellow author and speaker was Lucinda Dickens-Hawksley, the great, great, great granddaughter of

Charles Dickens and one who could rattle off a veritable plethora of famous forebears. Then there was the young man in a school in Harrogate who told me he had much to live up to, being the direct descendant of Scott of the Antarctic.

My father-in-law has traced his family back several generations and has found a number of illustrious ancestors, including the Methodist preacher and theologian Joseph Bentley, author of *How to Sleep on a Windy Night*. I can certainly vouch for the veracity of the title; the collection of sermons put me to sleep in minutes.

I did once think I might be related to the great and the good when I received a letter from a Miss Marjorie Mangham-Phinn, in which she claimed kinship. Having researched her own family history, Miss Mangham-Phinn had discovered that one of her most famous ancestors was Thomas Phinn, an eminent Victorian philanthropist and worthy. She maintained that Trollope based his character Phineas Finn, the decent, strikingly handsome young heartbreaker who charmed himself into polite society, on her distinguished ancestor. Thomas Phinn, she informed me, was the Member of Parliament for the elegant city of Bath from 1852 until 1855. She had an idea we might be related since Phinn is a most unusual name.

When I was asked to speak at the Bath Literary Festival, in the magnificent Guildhall, in 2005, I had the opportunity of meeting my supposed ancestor. His marble bust had a prominent place in the entrance of the Guildhall. Styled as a Roman statesman with luxuriant curls, large honest eyes and prominent nose, he did bear a striking resemblance to my brother, Alec. I was introduced to my audience, on this occasion, by the present MP for Bath, Don Foster. Later, he very kindly researched Thomas Phinn for me in the archives of the Houses of Parliament.

Thomas Phinn. Hall – Staircase, Inner Temple, London. 41 St James's Street, London. Brook's and Reform. Born at Bath

1814, the son of Thomas Phinn of Bath, Surgeon, by Caroline, daughter of Richard Bignall, Esq. of Banbury. Unmarried. Educated at Eton and Exeter College, Oxford where he was 1st class in Classics 1837. Was called to the bar at the Inner Temple in 1840 and joined the Western Circuit.

The impressive entry in *The Who's Who of British Members of Parliament, Volume 1, 1832–1885* continues to describe the glittering, if rather curtailed, political career of Thomas Phinn, QC, Liberal Member of Parliament, Secretary to the Admiralty, who was fiercely in favour of 'vote by ballot and the fullest development of free-trade principles'. It was he who voted for an inquiry into Maynooth, the Irish seminary from which so many missionary priests came over the water to England, so I guess he must have had some Irish connections.

The entry in *The Times*, 1 November 1866, announced, with great regret, the sudden death of Thomas Phinn:

> He was yesterday apparently in his accustomed excellent health and spirits, but on returning to his chambers in Pall-mall about 7 o'clock he complained of a pain in the region of his heart, and after a few minutes expired.

Much as I would like to claim the eminent Thomas Phinn as an ancestor, and perhaps lay claim to his fortune and that wonderful marble bust, my sister Christine, guardian of the family archive (a few scribbled letters, birth and death certificates and a battered album of faded sepia photographs), gave me the low-down on our branch of the Phinns. On the distaff side of the family, I am descended from the Brothers of Portumna, County Galway, whose notoriety was that they made coffins for the victims of 'The Great Irish Potato Famine'. On my father's side were the Macdonalds of South Uist, who eked out a living on that bleak island of great melancholic stretches of heather-covered moors and bog land in the Outer Hebrides. The headstone of an ancestor, one Ranald Macdonald, is somewhat ambiguous in its dedication. Perhaps he had a reputation for untrustworthiness or was a noted sheep-rustler, for the inscription on his gravestone reads:

> Let all the world say what it can,
> He lived and died an honest man.

I felt it politic not to delve further into my ancestry.

A Father of the Old School

'Education, education, education.' This was my father's mantra well before Tony Blair made it his clarion call. My father, a steelworker for most of his life and with little formal education, but with a sharp intelligence and lively sense of humour, was ruthless in his determination to provide for and protect his family. He recognised that the central factor in achieving any sort of real advancement in life was 'a good education'.

My father once told me that he had passed his scholarship examination to attend grammar school, but his step-father felt it was best for him to leave school. Like many a youngster at that time, largely because of lack of the necessary money to pay for books, equipment and the uniform, he was denied the opportunity to continue his studies. At fourteen, when his mother died, he went to live on an uncle's farm, before joining the army on his seventeenth birthday to become a despatch rider. Although he never said so, I guess my father deeply regretted not having had the opportunity of a good 'schooling', but he never saw education as a possible route to better things for himself. He perhaps knew by the age of thirty, with a wife and young family, that it was too late for him. He believed, as did my mother, that the key to success lay not in wealth but in education. Education opened doors and he was determined that his children should take every opportunity to receive the best education on offer. He had seen first hand, during his army service and latterly working in the steelworks, what a gulf there existed in the world in opportunity, wealth and education – how the officers and the managers were set apart from others by dint of what he called 'their schooling'.

Following my father's death, when I broached the subject of his scholarship examination with my mother, she told me that my father was quite content with his lot in life and never aspired to anything more. He loved his family and provided for us, enjoyed the simple things in life but was unambitious. I cannot believe that. I cannot believe that he was happy working in the steel-works with all the noise, heat, oil, dust and dirt. As a boy, on my way to watch Sheffield United I remember well the bumpy bus rides from Rotherham to Sheffield via Attercliffe, past the dark and dirty place where he worked for thirty or more years. As I looked down from the top deck of the bus on that grim environment, as young as I was, I knew I wanted more out of life than this.

My parents were of 'the old school' when it came to education. Unless I was at death's door, I had to attend school, do my homework, listen to my teachers and do as they said, and if I were to get into any trouble at school I would be in twice as much trouble at home. Sometimes I felt they supported the school a little too much. I recall once, when I was about ten, I was presented with my school dinner on a plastic plate and wouldn't eat it. There was a slice of pale cold meat edged in fat, a dollop of cold mashed potatoes and sliced carrots swimming in greasy gravy. None of the healthy fare served up in schools today and none of the choices. I folded my arms and resolutely refused to pick up my knife and fork. I was made to remain in the corner of the hall when it had been cleared after dinnertime, with the plate on a table in front of me. I was told I would not be allowed to go until it was eaten. I finally did as I was told and then went to the boys' toilet and was promptly sick. When I relayed this dreadful injustice to my parents at tea time, my father, looking over his glasses, merely remarked, 'Put it down to experience, son. Now eat your tea.'

On the Road to Reading

Thinking over what gave me the most pleasure in my childhood, I should place, first and foremost, reading. My mother, a natural storyteller, taught me nursery rhymes and read from picture books. I knew all the old favourites – *Chicken Licken, The Gingerbread Man, The Giant Turnip, Rumpelstiltskin, The Magic Porridge Pot* and many more – before I started school. Most evenings, before I went to bed, she would read aloud with me snuggled up next to her. I loved listening to the story, following the words on the page as she read and feeling that special physical closeness. Sometimes she would change a word, take a bit out or add something, and I could tell and told her so. I might not be able to read those black marks on the page but I knew the stories so well. Later, when the story was told and the light turned off, I would close my eyes and dream of a world peopled with the magical characters I had encountered in the book.

My father too captured my imagination with his stories. He would bring back books from Rotherham Library to read, or buy a couple of old tattered versions of the classics from the market, taking out his finds from the brown paper carrier bag where they had been hiding between the vegetables and fruit. Once, he arrived from the market with a large hard-backed tome called *King of the Fighting Scouts*, which depicted on the front cover a garish illustration of a soldier on a rearing horse, hacking his way through a horde of savages. For several nights my father read a couple of chapters, only to arrive at the denouement to discover that the last few pages of the book were missing. Undeterred, he made the end up.

My father took over from my mother this nightly ritual of reading to me when I was eight or nine. He would read a chapter or two at a time, ending on a high note and thus whetting my imagination for more. I would be keen for the next instalment the following night and be up those stairs in my pyjamas, face washed, teeth brushed, ready and waiting. It was a really clever way of making me go to bed at night. Boys who have had this sort of upbringing, where fathers tell them stories, read to them and associate reading with great pleasure and affection, learn to love books. A magical world is opened up to them.

A Grandparent's Prerogative

The relationship between grandparents and their grandchildren is rather different from that between parents and their children. I know this to be true because I am told frequently enough by my own grown-up children that I am 'much softer' with Harry and Megan, my grandchildren, than I ever was with them. Of course I am. It's the grandparents' prerogative. We grannies and grandpas are more tolerant and patient; we are better listeners, less critical and, dare I say it, more indulgent than we were with our own offspring.

My mother and father were loving, supportive and dedicated parents. I was never slapped and rarely shouted at but they were firm and decisive in their treatment of their four children, insisting on best behaviour, no answering back and good manners. If we persisted in demanding something, my mother's predictable retort would be: 'I want, doesn't get.' My father's favourite expression was: 'I've warned you once, I won't tell you again.' Growing up, I knew the parameters.

One morning, when the family was on holiday in Blackpool, I bought a set of false teeth made out of pink and white rock with pink sugar gums. I was about six or seven at the time. Much to my father's irritation, I kept on clacking the teeth like castanets as we walked along the prom. Finally I was warned that, should I persist in the annoying clacking of the teeth, they would go in the sea. When I continued, the teeth were snatched from my hand and thrown over the promenade wall to disappear into the ocean. 'I did warn you,' said my father calmly, and strolled on. It was a good lesson to learn for a prospective teacher: if you warn a child you will do something, then do it.

When she became a grandma, my mother would often come around to our house for Sunday lunch. From her vantage point in the comfortable chair in the corner of the lounge, she would watch me attempting to bring up my children. One Sunday, I had occasion to chastise my son Matthew, then aged six, for his untidy bedroom. Stabbing the air with a finger, I ordered him, 'Up those stairs now, young man, and tidy your room. Do you follow my drift?'

'Your father used that expression,' my mother interrupted. 'I don't suppose you knew what it meant when you were a boy, and I don't suppose your Matthew knows what it means either.'

'Thank you, Mother,' I said, pompously. I turned back to my son. 'Go on, up those stairs and tidy your room or you'll go without your tea.'

Matthew at first looked suitably contrite. Then a small smile appeared on his lips, then a grin, to be followed by giggles and finally guffaws. I ballooned with anger. Then I caught sight of my mother in the mirror. She was sitting behind me, pulling the most ridiculous faces and wiggling her fingers in front of her nose.

'Mother!' I snapped. 'I am trying to instil some discipline. You are not helping matters.'

'Oh, do be quiet,' she said. 'You're not talking to teachers now.'

'Mother . . .' I began.

'Don't mother me,' she said. 'You sound like Hitler on a soapbox. He's a lovely little lad is Matthew. There are more important things in this world than an untidy room, you know. And, as I remember, your bedroom was a tip when you were a boy.'

My Irish grandmother certainly had a soft spot for me, the youngest of her grandchildren. When I was asked to submit a piece for the anthology *Grandparents*, edited by Sarah Brown in support of the charity PiggyBankKids, I wrote about this remarkable woman who had a profound influence on my life. Grandma Mullarkey took a particular interest in my reading and writing. One of my most vivid early memories of my grandma was when she read to me from a small hard-backed picture book, about the shrewd little boy who outwits the greedy tiger. I soon knew the story of *Little Black Sambo* by heart. This simple little story stirred my imagination. *Little Black Sambo* was the first black child I encountered in a book and I delighted in his sheer joy, courage and cleverness.

As an older child I would take along with me on my visits the book of the moment, and we would read quietly together. At other times she would read to me from one of the large illustrated books she kept on a shelf near her bed. One favourite was *The Swiss Family Robinson* with its garish coloured plates and big print. I loved the story, where all the members of the shipwrecked family worked happily together under the benign guidance of a father who was both strong and wise and who sported bulging muscles and a long chestnut beard.

When my grandma read, I thrilled at the sound of the words, the rhythms and the rhymes, and would sit goggle-eyed at the power of her voice and her extraordinary memory. She knew passages of verse by heart and had a natural feel for measure and stress.

It was my Grandma Mullarkey who bought me my first dictionary when I started secondary school, and the treasured portable Olivetti typewriter with the black and red ribbon. I would sit with it on my lap feeling like 'a real writer'.

Like many of Irish stock, my grandmother possessed that Celtic combination of levity and seriousness. Laughter and tears were never far apart. She was a keen and discerning reader, an avid letter writer and a fine storyteller. She delighted in telling amusing anecdotes, embroidering the stories with facial expressions and comic voices. There was the time, she told me, when the turkey arrived from her cousins in Ireland and had to be collected from Masborough Station on Christmas Eve. The bird, recently killed, had been stuffed in a cardboard box, fully feathered and still possessing its head and claws. Christmas dinner didn't take place until much later that evening and by then everyone had lost their appetites.

There was the story too of my Uncle Jimmy, her only son, who, instead of going to Mass on Sunday, would spend the time swimming in the Rotherham Canal, until the fateful day when he was caught red-handed by his father. A neighbour had seen young Jimmy and informed upon him. Grandfather Mullarkey, unseen by his son, collected the pile of clothes left on the bank and waited until the miscreant emerged from the smelly water. Jimmy didn't seem all that concerned that his clothes had gone and set off home in his wet underpants before his father emerged from his hiding place and confronted him. Grandma found the incident very funny and chuckled at the memory. Her husband, she said, was not amused.

I loved to listen to her tales and I had an inkling early on that some were just a little far-fetched. I remember once she told me of when a fellow parishioner went on a pilgrimage to Rome with the Union of Catholic Mothers. In St Peter's Square, amidst the throng, the woman was excited to hear from her friend that His Holiness himself would soon be making an appearance on his balcony to give his blessing. At that very moment, the Pope appeared. The woman was said to have remarked to her companion: 'Oh, speak of the devil.'

Grandma Mullarkey opened a door in my early childhood and changed my life for the better and, when she died, she left a great gap. When I was sixteen, I accompanied my mother to Doncaster Gate hospital where my grandmother, aged 81, was dying of stomach cancer. She told me not to look so miserable. 'Remember,' she said, 'a smile will gain you ten years of life.' She died the following day, clutching her rosary beads.

Penny for the Guy

As a youngster I looked forward to Bonfire Night with great anticipation. My friends and I would scavenge for combustible material and gradually build the pyramid of wood and old carpets, rags and cardboard boxes, on the allotment at the back of my house. We would keep a watchful eye on our construction, for other boys were known to steal what others had spent weeks collecting. The evening before the big night, we would keep vigil until we were summoned indoors by our parents. My father agreed to become a sentry when I had gone to bed.

We would make a Guy out of old clothes, stuff screwed up paper in the arms and legs, and paint a face on a piece of cardboard. He would be wheeled through the streets on a trolley made of pram wheels and two planks, and we would ask passers-by: 'Penny for the Guy?' With the money we collected, we would buy fireworks. Recently, I read about the two young lads with their Guy who had been moved on by the police for begging. It's a funny old world.

In October, fireworks were for sale at the newsagents and could be freely bought by children. I would buy a thin rectangular box, on the front of which, in garish reds and blues, was the caption, 'Light up the Sky with Standard Fireworks'. This small collection would be added to over the coming weeks, up to the Fifth of November. There would be Catherine wheels, blockbusters, squibs, jumping jacks, traffic lights, penny bangers, Roman candles, golden fountains, silver rain and rockets in brightly coloured cardboard tubes, with a cone on the top and a thin wooden stick down the side.

I remember my first Bonfire Night vividly, and it was not a happy memory. I must have been six or seven at the time, and walked from home with my father on a cold, clear night, with the air smelling of woodsmoke. We arrived at Herringthorpe Playing Fields in Rotherham to find crowds of people gathered around the great wigwam-shaped stack of wood. My father sat me high on his shoulders, and I watched the dancing flames and the red sparks spitting in the air. It was magical. Fireworks banged and rockets lit up the black sky, showering bright colours, and the fire was lit. My face burned with the heat. And then I saw him – the figure sitting on the top of the bonfire. He was forlorn and misshapen, and dressed in old clothes with a floppy hat perched on his head. I screamed and screamed.

'There's a man on top!' I cried. 'A man in the fire!'

Everyone around me laughed.

'It's just a Guy,' my father told me. 'He's made of rags and cardboard. He's not real.'

But I was sad and scared to see those clinging fingers of fire scorch the stuffed body, cracking the arms and swallowing up that wide-eyed pitiful face.

To this day, I still feel uneasy at the sight of a human form, albeit a dummy, placed on the top of a burning bonfire. I am not against Bonfire Night; it is an enjoyable occasion particularly for children, though I guess that the light-hearted festivities have little connection in most people's minds to the fanatical men who plotted the downfall of the Government in 1605. It is just that I do not like to see that burning figure on the top.

You might guess then that I am not that keen on the famous Bonfire Night celebrations in Lewes in East Sussex, where figures of the infamous – or just the famous – are set alight each year. In 1994, effigies included Margaret Thatcher, John Major on a dinosaur, taken from the film Jurassic Park, and the Home Secretary, Michael Howard, in the week of the unpopular Criminal Justice Bill, as well as a Guy Fawkes. On one bonfire, an effigy of the Pope is burnt annually.

I have an ally in a good friend of mine, who is a former scholar of St Peter's School, York, the *alma mater* of the most notorious of the powder treason conspirators – Guy Fawkes himself. The school, he tells me, retains the long tradition of interest in, and even has a certain affection for, their best-known former pupil, who was once tactfully described by a head boy at a school speech day as 'not exactly a role model'.

I guess my old history master, Theodore Firth, shared this fondness for his fellow Yorkshireman. I found my old history book the other day and have to say that Guy Fawkes doesn't sound, from the notes I took from the blackboard, like the villain most people think he was.

Guy Fawkes was, without question, a courageous, charismatic, if misguided, man, of impressive appearance. Slender, muscular and handsome, with long red hair, a full moustache and a bushy beard, he was a distinguished soldier and a good-humoured companion. He was also well read, intelligent and interested in discussion and debate. A fanatic he may have been, but he was exceptionally brave and capable of amazing stamina and endurance. He died a horrible death, which he faced bravely, after terrible torture on the rack.

So, next Bonfire Night I shall pop a penny or two for the Guy in the tin the little boy holds out when I pass him in the street (that is if he is not moved on by the police), I shall enjoy the spectacle of the fireworks and the sparklers, the over-cooked sausages and the sticky bonfire toffee, but I shall turn away when the figure on the top of the bonfire is consumed by the flames.

Bully for You

No childhood, it is said, is entirely happy. All children at some time in their young lives experience disappointment, failure, loss and hurt, and some have truly miserable and sometimes tragic upbringings. Bookshop shelves, under the heading 'Tragic Life Stories', are stacked with the heart-rending autobiographies of unbelievably unhappy childhoods – nightmare families, loveless homes, brutal parents – all described in vivid detail; of children beaten and starved, rejected and abused, bullied and tortured. Such accounts, where the authors describe how they have overcome the huge disadvantages of miserable upbringings, have become instant best-sellers, and the reading public appears to love them. Perhaps in doing so, the readers' own lives seem less wretched and more bearable. Perhaps they are heartened by these sad stories of children who have a shining spirit to survive, cope and forgive. For me, such memoirs are painful to read, for mine was a very happy childhood. I did not suffer from great poverty as a child, nor was I born into an affluent and privileged home. I was not smacked or told I was an unwanted child. I was not bullied by my brothers or told by my parents I was a disappointment to them. I felt loved and cherished. There was a short time in my young life, however, when I was desperately unhappy – the time I was bullied.

A couple of years ago, I met the bully again. He approached me after I had spoken at a formal business dinner in Sheffield. I had spotted him earlier, with a group of other men sitting directly in front of the top table. It was the laugh I recognised first, and it brought back unpleasant memories. As a lad, I remember this tall, fat, moon-faced boy with lank black hair and a permanent scowl, who developed an obsessive dislike of me. In primary school, I was a biddable, easy-going child. I enjoyed the lessons and readily volunteered answers and did as I was told. I was small for my age, not good at sports and of average intelligence so, I guess, I was vulnerable and the ideal victim for the bully.

I little thought that my behaviour would antagonise the large moon-faced boy, who was frequently outside the head teacher's room for misbehaving. He would delight in mispronouncing my name, much to the amusement of his two sidekicks. 'Gervarse! Gervarse!' he would shout, and mince down the corridor. He and his two fellow bullies would stop me going to the toilet, tip everything out of my satchel and spit at me when my back was turned. I had a dreadful two months until I moved to secondary school and thankfully never saw him again – until, that is, I attended the dinner. He hadn't changed much, except that he was now almost entirely bald.

'I was just telling those at my table we were at school together,' he said to me as he approached. He was smiling inanely.

'Yes, I know,' I replied.

'Really,' said the president of the association, who was sitting on my right at the top table. 'An old school friend?'

'Hardly,' I said. 'He bullied me.'

'I . . . I . . . don't remember that,' blustered the bully.

'Well, of course you wouldn't,' I said, looking him straight in the eye. 'Bullies forget but the bullied never do. You were vicious, cruel and you made my life a misery for two months and I have no wish to speak to you.' My heart was thumping in my chest.

He stared at me a moment, shuffled with embarrassment and opened his mouth about to speak, but he thought better of it. He then strode away angrily.

Bully

He shouts and swears and smokes and spits,
Pummels, pinches, pokes and nips.
He likes to kick, he likes to punch,
Call you names and steal your lunch.
But, have you ever wondered why
He likes to make another cry?
What makes a child turn out like you?

You see at home he's bullied too.
His father beats him, black and blue.

Having a Laugh

One afternoon, just before Christmas when I was ten, my father took me to see the pantomime at the Leeds City Varieties. We caught the train from Masborough Station and walked through the city, crowded with shoppers. It was one of the few very special occasions when it was just me and my father, no brothers or sister. The City Varieties is the oldest extant music hall in the country; an intimate, colourful and atmospheric little theatre, hidden between two arcades. All the greats of variety theatre have performed here: Charlie Chaplin and Houdini, Tommy Cooper and Hylda Baker, Marie Lloyd and Les Dawson and, of course, the legendary Ken Dodd, who takes some persuading to leave the stage once he's started.

I appeared there myself in 2006, in my one-man show. Before

my performance I stood on the empty stage looking down at the empty stalls and recalled a small boy sitting on a plush red velvet seat with his father, his eyes (as we say in Yorkshire) 'like chapel hat pegs', entering a magical world of the pantomime.

It was at Leeds City Varieties that I first saw the great Sandy Powell, who hailed from my home town of Rotherham, and when I heard his famous catchphrase: 'Can you hear me, Mother?' For a few weeks afterwards, I would imitate this catchphrase at home, much to the irritation of my family, until my father put his foot down and said: 'That'll be enough!'

Sandy Powell's comedy was clever, clean, inoffensive and hilariously funny. Part of his act was when he appeared on stage dressed in a soldier's scarlet tunic, pill-box hat askew on his head, and holding a particularly ugly dummy, which was dressed identically. He was a hopeless ventriloquist and his dummy would often fall apart in his hands. His act was interrupted by a posh-sounding member of the audience, in real life his wife, Kay.

'Tell me sonny,' he asked the dummy in a deep throaty voice, 'where do you live and where were you born?'

'I vass born in Volchergrankon,' replied the dummy.

'Where was he born?' asked the woman.

'Wolverhampton. Oh, I wish I'd have said Leeds. I'm glad it wasn't Czechoslovakia.'

My first sortie onto the stage was when I was thirteen and, at a school concert, I performed a song, an old Yorkshire verse, which Sandy Powell made famous. I was accompanied on the piano by Mr Gravill, the music master. At Christmas, I insist on singing this ditty at family gatherings, much to my children's embarrassment.

> When I was a right young lad
> My father said to me:
> 'Seems to me tha's growin' up,
> Now what's tha goin' to be?

It all depends upon thyself,
It's only up to thee,
I won't say much to thee ageean,
But tek a tip from me.
'Ear all, see all, say nowt,
Ate all, sup all, pay nowt,
It's a long time, remember,
From January to December,
So 'ear all, see all, say nowt,
Ate all, sup all, pay nowt,
And if ever thy does summat for nowt,
Always do it for theeself.'

When I watch the present-day comedians on the television, and hear their acerbic, cutting-edge and supposedly entertaining humour, usually peppered with expletives, how I wish a Sandy Powell would make a return. 'The golden age of British comedy has passed,' said John Cleese. How right he is.

I was attending a gala charity function the other week. The 'star' of the evening was one of these 'cutting-edge, alternative' comedians, who was 'guaranteed to make us roll in the aisles'. Well, I stayed firmly in my seat until I could stand no more and departed for the toilets. The material was, to my mind, uninspired, vulgar and relied for its dubious humour on poking fun at others who were in some way different. Of course, there was the usual string of inane and predictable Irish jokes.

One of the highlights of my holiday in Blackpool when I was a child was an evening at the pier show. I looked forward most to the appearance on stage of real comedians, and I laughed until my sides ached at the very best of the crop. Nearly all the stars at Blackpool came from the music hall tradition: big hearted Arthur Askey ('Hello Playmates'), Tommy Cooper ('Not like this, like that'), Richard Murdoch, Al Read ('Right Monkey'), Jimmy

James and Eli, Dickie Henderson, Freddie Frinton, Beryl Reid, Arthur Haynes, Joan Whitfield, Norman Evans, Professor Jimmy Edwards and Chick Murray ('I'm taking the dog to the vet to have it put down.' 'Is it mad?' 'It's no too pleased.'). There was Frankie Howerd, who managed to have people doubled up with laughter and he said nothing, but just spluttered and 'Ooed' and 'Aahhd', jettisoning any script he might have had and departing on some wild fantasy of his own.

My favourite was the great Hylda Baker, with her gormless and silent stooge, Cynthia. This small woman (four foot, eleven inches) characterised the fast-talking gossip and her catchphrases ('She knows, you know,' '"Be soon," I said,' and 'You big girl's blouse') became household phrases. It is reputed that when she appeared at the Stephen Joseph Theatre in Scarborough, Noel Coward observed after the performance he had 'endured' that, 'I would happily wring that woman's neck – if I could find it.'

In her moth-eaten fox fur, ill-fitting checked jacket, large handbag over the arm, and misshapen hat, she had the audience rolling in the aisles with her facial contortions and mangling of the English language. 'I don't think you've had the pleasure of me,' she told the audience as she came on stage, wriggling her small frame as if she had chronic worms. 'I can say this without fear of contraception,' she would continue. 'I went to the doctor and he was standing there, his horoscope around his neck. He said I'd got the body of a woman twice my age. "Get away," I said, "you flatterer, you." I was so excited I nearly had a coronary trombonist and fell prostitute on the floor.'

Then she would look up at her silent friend. 'Ooo,' she would mouth, 'Have you been with a fella? Have yooo? Have yooo been with a fella?' Cynthia would stare into the middle distance with a blank expression. 'She knows, you know,' Hylda told the audience. 'Oh yes, she knows, you know.' Simple, innocent, clean, inoffensive, silly material, but hilariously funny.

Hylda Baker was a direct descendant of Mistress Quickly and Mrs Malaprop and the precursor of Connie, the character who appears throughout my Dales books. She was one of those people who mangled and murdered the language with malapropisms and *non sequiturs* to great comic effect. She could mince words like a mincer minces meat.

Aged ten, I waited in the rain on the pier after a show to get Hylda Baker's autograph. She arrived at the stage door. 'Have you been standing there in the rain, you little tinker, you?' she said as she scribbled her name across the programme which I still have to this day.

I was enthralled when I attended a brilliant performance by the character actress, Jean Ferguson. In her one-woman show she was uncanny in recreating the comic genius of Hylda Baker, capturing the voice and mannerisms, the body wiggling, the facial contortions and handbag adjustments.

Sadly, Hylda Baker spent the last years of her life in a nursing home for retired variety performers and died alone in Horton Hospital in 1986, aged 81. Only eleven people attended her funeral. This great comedian has been largely forgotten, but not by one of her greatest fans who, as a child, remembers waiting in the rain outside the stage door on a wet Saturday evening in Blackpool for an autograph.

Stage Struck

On a recent Saturday visit to my home town of Rotherham, I met Miss Greenwood, my former infant teacher, in All Saints' Square. She is now over 80 years old, but still possesses the shining eyes and the gentle smile of the great teacher she was. I loved Miss Greenwood and those early years at school. I moulded little clay models, dug in the sand pit, played in the water tray, counted with little coloured beads, sang the nursery rhymes, danced with bare feet in the hall, made models with toilet rolls and cardboard boxes, splashed poster paint on large sheets of grey sugar paper, chanted poems, listened to stories and learnt to read. And how I loved those stories she read in the reading corner.

That Saturday I took Miss Greenwood for afternoon tea, and we reminisced.

'And do you remember when you wet yourself, Gervase?' she asked with a twinkle in her eyes.

'Of course I do. How could I ever forget?'

The time will remain ingrained in my memory. The curtains had opened on the Christmas Nativity play and there I had stood, six years old, stiff as a lamppost. I was the palm tree, encased in brown crêpe paper with two big bunches of *papier mâché* coconuts dangling from my neck, and a clump of bright green cardboard leaves in each hand and arranged like a crown on my head. My mother had knitted me a pale green woollen balaclava, through which my little face appeared. I had stared at all the faces in the audience and wriggled nervously. Then someone had laughed and it had started others off laughing too. It was the first occasion anyone had laughed at me and I had felt so alone and upset. I had looked for my parents and, seeing them in the second row, I had focused on them. They, of course, were not laughing. I had begun to cry and then, frozen under the bright lights and frightened, I had wet myself. It had seeped through the brown crêpe paper leaving a large dark stain in the front. The audience had laughed louder. I had been devastated. On the way home, my face wet with tears, my father had held my small hand between his great fat fingers and he had told me that I had been the best palm tree he had ever seen. My mother had told me that I was the star of the show. I knew full well at the time that they had not been telling me the truth, but it had been so good to be told. I felt so secure and so loved.

'And do you remember, Miss Greenwood,' I asked her, 'what you said to me when I came off the stage?'

'I don't,' she said. 'Remind me.'

'Well, I guess some teachers would have stabbed the air angrily with a finger and told that little boy what a silly child he was, and demanded to know why he hadn't gone to the toilet before going on stage.'

'And what did I say?' she asked.

'You put your arm around me and you said, "Don't worry, love, I used to wet my knickers when I was your age." '

There was a short silence. Then a small smile came to my former teacher's lips. 'Well Gervase,' she said, chuckling, 'it's funny how things come full circle.'

The Good Teacher

The child is initiated into what Kafta called 'The Lie': 'Education is but two things: first the parrying of the ignorant children's impetuous assault on the truth, and, second, the gentle, imperceptible, step-by-step initiation of the humiliated children into the Lie.' School, for him, was not a happy time. Indeed, many writers, describing their schooldays, dwell on their unhappiness at the hands of bullies and the cruelty at the hands of teachers. They speak of board rubbers thrown across the classroom, trouser bottoms smoking after a vicious caning, sarcastic, incompetent and sometimes sadistic teachers.

Andy Smith is a case in point. He undertook some building work at my house recently and I found him to be one of the most entertaining, imaginative and skilful people I have ever met. His schooling can at best be described as 'indifferent'. He was clearly a boy with a talent but one which was not recognised or encouraged by his teachers. On one occasion, after spending many weeks making a chair in the woodwork room, carefully fitting the joints, sanding and varnishing, the teacher, angry with him about something trivial, and in a mighty fury, smashed the chair to pieces before the boy's eyes. Andy was heart-broken. It was something he has never forgotten. He did, however, have the satisfaction of getting his revenge. He bided his time until he had the opportunity, some weeks later, of being alone and unobserved in the woodwork room. Carefully, he sawed two legs off the teacher's prized table, the one he used to demonstrate his own craftsmanship. Balancing the table top on the legs, young Andy scurried away. The following day, the teacher entered the room and threw a pile of books and his case onto the table, which immediately collapsed before him. He had an idea, of course, who the culprit was, but he had no proof so was helpless to take any action.

Sadly, schooldays for Andy and many more children were

not 'the best years of their lives'. Well, my schooldays were. I was very fortunate to have, on the whole, dedicated and hard-working teachers with an enthusiasm for learning and possessing a desire to help their students appreciate and explore the subjects they taught more profoundly. I was never caned or slippered, called an idiot or made to write out lines.

When I recall my schooldays, there were several teachers who stood out as exceptional practitioners. Ken Pike, who later went on to become a distinguished head teacher, taught me for my 'O' levels in English Language and English Literature. He was an inspirational teacher who infected me with a love of language and an appreciation of poetry and prose. He spoke with wonderful conviction and developed in me a passion for literature. As a school inspector, I often thought that if the material is appropriate to the age and maturity of the students, if the teacher manages to interest and challenge the students, and if they possess some sensitivity, understanding and have a sense of humour, then there would be far fewer discipline problems in schools. It is often when the lessons are dull, and the teacher lacklustre, that poor discipline emerges. Mr Pike had a great sense of humour. It is of inestimable importance that teachers do have a sense of humour – indeed, a sense of fun.

Alan Schofield taught me Geography for 'O' level. He was a sensitive, tolerant man, always willing to listen, but not a soft touch. He was never too preoccupied to talk informally to the pupils at break times, or too impatient to go over an explanation again if we were unsure. His classroom, decorated with great coloured maps, posters, newspaper cuttings, postcards and photographs was kept neat and tidy. We would line up outside in silence, file in, stand behind our desks, wish him a 'Good morning, sir,' and then be told to sit. Trained as a primary teacher, I guess he never possessed the letters after his name, but he was a natural teacher who enjoyed teaching, handled dissenting voices with humour and always made us feel valued. Those of us who have been teachers know only too well how daunting it can be to stand in front of a group of large, volatile adolescents not accustomed to sitting still and listening, and attempt to engage their attention and get them to do as they are told. It is important to appear strong and fearless, even if it is an act.

Many years later, Mr Schofield, then in his eighties, came to hear me when I appeared on stage at the Strode Theatre in Street. I sat in the bar after my performance with his wife and family, and we reminisced. Eventually, the manager of the theatre had to ask us to leave. Before he left, I held my former teacher in my arms and acknowledged him as the great teacher he was. I wanted to repay that fondness and respect that he had showered on me. Sadly, Alan Schofield died the following year.

Some would say that there is no room in education for the eccentric teacher. I would disagree. Mr Firth ('Theo') taught me history at 'O' level and was one of those individuals who are out of the ordinary, idiosyncratic and do not always follow the various directives, but he had a profound impact upon me in my schooldays; he brought history to life for me. Eccentrics, in my experience, are less inhibited, more imaginative and often more childlike in their approach to life than we 'ordinary' folk, and they do not care what other people think of them. As I walked into the playground on my first day at secondary school, there, standing like a great Eastern statue in the middle of the yard, was this barrel-bodied, balding man with little fluffy outcrops around his ears. He was wearing old black plimsolls and, instead of a belt, he had a piece of string fastened around the top of his baggy corduroy trousers. He looked like a character from Dickens. This was the much-feared Mr Theodore Firth.

In my experience, such non-conformist teachers as Mr Firth frequently have a greater impact than the more conventional teachers and are often remembered years later, when the 'ordinary' teachers have been long forgotten. Mr Firth was strict but he was scrupulously fair, totally committed but rather unpredictable and, provided you worked hard and were well behaved, he posed no problem. He insisted on every pupil's undivided attention, neat and accurate writing, and work completed on time. In answer to his questions, he expected the right hand of the pupil to be raised straight as a die and for the pupil to answer clearly and confidently. Like all great teachers, Mr Firth believed that all children mattered, whatever background or ability, and he built up his pupils' self-esteem and expectation. He was a bit of a showman, with unflinching opinions about the events of history, and above all a performer, always master of his audience and in command of the stage.

A Joyful Learning

I was massively fortunate in my schooling to have, for 'A' levels, two outstanding teachers: Miss Mary Wainwright and J Alan Taylor. Much of what I hold dear was first shown to me by teachers such as these – sensitive, supportive, patient and good-humoured – they inspired me, encouraged me, took an interest in me and convinced me that, despite my humble background and my average abilities, I could achieve anything.

I was in Thomas Hardy country recently, speaking at an education conference and staying overnight at The Casterbridge Hotel on the High Street in Dorchester. In the evening, I wandered around this delightful Dorset town, with its greystone churches and museums, and came upon the statue of its greatest writer. I stared up at the imposing figure and remembered fondly Miss Wainwright, who introduced me to the world of Thomas Hardy.

English Literature 'A' level was not offered in the boys' high school in Rotherham so I, along with several other large gangly adolescents, studied the subject in the adjacent Oakwood Girls' High.

Miss Mary Wainwright, head of the English department, was a diminutive, softly spoken woman dressed in a pristine white blouse with lace collar, which was buttoned up at the neck with small pearl buttons. She was swathed in a long, pleated tweed skirt, dark brown stockings and small leather brogues. The delicate embroidered handkerchief that she secreted up her sleeve would be occasionally plucked out to dab the corners of her mouth. Save for the large cameo brooch placed at her throat, she wore no jewellery and there was no vestige of make-up. She lined up her new students, a motley group of spotty, lanky boys, and peered up at us. 'I've never taught boys,' she said, and then, after a long pause and with a twinkle in her dark eyes, she added, 'but I've heard of them.'

As soon as Miss Wainwright opened the set text, *The Mayor of Casterbridge*, and started to read, I was in a world I came to love. Occasionally she would stop, make a comment, and smile with a curious wistfulness, as if there was something she recalled fondly from a distant past.

The first essay I handed in to Miss Wainwright concerned our initial impressions of Henchard, the main character in the novel, and I spent long hours in the central library in town, writing, rewriting and referring to various reference books. When the essays were handed back my heart leapt. Following a long and detailed assessment of my effort, written at the bottom of the page in small neat handwriting, I had been awarded a B+.

Miss Wainwright took me aside after the lesson. 'That was extremely promising,' she told me, smiling. 'It's a very good start. I am sure you will do well.' From then onwards, I gained in confidence, contributed in the lessons and achieved good marks.

What incredible good fortune it was for me to have had this remarkable woman for my teacher. Miss Wainwright, a woman of great learning and infinite patience, was passionate about her subject and had the ability to bring the works of any writer to life.

These days, teachers are having to adjust to yet more additions to the curriculum and, with such changes, will come the attendant paperwork. There will be new guidelines and planning documents, detailed policies and ceaseless evaluations with which teachers will have to deal. Sadly, more teachers will leave the profession, weary with the constant changes, the snowstorm of paperwork and the increasing pressures. I pray that one day the Government will understand that education is not about process and paperwork but about the quality of the teaching. At the very centre of the process of education are the teachers like Miss Wainwright, who infect their charges with a love of learning; enthusiastic, committed, good-humoured people, who enjoy the company of the young and give them the best they can give.

In writing about the highly successful teacher who commands the greatest respect and affection from his or her pupils, Edward Thring, the Victorian scholar, educationalist and former headmaster at Uppingham School, describes better than I the sort of teachers I was privileged to have:

The teacher makes the taught do the work and occupies himself in showing them how to do it and taking care that they do it. His work is to direct, suggest, question, enspirit; he adapts himself in every possible way to the individual minds, never resting until he had made them master of the skill required and seen them become capable of working on their own account. Teaching takes any shape whatsoever, is fragmently changing as the difficulties of the pupils minds change and disregards all precise plan, provided that a close, laborious and exact exercise of mind is the result. The teacher makes the pupils work and stands and falls by what they do.

Creatures Great and Small

When I was six, my father arrived home with a kitten. It was a scrawny little scrap of a creature of indeterminate colour, with great glassy eyes and half an ear. He had discovered the cat in the finishing shop at the steelworks where he worked. Christine, my sister, was given the job of looking after it, a task she soon abandoned after she was scratched when trying to stroke it. Whiskey, as the cat was to be called, was the first of many pets which we adopted. He grew alarmingly over the weeks, into a sleek, jade-eyed feline, the strange-shaped ear giving him a raffish look. Rather than showing any gratitude for being rescued from certain death, this feral creature scratched and bit and disliked being stroked. If he was approached, his back would arch and he spat and hissed. Many was the time he padded into the kitchen with a bird or a mouse in his jaws and, try as we might, he would not release his victim. He enjoyed playing with his prey until the final *coup de grace*. At night, he would claw at the back door until let out and not return until the next morning, when he would whine for his breakfast. During the night, when he was on his amorous adventures, we knew it was Whiskey who made the terrible noise in the garden to attract any passing female.

When the cat sharpened his claws on the back of the chair, my father exclaimed, 'That cat has to go!' But of course it didn't, and it continued to be tolerated and indulged and approached with caution. Then, one day, Whiskey never returned. We found a dead rat on the doorstep. Perhaps it was his farewell present. If he could have left a message it would no doubt have been: 'This life is a bit too tame for me so I must be off. In this heart of mine, you see, there burns the spirit of a savage blood.'

After our experience with Whiskey it might be thought that my parents would be disinclined to adopt another creature, but they did. When my brother Alec arrived home one day with a liver and white puppy, with doleful eyes and floppy ears, they merely took it in their stride, telling him that Dan, (the name given to the dog) was his responsibility. Neighbours had dogs – little snappy terriers, fat slobbering Labradors, fearsome Alsatians and frisky mongrels – but Dan was different. He grew to be an elegant, gentle-natured creature, a pure-bred German pointer. There were no threatening rumbles or sharp yapping, no growls or show of sharp teeth. He was such an amiable beast that we all grew to love him. At the park, few dogs could keep up with him. He would bound off into the distance but return immediately at the call of his name. He would snuffle in bushes and then, on scenting game, he would freeze. His tail would shoot up, his nose dip to the floor and he would raise one paw and 'point'.

Once, on a trip to Bridlington in my sister's VW Beetle car, we stopped in a lay-by for Dan to stretch his legs. The man in the car parked behind enquired what breed he was.

'He's a German Pointer,' I told him.

'And you're in the Volkswagen?'

'Yes.'

'Bloody patriotic, aren't you?' he said.

When I bought Lizzie, my daughter of seven, a hamster, my father gave her a little lecture on how to look after it, and warned her to make sure its cage was secure 'for these little rodents', he said, 'are expert escapologists'. He reminded me of the time when I was Lizzie's age and I volunteered to look after the hamster from school during the half-term break. It was a fat, pale brown, affectionate little creature called Oscar, but, one morning, I found his cage empty. He had somehow managed to escape. All day we searched the house, but to no avail. When Alec thought he heard a scratching under the floorboards, my father reluctantly pulled up a corner of carpet, levered up one of the planks and shone a torch into the darkness, but there was no sign of the hamster. All week we searched and, as the holiday came to an end, I became distraught. What would I say to Miss Greenwood, my teacher? I would never be trusted to look after one of the school's pets ever again. And how would I face the other children? On the Saturday before the start of school, my father arrived home with another hamster but it was smaller, thinner and a different colour.

'But it's different!' I cried. 'Everyone will know.'

'It was the only one in the shop,' my father told me, and then added, reassuringly, 'And anyway, the children will have forgotten what it looked like.'

I was not convinced.

The following Monday morning, I sat at my desk, glancing over at the cage in the corner. The new hamster had not emerged from its warm little den, but it chose playtime to make an appearance. When the children gathered around the cage and peered through the bars they were puzzled. 'Miss!' they cried, 'Oscar looks different.'

Miss Greenwood's eyes met mine. I must have looked close to tears. 'You know, sometimes children,' she said, 'hamsters do change colour with the seasons, and lose weight as well.'

'And shrink?' asked Margaret Johnson.

'And shrink,' repeated the teacher.

Of course, I knew that she knew and I could have kissed her.

The new hamster lasted a week. One of the children fed a piece of orange peel though the bars of the cage which finished the poor creature off.

As a child, I learnt a few of life's lessons from these dealings with animals. First, one should not expect that a kindness will necessarily be reciprocated or even appreciated. Second, one should never judge by appearances. Third, it is sometimes kinder to tell a lie, than to tell the truth and get someone into trouble. Finally, it is not a good idea to eat orange peel.

Opening Doors

There was a metaphor about life that my former headmaster, Mr T W 'Taffy' Williams, was fond of using. At the leavers' assembly, at South Grove Secondary Modern School for Boys, he asked us to think for a moment before we left the school for the last time.

'Whoever you are and whatever you do,' he said, 'as you walk down that corridor and out into the wide world, I want you to pause for a moment and remember one thing: life is like that corridor, lined with many different doors. Some few will be bolted and barred to you and, however hard you push and pull, strike and shout, they will remain forever closed. Some will be wide open and you can walk through with little effort and no hindrance. Some will be ajar and, with a little exertion and curiosity, you will be able to see what lies behind. Most doors, however, will be closed, but they will be seldom locked. These are the doors of opportunity, boys. The doors of opportunity. It is up to you which of those closed doors you choose to try and to discover what is behind, waiting for you –' he paused for effect – 'and which to pass on by.'

I guess, for many of the pupils in the school hall that heady July morning, the headmaster's metaphor was lost upon them, but for me, an ambitious, rather studious, idealistic sixteen-year-old, those words have remained a vivid memory. The closed doors in my own life have been rarely, if ever, locked, and I have been immensely fortunate that I have had caring, supportive, encouraging people all along the way who have helped me through them.

Throughout my life, I have been encouraged to open doors by my parents, my grandmother and my teachers, but many a time they have opened them for me and urged me through, building up my confidence to do so.

My grandmother's dictum was that life is short, and to make the most of it. She encouraged me to believe that every opportunity which comes my way should be taken; I should read books, take an interest in people and events, not be afraid of asking questions and expressing opinions. A favourite expression of hers was: 'Never be afraid of chancing your arm.' Then she would add: 'And don't take life too seriously – after all, nobody comes out of it alive.'

A Father's ABC of Life
Always remember my son to:
Act in a matter that you would wish to be treated,
Be considerate . . .
Choose your friends with care,
Don't take yourself too seriously,
Enjoy all that life offers you,
Follow your dreams,
Guard against bitterness and envy,
Harm no one,
Ignore the cynic,
Jog a little each day,
Keep calm in a crisis,
Laugh a lot,
Make the best of what you have got,
Never miss an opportunity of saying 'Thank You',
Open your heart to those you love,
Pay no attention to grumblers,
Question certainties,
Respect the feelings of others,
Stay true to your principles,
Take a few measured risks,
Use your talents wisely,
Value your family,
Work hard,
X-pect a lot of yourself – but not too much,
Yearn not for riches,
Zest for living should be your aim in this world.

'Don't You Have a Proper Job?'

Into the World of Work

My first interview for a job was a simple and informal affair. My girlfriend's father had a friend who was manager of a large bread factory on Greasborough Street, on the outskirts of Rotherham. I was looking for a job just after the sixth form and during the weeks before departing for college so, on his recommendation, I presented myself one Monday morning at the factory. The manager, a lugubrious-faced individual with thick, black-framed glasses, reached out and picked up a pencil which was lying on the desk, and twirled it between his fingers.

'Work hard, be punctual, do as you are told, wash your hands and don't steal the bread, and you'll be fine.'

And that was it.

Chuck, the foreman, a bald-headed, rotund little man with a stomach as solid and round as a football, tight in his white overall, looked me up and down.

'Another bloody student,' he mouthed. 'I hope you last longer than the last one. He nearly fell in the bloody dough and was baked with the bread.' He held up a hand. Two of the fingers were missing. 'And be bloody careful if you're on the slicers,' he said.

I learnt a great deal about life, work and human nature in that bread factory.

I learnt about getting up before it was light and catching the early bus, enduring the hot dry and noisy atmosphere of a factory, about boredom and monotony and weariness and sheer hard work. I also learnt to be wary of my fellow workers.

Chuck, aided and abetted by some old hands, took delight in playing tricks on the students. I guess it was because a life baking bread, after the initial fascination, became incredibly tedious and predictable, and these clever ruses lightened the monotony. But there may have been more to it than that. It may have been born out of resentment – the fact that these bright young things would earn a bit of pocket money over the holidays and then swan off to university and end up with fat salaries and company cars. It they ever did return to the bread factory it would be as pen-pushing managers and company accountants, engineers or directors. They needed bringing down a peg or two, showing everyone they were not that clever.

The perpetrators must have thought their antics were hilarious. Most of them were harmless, such as hiding essential tools and equipment, removing the toilet paper from the lavatory or putting salt instead of sugar in the students' tea. Some went too far though. One student discovered a dead rat underneath his sandwiches in his snap box and spent most of the shift retching in the lavatory. Another had his bike loaded onto a van with the bread and had to walk all the way home.

One poor lad, a pale-faced boy with a wispy beard and large glassy eyes, who is now probably an eminent doctor or a university professor, spent the whole of the morning with a tea towel wrapped around his head after following the foreman's instruction not to enter the factory without covering all facial hair. He only discarded the cloth when the manager, on his daily walk around the factory, asked him if he had a sore tooth.

I was not immune from the tricks. My first job was to wheel the bread from the factory to the vans, for loading. The loaves would be stacked on sliding metal shelves, on a tall trolley with heavy rubber wheels. At the very bottom was a locking device, triggered by a push of the foot. Of course, Chuck never mentioned the lock and, on my first trip down the long ramp, observed by the foreman with his arms folded over his chest, the trolley gathered speed, then careered out of control, collided with a van and spilt its load. I was panic-stricken and began frantically picking up the bread.

'Bloody marvellous, that!' shouted Chuck, drawing everyone's attention to my distress and embarrassment.

'Bloody students don't know their arses from their elbows. All that bloody learnin' and he can't push a bloody trolley wi'out dropping all t'bread. Comes out of tha wages that, tha knaas.'

On the next occasion I was let loose with the trolley, Chuck sidled over, surreptitiously activated the locking device with a secretive flick of his foot and then sauntered off, with the words: 'And watch what tha're doin' this time.' I spent the next five minutes pushing and pulling to get the trolley moving.

One of the students who had worked at the factory the previous year, warned me to never, under any circumstances, go down to where the confectionery was prepared by the women, under the supervision of an Amazon of a forewoman called Dora. If I did, it was likely that I would have discarded cakes and pastries stuffed down my overalls or, even worse, be squirted all over with whipped cream.

One morning, Chuck sidled up. 'Go down the confectionery and ask Dora for a triple, screw-top, flange extractor,' he instructed me.

I set off but spent the next five minutes hiding in a cubicle in the lavatory. I then returned. 'Dora told me to tell you that she needs a note from you,' I informed Chuck seriously. 'She said that the last triple, screw-top, flange extractor she sent up here has gone missing.'

'Clever bugger,' mouthed Chuck, ambling off down the factory. 'I reckon from t'first time I clapped eyes on thee, tha'd end up a bloody teacher. Too clever by 'alf.'

It was never my ambition to become a teacher. It was another contact who put me in line for the job as a trainee accountant. Mrs Gill, my mother's best friend, was Company Secretary at Thomas Wilde and Son, in Sheffield, and she arranged for me to have an interview with a senior partner at Hart, Moss and Copley, Chartered Accountants. I had presented myself at the plush offices on Moorgate Street, in a new suit, white shirt, school tie, hair short and slicked back and highly polished black shoes, and sat before one of the senior partners. He appeared every inch what I imagined an accountant would look like in his dark pin-stripe suit and waistcoat and with a pair of half-moon spectacles perched on the end of his nose.

Having satisfied himself that I had the necessary qualifications, he sat back on his chair and asked me a few general questions before leaning over his desk.

'Well, young man,' he said, after a long pause. 'Go ahead. Sell yourself.'

I must have acquitted myself reasonably well because he nodded approvingly after each answer.

'Can you can start in September?' he asked.

'Yes, sir.'

'Welcome to Hart, Moss and Copley,' he said, smiling.

I never did train as an accountant. Three days after the interview, I received a letter inviting me to attend Rotherham Education Office to see Mr Bloomer, the Director of Education. I had never met Mr Bloomer, but knew him to be a very important man, in charge of all the schools in the town. I reported to the reception desk at the Education Office, on the appointed day and at the appointed time, and waited in the outer office. I couldn't understand why he would wish to see me. After a short wait, I was shown into Mr Bloomer's office. I entered a large, dark-panelled room. Great glass-fronted bookcases full of leather-bound tomes lined one wall and framed pictures and prints, no doubt drawn and painted by the town's children and students, were displayed on the other.

The Director of Education had been contacted by my headmaster, Mr Williams.

'Your headmaster,' said Mr Bloomer, 'has had a word with me, and he is of the opinion that you ought to stay on and do your 'A' levels. He thinks you would make a very good teacher.'

'Yes, sir,' I replied, not really knowing what to say.

At the time, I didn't think it was particularly unusual for the Director of Education to take a personal interest in just one student, to summon him to his office and give him the benefit of his advice, but now I know that it was. I took the advice, stayed on for 'A' levels, and then trained to be a teacher.

Fun and Games

When training in the profession, I went on teaching practice to St Augustine's Roman Catholic Secondary Modern School, in Huddersfield. Being young and reasonably fit, I was given two lessons of games to teach each week. The head of the PE and

Games department, a large, amiable Scot I shall call Gus, told me to buy a tracksuit and football boots and report to the boys' changing rooms the following week. I duly did as I was told.

Forty-five large, gangly adolescents were waiting outside the changing rooms when I arrived. Gus, attired in an old tracksuit heavily decorated with various colourful athletic badges, was standing at the head of the queue, jangling a huge bunch of keys.

'Right lads,' he shouted, 'get changed quickly and quietly, quickly and quietly.'

I accompanied him into a small teacher's office, where I was presented with a whistle. He poked his head around the door.

'Keep it down, lads, keep it down!' he shouted, and the hubbub immediately subsided.

Out on the fields, he told me he would lead the pack on a jog around the perimeter and that I should follow up the rear.

Having all 'limbered up', Gus ordered: 'Get the poles!' Was this some sort of arcane ritual in which the boys attacked their Polish peers? Four boys appeared, with large white poles, and were instructed by the teacher to stick them in the grass, spaced out evenly for skills practice. 'Balls!' shouted Gus, and four more boys appeared with the footballs. The pupils dribbled and wove for ten minutes before being told to form four teams.

'I'll referee one match, Mr Phinn,' said Gus, 'and you the other.'

During the game, which I refereed, despite my giving various dubious rulings, none of the boys questioned my decisions.

At the end of the lesson, the boys showered, changed and lined up quietly to be dismissed.

I joined Gus later that lunchtime.

'That was a really good lesson this morning,' I told him.

'Aye.'

'You know I have an idea I might change from English and teach Games.'

'Oh, aye?'

'I mean,' I continued, 'it's so much easier, isn't it?'

'Is it?'

'You don't have all the preparation to do, the homework to set and the examinations to mark.'

'Bit of a doddle really,' observed my colleague.

The following week, before the lesson, Gus approached me in the staff room.

'You'll be all right on your own for ten minutes this morning, won't you?' he said. 'Get the lads started. It's just that I have something to take care of.'

My heart sank down into my shoes.

'On my own?' I repeated.

'Aye. The lads know the routine.'

I arrived at the changing rooms, my heart thumping in my chest. I jangled the keys.

'Right lads,' I said, lowering my voice a couple of octaves, 'get changed quickly and quietly, quickly and quietly.'

I disappeared into the teacher's office, emerging a moment later with my whistle around my neck.

'Keep it down, lads, keep it down,' I told the boys, and the hubbub immediately subsided.

Out on the field, we jogged around the perimeter, with no problems whatsoever.

'Get the poles!' I ordered, and four boys disappeared to get the white poles. I pointed to a piece of grass a distance from the football pitches. 'Stick the poles in over there,' I told them.

'There, sir?' questioned a bear of a boy with a round red face, legs like tree trunks and hands like spades.

Here we go, I thought – a confrontation. Keep calm. Look confident. Don't show your fear. 'Yes, over there!' I raised my voice.

'Are you sure, sir?' he asked.

'Yes, I am sure! Do as you are told and be quick about it!'

The boy shrugged and did as he was told.

When Gus arrived, the boys were dribbling and weaving around the poles. He surveyed the scene.

'That, Mr Phinn,' he said, 'is masterful.' I ballooned with pride. 'Masterful.' Then, after a deep in-drawing of breath, he added, 'They've stuck the poles in the middle of the bloody cricket square!'

The Nun's Story

I visited the Bar Convent in York recently. Situated just outside the city walls at Micklegate Bar, the original 17th century house was purchased by Francis Bedingfield in 1686 and was replaced in the 18th century by the spectacular Georgian building now listed as Grade 1 by English Heritage. The building remains the home of the York Community of the Congregation of Jesus and is open daily for interest, education and enjoyment. This is one of the county's hidden gems and houses the most fascinating collection of artefacts, paintings, religious relics and historical documents, a stunning Maw tiled floor, a Winter Garden, a priest hole and a superb and beautifully preserved neo-classical Chapel, hidden from view.

The museum tells the story of how the sisters of the Community lived and worked in secrecy during the reign of Elizabeth I, to preserve their way of life in a time of terrible persecution and lack of recognition of the value of education for girls and women and the contribution they could make to society.

I had visited the Bar Convent before, in rather different circumstances. It was a good forty years ago, when I was training to be a teacher. My flatmate was on teaching practice at the convent, which then housed a girls' school, and he was intending to accompany the teachers and students to Stratford-Upon-Avon to see a production of *King Lear*, but he was ill. Sister Margaret Mary suggested I might like to take his place.

After a couple of hours on the coach to Stratford, I became increasingly uncomfortable. I had drunk a few cups of coffee that morning and now wanted to go to the toilet. I kept crossing and uncrossing my legs to try and ease the pain in my complaining bladder.

'All you all right, Mr Phinn?' asked the nun sitting next to me.

I pulled a pained expression. 'I'm fine,' I lied.

The discomfort got worse and worse. I just had to go to the lavatory or I would burst.

'I suppose we'll be stopping for lunch soon,' I said casually to my companion.

'Oh no,' she replied. 'We shan't be stopping now until we get to Stratford.

The pain in my bladder was becoming unbearable. I just had to go to the lavatory. Then I thought of the most horrendous scenario: me, standing by the side of the road, doing what I had to do, with thirty girls and four nuns staring out of the coach window in amazement. The embarrassment, the indignity, the shame! No, I would have to think of something.

I eased myself down the aisle of the coach to speak to the driver.

'I have to go to the toilet,' I whispered in his ear

'Toilet!' he exclaimed loudly.

'I have to go,' I said. 'I'm desperate.' There was a pathetic pleading in my voice. 'Please.'

'Well, I'll tell you what I can do. I'll get off and go via Coventry. There's a car park and toilets in t'cathedral precincts.'

'Oh, thank you, thank you,' I said.

'But you'll have to clear it with the teachers back there.'

I tiptoed down the aisle and returned to my seat. 'I was just talking to the driver, Sister,' I said casually, 'and he says we are in very good time. I think it might be a good idea to break our journey at Coventry and see the wonderful cathedral.'

'What an excellent idea,' she said. I said a silent prayer of thanks.

Ten minutes later, the longest ten minutes of my life, we pulled into the car park by the cathedral. I nearly cried when I saw the GENTS sign. As soon as the coach came to a halt, I leapt down the steps and shot off, like a man pursued by a charging rhinoceros. To my dismay, I heard the nun's voice behind me.

'Follow Mr Phinn, girls. Follow Mr Phinn. He's heading for the cathedral.' I turned and to my horror saw thirty girls running across the car park in my direction.

That Will Teach You!

I was presenting the certificates to newly qualified teachers. Each new member of the teaching profession attending was accompanied by their mentor, an experienced and senior member of staff, who had monitored progress and advised them during their first induction year. It was good to hear that they had received such support and encouragement.

At a conference, some weeks earlier, I had learnt that there was a haemorrhaging of teachers; after spending only a few years in the job, as many as one in seven newly qualified teachers decided to leave and do something else. The mountains of paperwork they had to deal with, the constant changes, new government initiatives, disruptive children and awkward parents were all cited as causes for them to leave the profession, but one other reason was that some felt they received little help and support from colleagues. There was the young woman who sought the advice of her head of department after a particularly difficult lesson with a group of disruptive pupils. 'Well, they were all right when I taught them last year,' he told her haughtily. Another mentioned the head teacher who, commenting on the display that she had spent hours mounting on the wall down the corridor, said that she had used too many staples. Then there was the primary teacher who shared an amusing anecdote with her older colleague in the staff room, only to be told that she was too enthusiastic and that she would soon learn that teaching wasn't a bed of roses. The cynic continued to tell her that she wouldn't teach if she had the chance again, and certainly wouldn't encourage any of her own children to become teachers.

'Good teachers,' said Bishop Samuel Wilberforce, 'take on the most important role in society for they change lives', and Seneca, who possibly had the most challenging job of all as the tutor of Nero, said that 'part of my joy in learning is that it puts me in a position to teach and nothing is of any value to me unless I have someone to share it with.'

I was fortunate, growing up, to have the very best teachers: the great majority were keen, enthusiastic and dedicated, and possessed of a sense of humour, indeed, a sense of fun. I was also immensely fortunate, in my first year as a teacher in a large comprehensive in Rotherham (it was called 'the probationary year' in those days), to work for a visionary and compassionate head teacher, Dennis Morgan, and a deputy head teacher, Roy Happs, both of whom gave such valuable advice, support and encouragement, and who never missed an opportunity to show recognition for what I did. One of Mr Morgan's maxims was that teachers new to the profession should have the option to fail and power to succeed.

I have to admit that in my first year, I failed a fair bit. I was reminded of one of my *faux pas* recently by a former pupil of mine. I, a green probationary teacher, took a group of students to the swimming baths for the weekly lesson. In those days, it was obligatory for girls and boys with long hair to wear bathing caps. One small, nervous little girl, having forgotten her cap, was told off by the swimming teacher and told to sit on the side. Next to her sat another girl, who was laughing at the distressed child.

'And what do you find so funny?' I asked.

'Nothing sir,' she replied.

'I don't think it's very nice to laugh at somebody else,' I told her. 'Anyway, why aren't you in the water?'

'You know, sir,' she said.

'No, I don't know,' I replied. 'I'm not psychic.'

'You know, sir,' she repeated.

'No, I do not know!' I snapped. 'Why are you not in the water with the others?'

'Time of the month, sir,' she said.

'Oh,' I said, colouring up. Then I used the teacher's stock-in-trade response. 'Well, don't do it again,' I said, walking quickly away.

Silence in the Library

I have always been a passionate supporter of school libraries. I suppose, as a former President of the School Library Association, I would be expected to say as much. When I was inspecting secondary schools, the first port of call was always the school library. I always hoped that I would find a cheerful, optimistic, bright facility, stocked with glossy paperbacks, contemporary and classic novels, poetry and picture books, up-to-date non-fiction material, quality hardback reference books and dictionaries, and magazines and journals that appealed to the young and helped them in their learning. I also hoped to see the tables fully occupied by quiet and dedicated students.

Sadly, this was not always the case. In one old, established grammar school, I was shown into a bare, cold, featureless room with a few ancient tomes and dog-eared textbooks scattered along the high wooden bookcases. The atmosphere carried a warm, pervasive smell of dust, and the grey walls did not help. This was the supposed central learning resource, the foundation of the curriculum and the place of academic study, reading and research. The books on the shelves bore witness to the fact that there had not been a full audit or clear-out of the old and inappropriate material for some time. There were books entitled *Wireless Studies for Beginners*, *Life in the Belgian Congo*, *Harmless Scientific Experiments for Girls* and *Our King: George VI*.

As a young teacher, I was given charge of the school library. Mr Morgan, the head teacher of the secondary school where I taught, stopped me in the corridor at the conclusion of my probationary year and asked me if I 'wanted the school library'. There would be an allowance to go with it. Of course, in those bygone days in education, any teacher who was warm and breathing after his or her first year expected to be given a scale salary point. I readily agreed to become 'teacher in charge of the school library' and, after a week's course, and fully equipped with new ideas and lots of enthusiasm, I set about transforming the place. I prevailed upon the head teacher to invest in new tables, easy chairs and attractive wooden shelving. I covered the empty walls with colourful paintings and prints, and arranged pot plants on the windowsills. Not for me the staff room at breaks and lunchtimes; I manned the library, surveying my domain from the small office with great pride and making sure anyone entering this hallowed place did so silently, and that they returned any borrowed books to the prescribed shelves. I chased up overdue books with the zeal of Torquemada and issued directives banning any student who had infringed the rules, which were displayed prominently on the door.

Then Her Majesty's Inspector arrived. Mr Dickinson complimented me on the state of the library. Particularly impressive, he said, were the unblemished carpet, pristine polished tables, immaculately tidy shelves and the fact that there were very few books for which I could not account.

'This is,' he told me, 'without doubt the most attractive school library I have visited in a long time – so clean, comfortable and ordered.'

I swelled with pride.

'There is just one small thing,' he continued, 'which you may feel somewhat trivial but I feel I do need to ask.'

I looked at him expectantly. 'Yes, of course.'

'Where are the students?' he enquired, smiling.

Bridge Over Troubled Waters

I do feel sorry watching the poor contestants facing the sour-faced, sneering Anne Robinson on *The Weakest Link*. Is it any surprise that they fluff the answers?

Anne Robinson: 'In English literary relationships, Mary Wollstonecraft Godwin, who wrote *Frankenstein*, married the poet, Percy who?'

Contestant: 'Thrower.'

Anne Robinson: 'The film starring Fred Astaire and Ginger Rogers was called *Flying Down to* . . . Where?'

Contestant: 'Halifax.'

Anne Robinson: 'What "X" is the fear of foreigners?'

Contestant: 'The X-Factor.'

I would hate to be up there in the glare of the lights, facing that virago with thousands watching me.

I hate quizzes. When the family gather around the table on Christmas Day for the ritual game of Trivial Pursuit, I skulk away to my study. I hear them downstairs, discussing the questions and answers, and I am pleased to be away from it all.

My aversion to quizzes stems from when I was a teacher and I represented my school house at the annual 'Inter-House Quiz'.

Four housemasters sat on the stage, in front of the entire school, to answer a series of general knowledge questions put to us by the Head of the Lower School. The 'Inter-House Quiz' afforded the quizmaster the perfect opportunity to get his revenge for a trick I had played upon him.

Some weeks earlier, I had amused myself with what I thought was a harmless prank. Each Friday lunchtime, the Head of the Lower School and three male colleagues would ensconce themselves in the corner of the staff room to play bridge. The four teachers took the game extremely seriously and would discuss in detail, at various times during the following week, the strategies and outcomes. These post-mortems were extremely tedious to have to listen to, so, when the fire alarm sounded one Friday lunchtime and we all had to vacate the school, I remained behind in the empty staff room with just enough time for me to swap a few of the cards around. When the game was resumed, the arguments that arose very nearly ended in violence, so I had the good grace to own up to what I had done. The four players were not best pleased.

The Head of the Lower School bided his time until he could get his own back. That time was when the 'Inter-House Quiz' took place. I sat under the bright lights on the stage, in front of the entire school, ready and confident to field the questions.

'Question one, for the first housemaster,' said the quizmaster, 'is: "What is the national flower or plant of England?"'

'The rose,' came the answer.

There was thunderous applause from those pupils in his house.

'Question one for the second housemaster,' said the quizmaster, 'is: "What is the national flower or plant of Scotland?"'

'The thistle,' came the answer.

This was followed by wild clapping from the pupils in *his* house.

'Question one for the third housemaster,' said the quizmaster, 'is: "What is the national flower or plant of Wales?" '

'The leek.'

Again, there was a lively response from those in *his* house.

Then it came to my turn. I had the word 'shamrock' on the tip of my tongue.

'Question one for the fourth housemaster,' said the quizmaster, a strange little smile playing on his lips, 'is: "What is the national flower or plant of South Africa?" '

'What?' I spluttered.

'Answer the question, Mr Phinn,' the Head of the Lower School told me.

'I've not the slightest idea,' I replied.

'It's the Giant or King Protea,' said the quizmaster before adding, 'I thought everyone knew that.'

There followed further humiliation as all the questions directed at the other contestants were pitifully easy and mine incredibly hard.

Question one for the first housemaster: 'Who wrote *Treasure Island*?'

Question one for the second housemaster: 'Who wrote *Oliver Twist*?'

Question one for the third housemaster: 'Who wrote *Macbeth*?'

Question one for the fourth housemaster: 'Who directed the film *A Bridge Too Far*?'

Next day, I was teaching the very bottom form in the fifth year. As I approached one of my pupils he tut-tutted, and remarked, 'I see now, sir, why you teach *us*.'

'Why is that, John?' I asked.

'Why, you're as thick as we are, aren't you?' the boy replied.

A Bird of a Feather

We have a brace of pheasants in our garden. They appeared last week and have commandeered the bird table, where they peck away, oblivious to everybody and everything, before pottering between the flowerbeds. They disappear at night but return the next day for breakfast, watched hungrily by a tree full of blackbirds and starlings.

Each time I see a pheasant, I think of the 'incident' when I was in my first week as a school inspector in North Yorkshire. It was a glorious drive from Settle to York. The sun was shining and cloud shadows chased across the undulating green of the Dales. A magpie strutted along a silvered white stone wall and a pigeon flapped across the road, just in front of the car. A fox appeared, stepping delicately across the road ahead of me, his brush down and snout up, unafraid, unconcerned. In the fields, the sheep grazed lazily; lambs would start to arrive in a month or so. This, surely, was the best of seasons. Suddenly, a large hen pheasant shot straight out in front of the car, and I heard a thud as it hit the bumper. I quickly pulled over and jumped from the vehicle to see its prone body in the middle of the road, eyes closed and legs sticking skywards. All around me was silent and still. Not a person to be seen. I picked up the bird, popped it in the boot of my car and thought of the wonderful roast game I would be having for my Sunday lunch.

At 4.30 that afternoon, I arrived at the York Teachers' Centre, where I was to direct a creative course for teachers. I opened the boot of the car to take the books and equipment into the Centre – only to find everything a complete jumble. In the very middle of the mess crouched the pheasant I had run over, and had assumed was dead. It was, to my amazement, very much alive and kicking.

The teachers began arriving for the course just in time to see something squawking and pecking and fluttering its wings madly. I had stunned the creature, not killed it; now fully recovered, it was not at all pleased to have been incarcerated in the cramped dark boot of a car for a couple of hours, bumping along, mile after mile.

'Shoo!' I cried, trying to encourage the bird to leave the boot, but every time my hand came within pecking range, it lunged at me. 'Shoo! Shoo!' I exclaimed again. Then, turning, I realised I had attracted a crowd of interested teachers, who stood in a half circle, watching proceedings.

'Is it a visual aid?' asked one teacher, mischievously.

'No, it is not!' I snapped.

'Are we going to write bird poems,' asked another teacher, chuckling, 'from first-hand experience?'

'No, we are not!' came my angry reply.

'You'd have been better off with a stuffed one,' ventured another.

'Well, I don't want it in the Centre,' said the caretaker, who had arrived on the scene, jangling his keys and shaking his head. 'I'm not cleaning up after that.'

'It's not going in the Centre,' I said, getting as flustered as the bird. It made another loud, plaintive squawk, and beat its wings and thrashed its tail.

Eventually, the bird flapped forward and took off, landing on the enclosing wall. Then, with tail proudly stuck up in the air, it strutted off towards York Minster.

Needless to say, the creative wrting course was a lively affair.

The School Inspector Calls

At the first secondary school I visited after becoming a school inspector with OFSTED, I met Bianca in the library before the start of school. She was fifteen, a tall, morose-looking girl with lank hair and a long, pale, unhealthy-looking face, and was dressed in an exceptionally tight blouse, very short skirt and huge platform shoes. She looked very different from the students on the front of the glossy folder which I held in my hand.

'So whatcha gunna be doin', then?' she asked, in a weary, apathetic tone of voice, which she had clearly cultivated over the years for use when talking to adults in authority.

'I am going to be joining you for all today's lessons,' I explained.

'Eh?'

'I said, I am going to be joining you for all today's lessons. I shall observe the teaching and also be talking to the students.'

'Wha' for?'

'Because that's my job.'

'Who are you, then?'

'I'm a school inspector.'

'A what?'

'A school inspector,' I repeated.

'And you just watch teachers?'

'That's right.'

'And sit in classrooms an' that?'

'Yes.'

'Don't you have a proper job then?'

Following the inspection, I met with the governing body in the school library, to give my report. The serious-faced group sat before me, all eyes trained in my direction. The chair of governors, a florid-faced man with huge ginger eyebrows which curved into question marks, eyed me suspiciously with pale watery eyes.

'We're 'ere for the report from the school inspector,' he announced. 'This is Mr Flynn from OFFSET.'

'Off what?' enquired a plain-faced little woman with a pursed mouth and small black darting eyes.

'No, no, that's the water, Doris. Mr Flynn's from OFFSET.'

'OFSTED,' I corrected him, 'and it's Mr Phinn.'

'OFSTED?' he repeated. 'Is that what it is?'

'OFFSET is, as I remember, a machine which prints paper,' I said, smiling.

'Oh,' said the chair of governors, addressing his colleagues. 'Well, you get so confused these days don't you, with "off this" and "off that"? Anyhow, Mr Flynn's here to tell how we've done in the inspection.' He turned his attention, and his eyebrows, back to me. 'And I should say, Mr Flynn, that we like things plain in Yorkshire, straight to the point. We don't put inspectors and the like on pedestals, for, as my sainted mother used to say, "they nobbut wants dustin".'

'Phinn,' I said. 'It's Mr Phinn.'

'This is all very confusing,' remarked the plain-faced little woman with a pursed mouth. 'We've not even got to the report yet and we're having differences. We'll be here all night at this rate. Can we make a start?'

'Well, I don't want to be too long,' said a cheerful-looking cleric. 'I do have another meeting in a couple of hours.'

'I'm sure it won't take that long,' said another governor, before glowering in my direction. 'Will it?'

'Aye,' said the chair of governors, his huge eyebrows twitching, 'let's get on. How's our little school done then?'

The governing body leaned forward, craned their necks and fixed me with stares which would curdle milk.

I placed the thick OFSTED handbook in front of me with the various additional updates, guidance booklets, questionnaires and school documents, before arranging piles of various lists, statistics and summaries to pass around. When I looked up, I faced a sea of faces staring at the mountain of paper in disbelief.

'Well, before I begin I would like to talk a little about the context of the inspection . . .'

I was cut short. 'I think I was right fust time with OFFSET, Mr Flynn,' announced the chair of governors. 'Talk about churning out paper. I reckon when you do your inspections, a forest falls.'

Eating with the Infants

I once visited an infant school in a deprived area of the town, with a very elegant education officer. I commented on the long, pale, pink scarf she wore.

'Actually,' she said, 'it's a pashmina.'

'I thought that was a breed of dog,' I said mischievously.

She gave a slight smile.

Being someone who is interested in words, I did a little research at home that evening, and discovered that 'pashmina' is a Persian word meaning 'cashmere'. Pashminas now describe those colourful silk shawls which, for many years, have been draped elegantly over the shoulders of the richest women in the East. Now they have become very popular throughout the world, although I can't say as I have seen many women walking through

Doncaster town centre with pashminas around their shoulders. When I was young, my grandma had a coloured shawl but, rather than elegantly draping it over her shoulders, she knotted it tightly around her neck like a football scarf.

My colleague and I were asked by the head teacher if we would care to stay for lunch, to which we agreed. We thought perhaps that we were to join her for a sumptuous repast in her room, but we were shown into the school hall, where we were each given a green melamine tray and asked to join the queue of infants.

The dinner ladies were over-generous with the portions and piled high our trays with whole hands of fish fingers and mountains of baked beans and chips. We were both given sizeable bowls of strawberry yoghurt and small plastic tumblers of water.

I very much enjoyed watching my colleague's discomfiture as she sat on a long wooden bench designed for small children, sandwiched between two rather messy little infant eaters who chattered without pausing, liberally spitting out food. She managed to force down half a fish finger and two chips before placing her knife and fork together.

'Are you 'avin' them fish fingers?' asked the little girl on her right.

'No, dear, I'm not,' replied my colleague.

'Can I have 'em?'

'Please do.'

'Are you 'avin' yer chips?' asked another child.

'No, dear.'

'Can I 'ave them?'

'Yes, you may.'

'Are you 'avin' your beans?' asked a third child.

'No,' replied my colleague.

'Can I 'ave 'em?'

'Please do.' The fish fingers, chips and beans were quickly commandeered.

A small girl sitting directly opposite my colleague asked shyly, 'Could I have your yoghurt, Miss?'

'Of course, dear,' came the reply.

'Well,' said my colleague, 'if you will excuse me, I need to freshen up.' She turned to the child who had just scooped out of the bowl a great spoonful of pink yoghurt. 'Could you tell me, dear, where the staff toilets are?'

'Over there,' replied the child, waving the spoon in front of her and, in the process, spattering strawberry yoghurt in all directions.

My colleague bore the brunt of the swinging spoon and the front of her jacket received the lion's share of the sticky substance. She rose solemnly from the bench with surprising equanimity, stared for a moment at the thin pink line which ran across her pale cream suit, with matching accessories, and took a deep breath. 'Thank you, dear,' she said, with a sour smile. 'Thank you so very much.' Then, wrapping the pashmina around her to cover the offending stain, she departed for the toilets.

Some weeks later, I met my colleague in a corridor at the Education Office. She was beautifully dressed, this time with a gossamer-like shawl around her shoulders. I could not help but smile at the memory of our school visit.

'Another pashmina?' I commented.

'Actually,' she told me, coolly, 'it's a shatoosh.'

I didn't say anything.

The Vicar's Story

When the school leaving age was raised in the 1970s, and the youngsters who had looked forward to starting work at fifteen now had to stay on for an extra year, there was a deal of anger and resentment. They had had quite enough of school and wanted to get out into the world.

In an effort to make the curriculum of the ROSLA (raising of school leaving age) group in the school I was teaching in at the time that bit more interesting and relevant, I invited a range of people into school to speak about their lives and work. The pupils were involved in the selection but were somewhat ambitious in their choices of pop stars, fashion designers, film directors, footballers and television personalities, none of whom replied to their letters of invitation. Over the year, there were visits from, among others, a member of parliament, a MEP, a doctor, a woodcarver, a woman police officer, a soldier, a fire-fighter, a farmer, an environmentalist and a vicar. The vicar was the least popular when I suggested him but, following his visit, he emerged as the most entertaining and the most memorable.

He recounted the story of a farmer who was so large that a special coffin was made for him and the gravediggers paid extra because of the size of the hole they had to dig. The coffin was lowered into its final resting place, and the words of interment intoned, before the undertaker hissed: 'It will have to come up, vicar. I've dropped my glasses down the hole and they're on top of the coffin.' The coffin was heaved half way up, and then lowered again as the pall bearers failed to lift it. There were several more unsuccessful attempts and only after more help was enlisted was the coffin finally raised sufficiently high enough for the glasses to be retrieved. At the funeral tea, the widow approached the vicar. 'I thought nothing to that,' she said, tight-lipped. 'My husband was up and down like a ruddy yo-yo.'

In a primary school assembly I attended, a young curate related the parable of the Prodigal Son. He described how the younger son had squandered all his father's money and then had returned home penniless, ashamed and repentant, with his head held low. He told them how the father, with great happiness in his heart and tears of joy in his eyes, had run to meet his son, and how he had put his finest robe around his shoulders, sent his servant for his best sandals and ordered the fatted calf to be killed for a splendid feast to celebrate his son's homecoming. When the elder son heard the sound of the music and laughter and the news that his brother had returned, he was not pleased, and would not enter the house. 'I have worked like a slave all these years for you, yet you have never even offered me as much as a goat for a feast with my friends. Now my good-for-nothing brother, who has spent all your money, turns up and you kill the fatted calf for him.'

'Now, children,' said the curate, 'who do you think was the happiest of all?' There was a forest of hands. He picked a small girl in the front row.

'The father!' she cried.

'That's right, and who do you think was the saddest and most disappointed about the son's return?'

Before he could pick anyone, a boy at the back shouted out, 'Well, I reckon t'fatted calf can't 'ave been too 'appy.'

The Good Little Reader

I discovered Esther, aged six, in the reading corner at the infant school. Her teacher had described the little girl as a gifted child, with a reading age well above her actual age. 'Quite the best little reader I have ever come across,' she had informed me. I have heard many a child described thus, only to discover that the boy or girl in question is bright, but rarely gifted.

'Hello,' I said to Esther.

The child looked up and examined me as one might view a strange object in a museum case. 'Are you the school inspector?' she asked.

'I am,' I replied, smiling.

'Mrs Smith said you would probably want to have a word with me.'

'Your teacher tells me you are a very good reader,' I said.

'I am,' she replied.

'Would you like to read to me?'

'I don't mind,' she said. 'I like reading. I have lots and lots of books at home. I have my own library in my bedroom.'

'I'm sure you have,' I said, 'and I bet you have a bedtime story every night, as well.'

'I do. Daddy and Mummy take it in turns. I have a cuddle and a bedtime story every night. Daddy says stories are very good for children.'

'Your daddy's right,' I told her.

'Daddies always are,' she told me, pertly. 'Shall I get my reading book?'

'No,' I said, 'perhaps you would read one of mine.'

I carry around with me in my briefcase various documents and books: standardised reading tests, non-verbal assessment sheets, word recognition lists and also a few books of varying difficulty to test children's reading ability. The reading scheme books, with which the children learn to read, have familiar characters and settings, and repeated words and phrases to give children confidence and security, but the good reader is able to be confronted with an unknown text and read and understand it. I presented little Esther with a book suitable for a seven-year-old.

'This looks too easy,' she told me, examining the cover and flicking through the pages.

'Easy?' I repeated. 'I'll be very surprised if you manage to read it.'

The child gave me the kind of melancholy smile a Mother Superior might bestow upon an erring novice. 'May I have a harder book, please?'

'OK,' I said, reaching into my briefcase, 'let's try another one.' I selected a book suitable for a nine-year-old. 'Now, if you find this a bit hard, don't worry. It's a book for older children.'

She stared at the cover for a moment. 'Shall I start from the beginning?' she asked.

'Yes please.'

'From the very beginning?'

'From the very beginning,' I repeated.

The child tilted her head, stared at the large black stamped box at the very top of the cover page and then read: 'Property of the West Riding of Yorkshire County Council, Education Department, Libraries, Archives and Resources.'

I shook my head and smiled.

Speech Day

I received a letter from the new head teacher of a grammar school, asking me if I would be willing to speak and present prizes and certificates at the school's awards evening the following December. At a time when children get such a bad press, it is important to know and to recognise that there are many young people from caring and supportive homes, who are taught by dedicated and enthusiastic teachers. It is always a pleasure to be part of such an event which celebrates the achievements and the talents of the young.

I have attended some memorable speech days over the years. Rather than just shaking hands with the recipient of each award, I do like to have a few words, particularly with those who have done exceptionally well or have persevered and achieved against the odds. At a girls' high school, one young woman gained a remarkable five top grades at 'A' level. I congratulated her and asked to which university she was going. She was a chatty and articulate young woman, and our conversation continued. The headmistress, a formidable and striking-looking woman, in a most colourful academic gown, indicated discreetly with a small nod of her head and a knowing look that I should move on. Mischievously,

I continued chatting to the student, much to the amusement of the audience. Later the chairman of governors remarked, tongue in cheek, that it was the first time in the history of the school that a speaker had ignored the headmistress on her own stage.

At one speech day, the chairman of governors informed the assembled parents and students that, over the previous year, the school had experienced its share of problems, not least the somewhat critical school inspectors' report. 'We are,' he informed the audience, 'on the edge of a precipice but, with the appointment of the new head teacher, we are now moving forward with confidence.'

One rather pompous headmaster informed the parents at speech day that he was like the captain of a ship, standing proudly on the bridge, scanning the horizon, heading for the land of opportunity and the harbour of success. 'Sometimes,' he said, 'we are buffeted by the stormy gusts of educational change. Sometimes we are carried off course by the cold currents of government policy. Sometimes we face the hurricanes and gales of school inspection. Sometimes a heavy downpour of yet more documents from the Ministry of Education inundates us. Sometimes we are becalmed by the shortage of the necessary resources. Yet we always keep a steady course, with a firm hand on the tiller, for the land of opportunity and the harbour of success.' The headmaster paused to sweep his hand before him. 'You know well, students,' he said, 'the name of this, our ship, a name that stands for history, for tradition and for the highest possible standards. What is the name of this, our ship, I ask?' The headmaster's eyes came to rest on a small boy in the front row who stared up from behind thick-lensed glasses. 'Yes, you, boy,' the headmaster commanded. 'Tell us the name of this ship of ours.'

'Is it the *Titanic*, sir?' enquired the boy.

The most memorable speech day took place in a large inner-city comprehensive school. The Lady Mayor was the guest of honour and was charged with presenting the prizes and giving a short address. She was a large jolly woman in a tight-fitting, powder blue suit, her magnificent golden chain draped around her ample bosom. As she bent to pick up a silver cup, she broke wind extremely loudly. The young people and teaching staff tried valiantly to suppress their mirth. The Lady Mayor smiled widely, approached the microphone and announced, 'Hark at me,' and then joined in with the uproarious laughter.

The Musician

I was once dragooned into inspecting music in a secondary school. The lead inspector, an HMI (Her Majesty's Inspector) with a science background, asked me if I would take on the task, explaining that our music specialist colleague was ill and could not join us, and there was no one else on the team sufficiently confident or capable enough to inspect the music department.

'Neither am I,' I told him.

'But you play the piano.'

'Yes, but –'

'And you have directed musicals in schools.'

'Yes, but –'

'And have performed yourself in comic operas.'

'I know, but –'

'And enjoy classical music.'

'That does not mean –'

'The thing is, Gervase,' he explained, 'I did tell the head teacher that there was no music specialist on the team, and she said the head of department would be very disappointed that no one would be observing his lessons. It is his last term and he so wanted to be inspected before he retired.'

Well, that is a rarity, I thought – a teacher actually wishing to be inspected.

The lead inspector continued: 'Clearly, the head of music is a very able man, a very popular and committed teacher and the students perform really well in the examinations. He's been in the school all his professional life. The head teacher feels that his is one of the best departments in the school and it would be a pity if some mention was not made in the final report. And, of course, it would be good for the head of music to retire with a confirmation from OFSTED of his excellent teaching – to leave on a high, so to speak.'

Reluctantly, I agreed and, having studied the section on music in the *Framework for Inspection*, the following morning I observed the first music lesson of the week. The classroom was bright, orderly and well equipped, the students were attentive and knowledgeable, and the teaching was excellent. I had no reservations in assessing the lesson as one of the very best.

'I am so pleased I got someone who knew what he was talking about,' the head of music told me later in the staff room. 'You hear all these stories of school inspectors with little or no idea of the subjects they are inspecting.' I smiled weakly. 'Were you at the Royal College of Music, by the way?' he asked. 'That's where I studied.' I shook my head. I felt it politic not to inform him that my expertise in his subject was gleaned from a Grade 3 pianoforte examination and from the fact that I could play any tune in the key of D. I also knew four chords on the ukulele and, at a pinch, could play 'When I'm Cleaning Windows'.

The team of inspectors attended the head of music's final concert, a rousing and an emotional affair. Prior to the performance, we were detained by the head teacher until the school hall was full with parents, staff and students, and the instrumentalists had assembled on stage. Then, as we were led by her down the central aisle to the front, to sit on the front row, the band struck up with 'Colonel Bogie'. The head of the music department glanced in my direction and smiled. I have an idea the march was in the key of D.

Behind the Staff Room Door

The head teacher asked me to wait in the staff room.

'I need to see a parent,' she explained, 'but I will be with you directly.'

I was at the large inner-city primary school to collect various documents to read over the weekend, prior to my inspecting the school the following week. The staff room was uncomfortably warm and cluttered, the walls full of various dog-eared charts, posters and guidelines. Unwashed crockery filled a bowl in the corner sink, above which hissed and bubbled an old geyser. There was an assortment of shabby hard-backed chairs arranged around a coffee table, the top of which was hidden beneath an untidy pile of exercise books, magazines and folders. A larger table, free of clutter, occupied a space near the window. My first impressions were not good ones. I sat in a threadbare armchair.

The bell sounded for morning break. The first person to enter the room was a tall thin woman with a pale melancholy beaked face. Her prim white blouse was buttoned up to the neck and she wore a grey pencil skirt from which protruded skeletal legs. Thick white hair was twisted up untidily on her head and speared with what looked like wooden meat skewers. She stared at me for a moment before speaking. 'Would you mind moving?' she said. 'You're sitting in my chair.'

'There are many chairs,' I replied pleasantly.

She bristled. 'I am aware of that,' she said, drawing in her breath, 'but that is my chair. I always sit in it.'

'I see,' I said.

'I have been a teacher in the school for twenty years,' she told me, 'and I always sit in that chair.' When I remained where I was, she fixed me with a piercing stare. 'So will you move?' she said, petulantly. I slowly got to my feet and sat in the adjacent chair. 'And don't set your books up on that table,' she continued, sitting down. 'We have our coffee on there.'

'And who do you imagine I am?' I asked.

'You're the book rep, aren't you?'

'No,' I replied. 'I'm the school inspector who will be observing lessons next week.'

If she was surprised she didn't show it, and she shuffled in her seat. 'Well, I assume you know what sort of children we have in this school?'

'I've read a little about them,' I told her.

'We have quite a number of council-estate children and travellers in our catchment area, and all the social problems they bring with them.'

'I beg your pardon?'

'Council-estate children and travellers,' she repeated. 'You know what they can be like.'

'Do I?' I asked.

She sighed. 'Have you taught these sort of children?' she asked, truculently.

'I have,' I told her. 'And they are like any other group of children, aren't they? They can be delightful, good-humoured and well behaved and sometimes can be difficult and challenging.'

'You will find ours fall into the latter category,' she said. Her tone was peevish. 'We have a great many problems with the estate children and travellers. The standards of reading and number work are poor and their achievements very low. I hope you are not expecting a great deal of them.'

'I am of the opinion that is exactly what teachers should do,' I said.

'What?' she asked, tight-lipped.

'Expect a great deal of the children they teach,' I told her, 'however disadvantaged and demanding they might be.'

She allowed herself a small smile. It was not a pleasant smile. 'Really,' she said and rose from her chair, like a queen from her throne, to make herself a cup of coffee.

Had I had the power, I would have taken the woman and her chair and left her in the playground. No children, however ill-favoured, damaged or badly behaved, should be written off by a teacher. Children are too precious to be tarnished by such sour empty critics who expect little of their charges and tarnish them with a rusty cynicism. As Bishop William Temple wrote:

> Until education has done far more work than it has had an opportunity of doing, you cannot have society organised on the basis of justice . . . Are you going to treat a man as what he is, or as what he might be? Morality requires, I think, that you should treat him as what he might be, as what he has it in him to become . . . That is the whole work of education. Give him the full development of his powers; and there will no longer be that conflict between the claim of the man as he is and the claim of the man as he might become.

The Point of Education

One of my favourite quotes about the very purposes of education is contained in a letter which Haim Ginott, when he was principal in an American high school, sent to every new teacher to help him or her understand the school's ethos:

Dear Teacher

I am the victim of a concentration camp. My eyes have seen what no man should witness: gas chambers built by learned engineers; children poisoned by educated physicians; infants killed by trained nurses; women and babies shot and burned by high school graduates. So I am suspicious of education. My request is this: help your students to become humane. Your efforts must never produce learned monsters, skilled psychopaths, educated Eichmanns. Reading, writing and mathematics are important only if they serve to make our children more humane.

At a time when the Government seems obsessed with league tables and targets, SAT results and risk assessments, OFSTED inspections and ceaseless teacher evaluation, and intent on covering schools with a snowstorm of paperwork, it is good to know that some schools go beyond the statutory curriculum, involve the pupils in exciting and innovative projects and endeavour to do what Ginott exhorts – to help young people to become more compassionate and caring.

I was asked to launch the splendid book *Ending the Slave Trade with William Wilberforce of Hull* at the Hull Street Life Museum. Supported throughout by the writer and lecturer John Haden, the children at St Nicholas Primary School researched, wrote and illustrated their own accounts of the slave trade, and narrated the story of the life and work of the city's most famous son. In undertaking such a project, they gained a real insight into the dreadful trade and learnt about the part Wilberforce played in bringing it to an end. They also learnt that slavery is still big business around the world (there are more slaves today than were seized from Africa in four centuries of the trans-Atlantic trade) and that slavery does not just exist in far-off places like Brazil, where children are sold into servitude, but that there is people-trafficking in this country.

At the launch, teachers, parents, education officers and invited guests listened in silence as the children sang a selection of traditional slave songs and laments. They heard about the horrors of this shameful trade and of the courage, dedication and persistence of William Wilberforce, who spent his life working for its abolition. It was an immensely powerful and moving experience.

'The Happiest Days of Your Life'

Schooldays

'George, Don't Do That!'

On a visit to the Doncaster Civic Theatre, my wife Christine and I lost ourselves in a wonderfully nostalgic evening filled with a gentle humour we so much enjoy. Caroline Fields, from the BBC Radio 2 programme, *Friday Night is Music Night*, delighted her audience with sketches and songs written and once performed by the inimitable Joyce Grenfell. There was the brilliantly written 'A Terrible Worrier' and the hilarious 'Old Girls' Reunion', but the show-stopper for me was the unforgettable 'Nursery School Sketches', delivered superbly by Caroline.

Joyce Grenfell's perfectly observed nursery school teacher keeps a simmering control over her temper when trying to deal with the recalcitrant infants. As the children's behaviour deteriorates, the teacher's tone becomes jollier and falser, or, as Joyce herself writes: 'the bright, bluffingly calm, cheerful encouraging manner becomes increasingly desperate.' Those of us who have spent a lifetime in the company of children know only too well how she feels, faced with the little Shirleens and Chardonnays, the Georges and Sidneys of the world.

Joyce Grenfell loved what she called 'young children's observations, discoveries and individualities', and was fascinated by the way that 'young children can invariably surprise, confound and delight'.

I have met many an anarchic infant like Sidney and Chardonnay on my visits to schools. One rosy-faced little boy, called Duane, certainly surprised and confounded the teacher at Story Time, but 'delight' is not the word that immediately sprang to mind.

'This morning's story, children,' began an infant teacher, 'is the story of 'The Three Little Pigs'.'

'I've 'eard it,' said Duane, exploring his nostril with an index finger.

'Really, Duane, that's nice,' said the teacher, in true Joyce Grenfell fashion.

'It's all abaat this wolf what gobbles up all these stupid pigs.'

'Just listen, Duane,' said the teacher, smiling wanly.

'Little pig, little pig,' began the infant, in the voice of Tommy Cooper, 'let me in or I'll 'uff and I'll puff an' I'll blow yer 'ouse in.'

'Duane,' interrupted the teacher, '*I'm* telling the story.'

'But I've 'eard it.'

The smile on the teacher's face was fixed. 'Well, now you are going to hear it again.'

'Burr I know wor 'appens,' the child told her.

'So you said,' observed the teacher, *sotto voce*.

She continued with the age-old story of the foolish pigs that built their houses of straw and sticks and were then gobbled up by the wolf.

'Then the Big Bad Wolf came to the house of bricks. He crept down the little path on his bristly grey legs and came to the door and scratched on it with his long sharp claws. "Little pig," he growled, "little pig, let me in, or by the hair on my chinny, chin chin, I'll huff and I'll puff and I'll blow your house in."'

''E dunt gerrin,' volunteered Duane.

'Thank you, Duane,' said the teacher trying to stay calm.

''E tries gerrin in t'winder burr 'e can't gerrin.'

'Duane,' said the teacher sharply.

''E gus on t'roof,' said the child.

'DUANE! Listen to the story!' snapped the teacher.

'Burr I know wor 'appens,' the child told her again.

'If you are a really good boy,' the teacher told him, 'you can tell us all what happens, but you must be quiet until near the end. The wolf climbed on the roof . . .' she continued.

'I said that,' added Duane.

The teacher decided to ignore the interruption. 'He looked down the chimney into the sooty darkness. "Little pig, little pig," he growled, "I am coming down the chimney to gobble you up."' The teacher paused. 'Now, Duane, what would you do if a wolf came down your chimney?'

'I'd shit myself,' replied the infant.

A Life in Rhymes

I had another long letter from Liam recently. Liam, aged thirteen, is a student at a college for the blind, and he wrote in Braille (with a translation) that he is really enjoying life there and doing well in his studies. He sent me his first published collection of poems, *My Life in Rhymes*, an inspirational anthology which makes the reader smile, think and sometimes feel a little sad. It was two years ago that I received his first letter with some of his excellent poems. The poems were heartfelt and sincere and inspired by his experiences of living with blindness and deafness.

In that first letter, he wrote: 'I am not enjoying school because I am being separated in most of the lessons. My favourite subject is science but it's impossible for me to learn. The experiments aren't accessible for me where you have to use sight to determine so much and handle dangerous equipment. The teachers use gestures and pictures and signs on the whiteboard and I cannot see these so learn little. I am excluded from cricket and rounders – health and safety issues they say. At break and lunchtimes all I do is walk around the playground with a support assistant. I have not had a friend since I started mainstream school.' Liam asked me if I could help realise his ambition to attend New College.

Along with his determined parents, Liz and Dean, his doctor, his psychologist and many other supporters, I wrote with my backing and, eventually, Liam was successful. I knew that Liam would be happy and would thrive at New College because I had inspected the establishment some years before.

I had visited New College with a team of HMI, and the OFSTED report we produced was excellent. Twenty years ago, blind students would no doubt would have been making lampshades and weaving baskets. Now they achieve as well, and often better, than their sighted peers, as a former Home Secretary and Secretary of State for Education from Yorkshire will vouch.

I remember meeting Ruth. She, like Liam, had been desperately unhappy during her time in a mainstream girls' high school. A clever, enthusiastic and good-humoured young woman, she had experienced a catalogue of indifference and unkindness from some of the other students. Chairs were deliberately placed in front of her so she would stumble into them, her greeting of 'Good morning' when she entered the classroom would be greeted by silence and few helped her as she went around the school. Ruth had no friends and led a lonely, unhappy life. Some of her teachers were sympathetic and the deputy head teacher frequently asked how she was getting along, but others were blatantly unfeeling and were irritable and lacked understanding. Someone suggested that Ruth really should not bother going on the Geography field trip because, she was told, 'you won't be able to see anything'. When her classmates were asked by the form tutor what were the most irritating things about being in the school one girl remarked, 'the blind girl with her white stick'.

At the college for the blind, Ruth had flourished, and was studying for four 'A' levels and hoping to study English at Cambridge. Her work was of a quite exceptional standard, as this poem, which I published in a collection, reveals:

I see with my ears.
I hear the leaves in the tall trees, whispering in the night.
I hear the sea, dark and deep, and the splash of the dolphin's
   leap.
I hear the flames crackling and the window frames rattling in
   the wind.
I see with my ears.
I see with my nose.
I smell the blossoms pearly-grey and hay new mown.
I smell the ploughed earth, cows in the byre, the smoky fire.
I smell Grandpa's pipe, Gran's lavender room and Mum's
   faint perfume.
I see with my nose.
I see with my mouth.
I taste the strong black coffee and the thick brown toffee
   between my teeth.
I taste the yellow of the lemon, the green of the melon and
   the red of the tomato.

I taste the orange of the carrot, the purple of the plum, the
    gold of the sun on my face.

I see with my mouth.

I see with my hands.

I feel the sharp edges, slippery floors, smooth ledges.

I feel lemonade in cold canisters, hard wooden banisters.

I feel hands to hold, arms on shoulders, faces to touch.

I see with my hands.

On Report

My mother was a hoarder, and I am so glad she was. After
her death, I discovered a treasure chest of letters, postcards,
swimming medals, badges and, to my delight, my school reports.
I guess I share with many others the common experience of
finding (with something of a shock) that my school reports
were by no means exceptional, but pretty lacklustre. My leaving
report from Broom Valley Juniors had the pithy and somewhat
ambiguous comment from J Leslie Morgan, the headmaster:
'Gervase is a little trier.'

School reports of the past make much more interesting reading
than present day examples. Modern school reports are often
produced from a standard 'Statement Bank', with key words and
phrases helpfully provided for the frazzled teacher, who has to
complete a comprehensive booklet on each pupil's attainment,
progress, conduct, contribution to school activities and significant
achievements, and fill in a whole grid of predicted grades. Such
earnest and restrained documents are anodyne compared with
those written in the past. Perhaps it is a good thing that the
funny, acerbic and sometimes brutal judgements have gone, but
they were much more entertaining.

In this litigious age, no teacher would dare write in such an
unprepossessing and sardonic manner as David Owen's master

at Bradfield College, who described the future political grandee as 'a scruffy urchin', or John Lennon's teacher at Quarry Bank School in Liverpool, who predicted that one of the world's most talented composers is 'certainly on the road to failure . . . hopeless . . . rather a clown in class'. Eric Morecambe's teacher at Lancaster Road Junior School forecast that the future great comedian 'will never get anywhere in life', and Jilly Cooper's teacher at Goldophin School in Salisbury resorted to sarcasm, something which was often favoured by the teachers of the past, when she wrote that 'Jilly sets herself an extremely low standard which she has failed to maintain'.

Some teachers predicted their pupils' future successes with great accuracy; others got it startlingly wrong. Winston Churchill's teacher at St George's, Ascot, asserted that the boy 'has no ambition' and the headmaster of Westminster, where Peter Ustinov spent his schooldays, remarked of his pupil: 'He shows great originality, which must be curbed at all costs.' Princess Diana's teacher at West Heath School recommended that, 'she must try to be less emotional in her dealings with others', and Judi Dench's teacher at The Mount School in York observed that she 'would be a very good pupil if she lived in this world'.

Recently, when I spoke at the Bradford Grammar School Old Bradfordians' Dinner, the president's wife said she well remembered the final, wonderfully terse comment on her school report: 'Sally must bestir herself.' An inspector colleague recalls his report for mathematics: 'Exam result 4 per cent. Effortlessly achieved.'

I was told the story of the housemaster at a Yorkshire public school who struggled to find something positive to say about a new boy on his end of term report. He wished to reassure the parents but felt he had to be honest in his assessment of his pupil, and it was proving very difficult. The boy had made no progress in any of his subjects, took no part in sports, lacked any musical ability and rarely contributed in class. The medical that all pupils underwent after the first term revealed that the boy, rather than shooting up in height like many of his adolescent peers, had in fact shrunk by an inch. This helped the housemaster out of his dilemma and he could truthfully report that: 'Rupert appears to be settling down well.'

An Encounter

Now that I have got my bus pass, and wish to be a bit more environmentally friendly, I have decided to make greater use of public transport. The bus from the village where I live into Doncaster is comfortable, smoke free and regular, and, after nine o'clock, I can travel free of charge.

Last market day, I took the bus into town and was wandering around Market Place when a loud voice stopped me in my tracks.

'Hey up, Mester Phinn!'

It was a young man behind a large fruit and vegetable stall.

He saw the look of incomprehension on my face, so reminded me. 'It's me – Jason. Tha' use' to teach me.'

'Ah yes, Jason,' I said, recognising in the large bearded face the boy I used to try to teach English.

'I were no scholar, were I Mester Phinn? Left school wi'out a certificate in owt.'

'You were a good lad, Jason,' I said, remembering the good-humoured and friendly ex-pupil who caused me no bother.

'Come over 'ere, Mester Phinn, and I'll sort you out wi' some fruit.' He then proceeded to fill brown paper bags with apples and oranges, pears and plums. Then he held up a banana and laughed. 'Does tha remember t'incident wi' t'banana?'

I smiled at the memory. Jason's French teacher had a bowl of plastic fruit on her desk. She would hold up an apple and ask, '*Qu'est-ce que c'est?*', and students were supposed to shout back, '*C'est une pomme*'. Then she'd pick up a pear and ask, '*Qu'est-ce que c'est?*', and they would shout back, '*C'est une poire*'. Once, she had a plastic banana in her hand. '*Qu'est-ce que c'est?*' she asked, but caught sight of Jason talking at the back of the classroom and let fly with the visual aid. The banana arced through the air like a missile and hit the boy straight between the eyes. It then ricocheted off his forehead and flew back to her like a boomerang. The teacher put up her hand and caught it. All the class jumped to its feet and gave her a standing ovation. Jason was, of course, sent to me, but, having related the story of the banana, must have seen by my expression and the stifling of a smile how amused I was.

'So you're a greengrocer then, Jason?' I asked now.

'Aye, in a manner o' speakin'. I've six market stalls. "High Class Fruit and Vegetables". Started wi' one stall in t'outdoor market and built up ovver t'last few years. I 'ave twenty folk workin' for me now.'

'You've done really well.' I said. 'I'm really pleased for you.'

At this point, drops of rain began to fall.

'It's goin' to chuck it down in a minute, by t'looks on it,' Jason said, staring at the grey sky. 'Are you in yer car, Mester Phinn, or can I give you a lift?'

'I came into town by bus,' I told him, 'It's very kind of you to offer me a lift but . . .'

'Nay, not a bit of it, Mester Phinn,' he interrupted. 'I'm knockin' off for t'day any road. I can go that way 'ome.'

I made my way to a small white van with his name printed in bold letters on the side, but Jason called me back. 'Nay, nay, Mester Phinn, I'm not in t'van.' He opened the door of a brilliant white, shining sports car with tinted windows. My astonishment must have shown. 'I can see that tha' thinking, "What's a gret big bloke like 'im doin' driving a piddling little car like that?" Well, I'll tell thee. Wife's got t'Merc today, so I've got 'ers. Come on, Mester Phinn, before tha' gets soakin' wet.'

The Man in the Box

When I was a lad (I can hear my children wincing), my school seemed to be populated by eccentrics. There was 'Snotty' Wilson, the teacher who used to wipe his nose on the sleeve of his gown, having taken a generous pinch of snuff, and one nicknamed Dr Death, whose white skin stretched across his bony face to give it the appearance of a skull, a deeply frightening teacher who talked in whispers. There was 'Cliff' Davis, the chain-smoking head of PE, who put the fear of God into everyone, and 'Smiler' Simcox, who leered at you over steel-framed spectacles with a grin as wide as a frog's.

The great eccentric seems to have disappeared from education. None of these weird and wonderful teachers would survive OFSTED, which, of course, has ensured a conformity and uniformity in everything. And yet these colourful characters made for an interesting, if not entirely unchallenging, life in school.

There are still one or two about, however. Perhaps the most memorable was the primary teacher with the wild, woolly hair and permanently startled expression, who employed a most original way of encouraging children to read. At the end of a 'sound' lesson, with 'satisfactory planning' and 'clear objectives', the teacher asked his Year 6 charges to join him on the carpet in the corner of the classroom for Story Time. He then proceeded to place a large cardboard box, which had been adapted to resemble a television set, on his head.

There was a cut-away square (the screen) and various felt blobs (the knobs).

'Turn me on,' he said pleasantly.

A large, amiable-looking boy came to the front and made a clicking sound as he 'turned him on'.

'Hello children,' began the teacher, in the voice of the *Jackanory* storyteller. 'Welcome to the world of story. My story today is about the child who could not cry.

'Once, many many years ago . . .'

We all sat completely transfixed. When the story ended, the large, amiable-looking boy headed for the front and 'turned him off'.

'You see, Mr Phinn,' explained the teacher later, with a wide, innocent expression, 'children these days live in a television culture. The average eleven-year-old watches thirty hours of television a week. I find that if I pretend to be a television set, children listen better.'

I smiled, wondering just what to say. 'Before I give you the feedback on the lesson, Mr Smith,' I began, 'perhaps you might remove the box.'

Risky Business

'Why are you all wearing goggles?' I asked a boy, during playtime at a primary school.

'We have to wear them,' he replied. 'If we don't, we might get a bit of conker in our eye.'

'We've scrapped the sack race this year,' explained the head teacher in another school. 'A child fell over last year and hurt himself.'

'We decided not to go to the castle,' a teacher told me. 'We did a risk assessment and we felt there were too many potential dangers.'

'I never let my child cycle to school,' said a parent to me. 'It's far too dangerous on the roads.'

'I drop my daughter off at school on my way to work and collect her every day,' another parent informed me. 'You have to be so careful these days with all these strange people about.'

Over-anxious adults who wrap children in cotton wool are doing the young no favours. I know the world is a very different place to the one in which I grew up but, if children are to develop a degree of independence and confidence and become equipped to cope effectively in an adult world, then they must be given some freedom and allowed to take a few risks.

As a child, I had a freedom denied to many children these days. I used to climb trees, walk on walls, paddle in streams, make dams and dens, sledge, play cricket and cycle without a helmet, get crushed in a rugby scrum, light fires, drink water from a garden hose, suck a sweet which had been in my pocket for a week, swing from the arms of lampposts, play marbles in the dust, jump off the top block at the swimming baths, play leapfrog, propel my home-made bogie (a trolley made from two planks and four pram wheels, with a bit of rope to steer it) down the hill – and all without adult supervision. I guess many people of my generation did the same and we managed to survive. Perhaps also, when we fell out of a tree or off the wall, scraping a knee or breaking a bone, by experiencing danger and seeing what happens to people who don't take sufficient care, we came to appreciate our own limitations. By suffering the consequences of our actions, we felt more in control of our lives and developed a sense of judgement.

In *Paranoid Parenting,* the sociologist Frank Furedi describes a culture of fear that has led parents to severely restrict their children's independent outdoor activities. In 1971, he states, 80 per cent of eight-year-olds were allowed to walk to school alone. Now it is fewer than 1 per cent.

Children should be allowed to take a few measured risks. Of course, we need to warn them of the dangers and not encourage them to be reckless or irresponsible, but let us not mollycoddle the young and erect fences between them and the world. My revered father-in-law, the celebrated 'Legs' Bentley who played rugby union for Yorkshire, once told me that he played the game for sheer physical exhilaration. He has been knocked out a few times and come off the pitch sore and bruised and bloodied but, as he told me, 'if you confront risk and go in with your eyes open, you are very often safer in the long run'.

Life is full of risks. If you laugh, you risk being thought silly; if you weep, you risk appearing mawkish; if you ask a question, you risk sounding foolish; if you show your feelings, you risk revealing your true self; if you try, you risk failure; if you tell someone you love them, you risk not being loved back. But the risk is worth taking, because the person who risks nothing has a pretty tedious life.

Playing Around

Young people should have the experience of performing in plays. It is a great disappointment that, in some schools, drama has been marginalised in the curriculum in favour of more 'useful subjects'. Those of us who have taken part in school plays and directed them know only too well the value of drama, through which young people can gain in confidence, develop their spoken English and work together. School plays are also great fun.

My interest in the theatre flourished when I joined the South Yorkshire Theatre for Youth at the age of fourteen. This was an amateur dramatic society for young people, formed by the Head of the English Department at Wath Grammar School. Bill Hammond was a charismatic, larger-than-life figure – one of the world's enthusiasts, a brilliant teacher with a passion for theatre. Over the summer holidays, for two intensive weeks, he would give up a fortnight of his holiday to rehearse young actors from all over the south of the county for a production which would be staged the following September, in Rotherham and Doncaster.

I loved the rehearsals, the camaraderie backstage, the sharing of jokes and anecdotes, the assignations and the attention-seeking exhibitionism which surrounded me. I loved watching my fellow actors going through their paces, listening to the producer shouting out directions, the smell of the theatre, the bright lights, the mugs of hot sweet tea and the bacon sandwiches and fizzy lemonade in the dressing rooms. I have never before in my life felt so much a part of such a group of like-minded, entertaining people.

The single most enjoyable experience in appearing in that first play was the sense of elation before and after the performance. Every night, my heart would race with expectation and be high with happiness. There is something very special and exhilarating about being a part of a company of actors backstage, listening to their exaggerated stories and the accents they put on, how they try to outdo each other with anecdotes and jokes and, above all, feeling the warmth of their companionship.

I remember seeing a brilliant production of *Anne of Green Gables* in a secondary school I was inspecting. The lead part of Anne, played by a plump, red-faced girl with protuberant blue eyes, was undertaken with great enthusiasm and confidence. Dressed in a bright blue and yellow gingham smock, she dominated the stage. After the performance, I was taken by the head of the drama department and the play's director to meet members of the cast.

'You were very confident,' I told the girl who had played the lead, 'and you did very well to remember all those words. It was a really impressive performance.'

'I do a lot of drama, actually,' she informed me loftily. 'I go to a Saturday stage school and I have a main part in *Annie* next week at the local theatre.' She was already well on her way to becoming a drama queen, I thought.

Then I caught sight of the pale, slight girl who had delivered the opening lines of the play.

'You were excellent,' I told her.

'I only had a few lines,' replied the child, smiling coyly.

'Ah,' I said, 'but you were the first person to speak and it was you who set the scene. We heard every word clearly and if I had an Oscar to award – you know, the prizes that very famous actors sometimes get – well, I would give it to you.'

'That was kind of you, Mr Phinn,' said the head of the drama department later, 'and if you only knew what that will do for that young lady's confidence. She is such a shy little thing and it took some persuading to get her to take part.'

'She deserved an Oscar,' I said. 'Anyone who could go on

to the stage, before all the other actors, beneath all the bright lights, in front of a hundred people and deliver such lines without making one mistake, deserves an Oscar.'

The teacher looked at me quizzically. 'In what way?' she asked.

I consulted my programme. 'I wrote down the words she had to say,' I replied, 'and I guess many of us would have had some difficulty declaiming them with such clarity.' I read the lines: '"Is Farmer Hart's farm far from here?"'

I was told some years ago by Graham Allen, the distinguished former drama adviser for Wakefield, about a school production of *Macbeth*. The sixth former playing the lead was another massively confident and rather self-satisfied young actor. Seyton, an officer attending Macbeth, was played by a small eleven-year-old who only had a very few lines to deliver. In Act V, he was to come on stage to inform Macbeth, 'The queen, my lord, is dead,' whereupon the devastated king would declaim his famous monologue. On the Thursday night, the little boy's relations took up the entire front row and, when he made his appearance, there was an audible noise from his fans. 'Look, it's our Darren,' came a voice from the audience. Seyton, aware that his family was there, developed his part somewhat and began rubbing his eyes, wailing piteously and beating his breast. 'The queen, my lord, oh, oh, the poor queen is dead. She's dead! Dead! Dead!' Then, to applause, he exited stage right.

Macbeth was far from happy after the performance.

'Say your line and get off,' he shouted at the boy, 'and cut out all that other stuff, because if you start that tomorrow night I'll kick you off the stage!'

It was the last night. Macbeth, alone on the battlements, sees his world crumbling about him.

'Wherefore was that cry?' he asks plaintively.

Enter Seyton.

'The queen, my lord,' he announces, 'is making a remarkable recovery.'

I guess it is not true but it makes a wonderful story.

Seeing Red

I recently shared a literary platform with Lucinda Dickens-Hawksley, the great, great, great granddaughter of Charles Dickens, who spoke about her latest book, *Lizzie Siddal, The Tragedy of a Pre-Raphaelite Supermodel*. This wonderfully entertaining and informative speaker gave a fascinating insight into the lives of the Pre-Raphaelite Brotherhood, and how they changed the public perception of those with red hair by their depiction of beautiful, Titian-haired women like Lizzie Siddal. Sadly, public perception has not changed very much and those with red or auburn hair still suffer mockery.

The mother who complained to Tesco about the offensive Christmas card for sale in their stores – showing a ginger-headed little boy sitting on Santa's knee, with the caption: 'Santa loves all kids. Even GINGER ones.' – had every right, and I too complained when visiting my local store. Anyone with red hair knows only too well how hurtful are such taunts as 'ginger nut', 'carrot top', 'ginger ninja' and 'copper knob'. I recall once visiting a school and commenting on the beautiful auburn hair of a child. 'I hate the colour,' she told me. 'People call me names.'

There has always been this ingrained prejudice against those with ginger hair. It was thought that Judas had red hair and, in Victorian times, there were many superstitions surrounding people with hair of this colour. Some people would not board a ship if there was a red-headed person on board, because he or she was thought be a jinx, and many mistresses would not employ servants with red hair, believing them to be deeply unlucky.

Following an article I wrote about bullying for the *Yorkshire Post*, I received a number of letters. One, an immensely sad letter, spoke of the reader's unmerciful bullying at school because of his red hair and freckles. When he approached his teacher about it, he was told to ignore the name-callers and that they would soon get tired, and anyway, coping with this sort of thing was part of growing up and learning to take the rough with the smooth. Clearly, the teacher had never been subject to such cruelty from his peers when he was at school.

Schools are places where children acquire much more than the principles, ideas and processes of a subject. They are formative little worlds, where children develop their social skills, learn to get along with others, make friendships and sometimes enemies. They are places where rules circumscribe their every move, where they discover, are hurt, feel lonely and experience success and failure, and where teachers loom large. In the good schools, they learn about love, beauty, compassion, goodness, co-operation, care and other positive human emotions and feelings. Children, however, even in the good schools, also learn the hard lessons of life; lessons about injustice, humiliation and cruelty, and sometimes, if they are unlucky, they come across the bully.

A measure of rough and tumble in a school builds a degree of immunity, and teaches us to stand up for ourselves. One can't expect children to be permanently pleasant with each other. We have all been name-called and called others names ourselves, but systematic cruelty in the form of constant bullying is a very different matter.

Bullies seek out their victims – those who are likely to be in some way different. It might be skin colour, physical appearance, a disability, the colour of one's hair or the way one speaks. For me, it was my name that set me apart.

Children can be a delight but they can also be corrosively mean and spiteful, and those of us who become the object of the bully's unwelcome attention remember for a lifetime those periods when it was our turn to be picked on.

When I was a school inspector I would ask children what they thought made a really good school. The answer came back again and again: 'No bullying.'

Parked Around the Back

Some years ago, I visited Ampleforth College. I had been invited by the then headmaster to attend a school drama production and the VIP reception beforehand. I duly arrived in good time and parked my car (an old black Volvo estate) in front of the main building.

Two young students, dressed in smart sports jackets and flannels, approached me.

'Would you mind parking around the back, sir?' said one, as I emerged from the car. 'This area is reserved for the VIPs.' I didn't enlighten them that I was there for the reception and had been told to park in this spot, but drove the car to where I was directed.

'You are rather early, sir,' said one of the boys. 'Would you like to look around the college?'

'That would be splendid,' I replied.

The two boys took me on a tour around the college, one of them explaining that on entering the library we should keep our voices down. There followed a short history of the college and abbey, details of the old boys and the sporting successes, and was told that much of the furniture and fittings were by the famous woodcarver, 'Mouseman' Thompson.

'And how are you finding the Volvo?' asked the other boy.

I explained that, with four young children, it was ideal. It was roomy and comfortable, a little heavy on petrol but very safe and reliable. It was getting on a bit, but had a good few miles left on it yet.

The boy, clearly something of an expert on cars, then proceeded to suggest various other vehicles in which I might be interested should I be changing the car.

Eventually, I admitted that I was expected at the headmaster's reception. The two boys looked horrified and apologised for asking me to park in the general car park.

'Not to worry,' I said. 'We have had a most interesting conversation. You were excellent guides.'

Schools can have all the glossy brochures they like, but the best advertisements are the students, they way they speak and behave. These two young men gave a splendid impression to a visitor: confident, courteous and good-humoured.

Some five years later, I took part in a BBC radio programme and was asked for a favourite piece of music to end. The track I chose, *Panis Angelicus*, was one featured on the superb Ampleforth College CD, *Spiritus*, performed by two young brothers. Listening to the piece sung in such beautiful clear voices made the hairs stand up on the back of my neck. I arranged to visit Ampleforth again, in the hope that I could arrange for two of the younger boys to perform the piece on the radio programme.

I parked my car (a smart new Toyota Avensis) in front of the main building, and climbed out. Two senior students in smart grey suits were walking past. One of them smiled.

'I see you've changed the Volvo, sir,' he said, smiling.

Paying a Visit

When I first visited the comprehensive school which my sons attended, the head teacher, Tony Storey, who had the distinction of being the country's oldest serving secondary head teacher, asked me if there was anything I wished to ask, or anywhere I would like to visit. 'The boys' toilets,' I told him.

'You are either a school inspector or a plumber,' he replied, smiling. I told him I was the latter.

The toilets were clean, well kept and free of graffiti and litter. There were locks on the cubicles, soap, paper towels and adequate toilet paper. I knew then that this was no 'bog-standard comprehensive', to use that ill-judged description, and was proved to be right. It turned out to be a first-rate school and my sons and daughter all did very well.

That same week, I visited a primary school in Carlton-in-Snaith and found the amenities of the same high standard. The building I entered was a bright, cheerful and welcoming one. Children's work of a high quality enhanced a busy, workmanlike environment. The head teacher, Peter Holgate, who had spent thirty or more years in the profession, gestured to a veritable tower of folders and files in the corner of his room.

'I get guidelines, recommendations, policy documents, circulars, questionnaires, reports, handbooks, strategies and I don't know what else, every week. I do wish people would not waste their time and money producing what has been said so many times before, and allow teachers to provide the best environment for learning and to get on with their teaching.'

He was right, of course; so much advice sent to schools has been given before. *The Handbook of Suggestions for Teachers*, produced by the Board of Education in 1936, is a far more sensible, intelligible and interesting publication than many of the recently produced directives which schools receive. For example, on the school itself is the paragraph:

The school cannot perform its functions adequately unless the premises themselves are an example of what we naturally associate with a civilised life. The building should be dignified and pleasing as well as conducive to health. The internal decorations should be bright and attractive with specimens of good craft work and suitably chosen

*pictures placed to best advantage. The school, moreover, should give
an impression of order and cleanliness, reflected for instance, in the care
of books and apparatus, in the proper storing of clothes in well-kept
cloakrooms, and in the tidy appearance of playgrounds and offices. The
school should, in short, be a source of comfort and inspiration to the
children while they are young, as a place where, for an important part
of their day, they can pursue their studies in a friendly, healthy and
civilising atmosphere.*

I was thinking of this paragraph when I visited a secondary
school the following week. It was quite a contrast: a run-down,
shabby-looking Colditz of a place, enclosed within high redbrick
walls. The corridors were bare, save for a few dog-eared posters
on the walls, and the rain had seeped through the roof, leaving
dark brown stains on the ceilings. In the boys' toilets, which
were smelly and dark, and bereft of soap and toilet paper, there
was a long list of pupils' names stretching down the back of one
cubicle door. The heading read: 'Sign here if you think this place
is a dump.' I was very tempted to add my name.

Off By Heart

Poetry took centre stage in primary schools across the country
with the launch of *Off By Heart*, an exciting BBC poetry
competition to find the pupil who could best recite a well-
known poem from memory. The winner performed his chosen
poem at Oxford last year, and I was delighted to be asked to
be the lead judge in the northern finals. It is good to celebrate
children's talents and achievements, particularly when all we
seem to read about are difficult and disaffected youngsters. I
was also pleased to be part of this initiative because I am a big
believer that children should know by heart some of the well-
known traditional verse.

I can still recite some of the poems I learnt as a child: the nursery rhymes and riddles, tongue twisters and nonsense verse. I still recall with great pleasure the occasions when, as a small child, I stood with my father at the kitchen sink as we washed and dried the dishes (which we called the 'pots'), and he would launch into a funny poem or a monologue; I thought he made them up.

I cannot say I was very keen when, at school, we were compelled to learn poems by heart. Now I am glad I did learn pieces of verse. As I travel down the motorway at dusk and see the moon high in the sky, I find myself reciting part of a remembered verse: 'the moon was a ghostly galleon tossed upon cloudy seas'. As I stroll along a pebbly shore, the words of a poem I learnt at school, where 'the flung spray and the blown spume, and the seagulls crying', come to mind. Late at night, when I look up at the dark and empty sky I recall the words of Walter de la Mare's beautiful poem: 'Slowly, silently, now the moon, walks the night in her silver shoon'.

Children, I have found, do enjoy learning poems if it is not made too much of a chore. They love showing off their talents and performing the poems, particularly before their proud parents at school concerts. The young contestants who took part in *Off By Heart* were a delight to hear, and performed with wonderful expression, gesture, perfect timing and great clarity and confidence. It was such a pleasure to hear the words of the great poets – Rudyard Kipling, William Wordsworth, Edward Lear, Hillaire Belloc, William Blake, Lewis Carroll, Walter de la Mare, A A Milne, T S Elliot, W B Yeats and many more – brought to life by young voices.

An inspector colleague of mine once visited a large primary school in the middle of a dreadfully depressing inner-city area. He found a nervous little boy in the corner of the classroom. When he asked if he could examine his book, the child looked at him with such large, sad eyes and said very quietly: 'No.' My colleague tried to coax him but the boy was adamant, saying that his work was not worth looking at. He couldn't spell, his writing was untidy and he never got good marks for his work. Eventually, he was persuaded to show his writing. The work was indeed of poor quality.

Then, at the very back of the book, the school inspector came upon a piece of writing in small crabbed print. The pupil was asked if he had written it. He nodded. He was asked if he had received any help with it. He shook his head. 'This is a small masterpiece,' the inspector told him, and he read it aloud with great feeling:

> Yesterday yesterday yesterday
> Sorrow sorrow sorrow
> Today today today
> Hope hope hope
> Tomorrow tomorrow tomorrow
> Love love love

'What a wonderful little poem,' the inspector remarked.

The boy thought for a while, stared up at the visitor with those large, sad eyes and announced: 'They're mi spelling corrections, sir.'

Playtime

I am patron, along with Professor Fletcher Ranney DuBois, of Queen Street School, in Barton-in-Humber. I recently shared a platform with this eminent educationalist, speaking to the friends and volunteer supporters who have tirelessly restored this remarkable and unique Victorian school. The building had remained derelict for almost thirty years and was destined to be demolished to make way for a car park. Thankfully, the Queen

Street Preservation Trust was established and, with help from the Heritage Lottery Fund, Yorkshire Forward, English Heritage and various other bodies, it has been faithfully recreated as a unique infant schoolroom, with tiered seating, gas lighting, an open fire, blackboard, slates, old desks, Victorian privy, playground and garden. It is now open to the public and is a small gem.

A principal aim of those wishing to preserve Queen Street and restore it was to revive the reputation of the nineteenth-century pioneering educationalist, Samuel Wilderspin, whose work provided the model for infant schools in Europe and America, and who is credited with the invention of the playground. Wilderspin, at a time when discipline in schools was strict and sometimes brutal, believed passionately that a child should be encouraged to learn through experience and in the development of feelings as well as intellect. Children, he believed, were born inherently good and deserved the very best models of behaviour from teachers and parents. Schools should be, for the most vulnerable and impoverished children, what the home is for the most fortunate: a place where there is work but where there is also laughter; a place where there is law but also where there is grace; a place where there is justice but where there is also love. He also believed in the educational value of play.

I was saddened to read that a new school has been built with every conceivable electronic resource and energy-saving device, but without a playground, for, as the head teacher remarked, in the twenty-first century, better use could be made of the space and anyway, playgrounds are not really necessary in 'a learning centre'. Then there is the head teacher of the infant school who has done away with the play area in the infant classroom to concentrate on more formal teaching approaches. It is regrettable that the 'home corner', where children can dress up, get into role, practise talking, reading, writing and acting out parts, is regarded by some as merely decorating the margins of the serious business of study.

Play, as Wilderspin was at great pains to stress, is of great importance for the developing child. He knew, as good teachers do today, nearly 150 years after his death, that play develops the imagination, promotes creativity, thinking, fruitful talk, co-operation and much, much more.

In one infant school, I met a stocky six-year-old boy dressed in a large blue apron, standing outside his little café in the home corner. I seated myself at the small melamine table and looked at a blank piece of paper, at the top of which was written, in bold lettering: menu. The little boy sidled up, and stared at me intently. I looked up.

'What's it to be?' he asked.

'Oh,' I said, taking on the role of a customer, 'I think I'll just have something to drink.'

The boy disappeared, and returned a moment later with a small, empty, plastic beaker, which he placed before me. Then he watched intently as I drank the imaginary liquid, licked my lips and exclaimed: 'That was the nicest cup of tea I have had in a long while.'

'It's an 'arf o' bitter,' he told me bluntly, and walked off.

It would have brought a smile, I am sure, to Samuel Wilderspin.

With Onions

I was teaching a class of eleven-year-olds in a Dales primary school. I was using a selection of stuffed animals – badger, mole, rabbit, stoat and fox cub – as stimuli and hoped that, by the end of the morning, the children would have produced some short, interesting descriptive poems. I spent a good ten minutes talking about the creatures but it soon became clear that these children, mostly from farming backgrounds, knew a whole lot more about them than me.

The previous week I had taught the same lesson in a school in Harrogate, and the children had produced rather trite and sentimental pieces of verse about little, soft-furred moles, adorable little dormice, gambolling rabbits or playful squirrels. The poems the children wrote in the Dales primary school that morning were very different – blunt, realistic descriptions of the animals that they knew so much about. They clearly did not need stuffed animals to prompt them. There were images of 'fierce, sharp-toothed badgers', 'crows which picked at the dead animals on the road', 'fat, black rats that hid in the hay' and 'red foxes creeping behind the hen coop'. Thomas's effort was quite clearly the best:

On a frosty morning, my granddad
Takes his Jill to catch rabbits.
She has a little blue collar and a silver bell,
Tiny red eyes and creamy fur,
And she trembles in his hands.

'Thomas lives on the farm at the top of the dale,' explained his teacher, as we headed in the direction of the school hall for lunch. 'Like most farming children, he's been brought up to be unsentimental about animals. They are on the farm for a purpose, not as pets, and any creature which affects their livelihood is regarded as a pest. You should hear what he's got to say about foxes.' She paused for a moment, before adding:

'Thomas has a great deal to say for himself, hasn't he?'

At lunch, I sat between Thomas and an angelic-looking little girl. The boy surveyed me. 'Meat and tatey pie for lunch,' he said, rubbing his hands. 'My favourite.' He stared at me for a moment. 'I reckon you won't be 'aving any.'

'Why is that?' I asked, intrigued.

'You're probably one of those vegetarians. Me granddad doesn't like vegetarians. He says they take the meat out of his mouth. "There's nothing better than a good bit o' beef on your plate or a nice bit o' pork on your fork." That's what my granddad says. He doesn't like vegetarians, my granddad.'

Before I could inform Thomas that I was not, in fact, a vegetarian, the little angel sitting next to me whispered shyly, 'I like rabbits.'

'So do I,' I replied.

'My daddy likes rabbits too.'

'Does he?'

'And my mummy likes rabbits.'

'That's nice.'

She took a mouthful of meat and potato pie before adding quietly, 'They taste really good with onions.'

Sent to the Head Teacher

You again, Farringdon!

Yes, sir.

Can't you stay out of trouble?

I try, sir.

Well, you don't try very hard, do you?

I suppose not, sir.

Three times this week you have been sent to my room.

That's right, sir.

For getting into trouble.

Yes, sir.

You're a nuisance, Farringdon.

Yes, sir.

A teachers' nightmare!

Yes, sir.

A difficult, disruptive, disobedient boy.

Yes, sir.

A naughty, wayward, badly behaved young man.

Yes, sir.

A trouble, a torment, the bane of my life!

If you say so, sir.

I do, Farringdon! I do!

Yes, sir.

And when I leave next week, Farringdon.

Yes, sir?

I shall not be sorry if I never ever see you again!

I see, sir.

Well, what is it this time?

I've brought you a leaving card, sir — to wish you good luck in your new job.

'The Wonder Years'

The Magic of Childhood

To Be a Child

Young children are a delight. The small child knows nothing of skin colour, rank, status, religion, money and the many other things that are at the root of envy and discord. For the little one, everything in the world is fresh, colourful and exciting. Smile at a small child and invariably the smile is returned.

After forty years in education, as a teacher and school inspector, I have met countless numbers of children and been genuinely entertained, amused and, on occasions, greatly moved by them.

I recall the small child of six, with hair like a bristly lavatory brush, who mused, 'Have you ever thought that, when I'm twenty-one, you'll probably be dead?', and the child emerging from the infant school, informing the VIPs there to see the Nativity play that: 'It's off! Virgin Mary's got nits!'

There was the little angel with her dolly clutched to her chest, who told me when I approached her in the infant classroom, to: 'Go away! I'm breast feeding.' There was the four-year-old I came across in the nursery department at an infant school, inside a huge cardboard box. 'Brmm, brmm, brmm,' he went, and the box moved from side to side. I peered over the top and asked the child: 'Are you in your racing car?'

'No,' he replied seriously, 'I'm in a cardboard box.'

In a small primary school, I commented on the writing of a seven-year-old girl.

'Your writing is very neat and tidy at the top of the page,' I observed, 'but it goes all squiggly at the bottom.'

'I know,' replied the child, looking up. 'This pen's got a life of its own.'

'I know how to mek babies,' a young boy of nine informed me when I visited a school in Swaledale.

'Really?' I sighed.

'Do you know how to mek babies?' he asked.

'I do,' I replied.

'Well, how do you mek babies?'

'You go first,' I told him.

'I knock off the "y" and put "ies".'

I was inspecting a primary school in Wensleydale, and thought I would test a youngster on his number work. We looked out of the classroom window at the spectacular panorama before us.

'How many sheep can you see in that field?' I asked.

'All of 'em,' he replied.

Young children are nothing if not honest, and their honesty is invariably disarming and comical. At a time in the world where everything seems so gloomy and depressing and there is constant conflict and violence, the words of small children lift our spirits, they help us to feel good about ourselves and others and they make us optimistic for the future.

Out of the Mouths

I recently became a grandfather for the second time. Nina, my daughter-in-law, gave birth to a bonny little girl with large round eyes and a captivating smile. Her parents were intending to call the baby Scarlett. What a relief it was for me when they decided on the name Megan. Scarlett Phinn sounds to me like a disease of tropical fish. When I became a grandfather for the first time, my preferred name for the baby boy was Sebastian. Perhaps understandably, it was not my son and daughter-in-law's. 'One unusual name in the family is quite enough,' said my son Richard. I once heard Lord Sebastian Coe speaking at a dinner and he confided in the audience that: 'When you grow up in Sheffield with a name like Sebastian, you have to learn to run.' Well, what about being brought up in Rotherham with a name like Gervase? I could tell him a few tales.

Anyway, here I am in my sixties, a grandfather, and like a child myself. I have so many things planned for little Harry John Gervase and Megan Rose. We will walk along the beach at Bridlington, paddling in the sea, getting sand between their little toes. We will explore rock pools for crabs, collect shells and bits of smooth coloured sea glass, eat sticky candyfloss and feed the screeching seagulls on the harbour wall. They will snuggle up with Grandpa for a bedtime story, help Granny make gingerbread men, squeal with delight at the pantomime and do all the other things little ones so love to do. Everything for them will be bright and new and exciting.

Of course, my little grandchildren will also make the shrewdest observations as they grow older, as all young children tend to do: 'Grandpa, your face needs ironing', 'Oh, I do like the smell of old age', 'Daddy, that fat lady needs to go on a diet.' And they will confound me with the most difficult questions that innocent children frequently ask: 'Why are holes empty?', 'Why are bananas bent?', 'Why do you have to talk to God with your eyes closed?', 'Grandpa, who will fetch the fish and chips when you're dead?', 'Why can't *we* walk and wee at the same time like cows do?', 'Grandpa, why are there more idiots on the road when Daddy's driving?'

When Princess Diana visited the North, crowds came to see her. She knew young children well and had a great empathy with them. Seeing, among the children thronging to give her flowers, a rather sad little boy with hair like a lavatory brush and a small green candle appearing from a crusty nostril, she went straight to him. He was holding a single wilting bloom. She singled him out and, bending low, took the flower and ruffled the child's hair affectionately. 'And have you had the day off school to see me?' she asked the child, giving him one of her stunning smiles. 'No,' he replied bluntly, 'I've been sent home with nits!'

Something Colourful

I do like bright colours. Red, in particular, is such a cheerful, uplifting hue. Young children also like bright colours. One only has to see their paintings, so full of bold reds, vivid greens and bright blues, to appreciate this.

In an infant school, I once encountered a serious-faced little girl with more paint on herself than on the large piece of paper in front of her. She had drawn what I thought was a snake. The long, multicoloured creature curled and twisted across the page like a writhing serpent from a fairy story. It was a small masterpiece, with intricate patterning and delightful detail.

'That's beautiful,' I told her.

She looked up and eyed me solemnly. 'Is it?' she asked.

'Oh yes,' I replied. 'See how your snake wriggles across the paper.'

'It's not a snake,' the child told me, putting down her brush and folding her little arms across her chest. 'It's a road.'

'It looks like a snake to me.'

'Well, it's not,' she told me pertly. 'It's a road. I know because I painted it.'

'Ah, yes, I can see now,' I said tactfully. 'It's a magical road that twists and turns up into the grey sky and through ragged clouds and to the ice palace, where the Ice Queen herself sits on her crystal throne. She has a face as white as snow and long nails as sharp as icicles.'

The child stared at the picture for a moment and then at me. 'No, it isn't,' she said. 'It's an ordinary road.'

'It looks like a magical road to me.'

'Well, it isn't,' said the child. 'It's an ordinary road.'

'But it's full of greens and reds and blues. It looks like a magical road.'

'I've told you,' said the child, sighing. 'It's an ordinary road and it doesn't lead to any ice palace.'

'Why all the colours?' I asked, intrigued.

Her finger traced the curve of the road. 'Those are the diamonds and those are the rubies and those are the emeralds,' she explained.

'It *is* a magical road!' I teased.

'No, it's not,' the child replied, 'it's a jewel carriageway.'

It was during that school visit that I was joined on the team by a fellow school inspector from Lancashire. I had not met John before, and telephoned him prior to the inspection to say we would meet in the school entrance on the Monday morning at eight o'clock.

'And be sure to wear something cheerful,' I said. 'You know how young children like bright colours, and it is a little daunting for them if we all appear in grey suits and dark ties.'

On the morning of the inspection, Joyce, the inspector for mathematics, approached me.

'Gervase,' she said quietly, 'what did you tell that inspector from Lancashire to wear?'

'Why?' I asked.

'Well, I've just passed Coco the Clown in the entrance,' she told me.

John, I soon discovered, was dressed in a smart navy jacket with bright brass buttons, pristine white trousers, fuchsia pink shirt and a blue polka-dot bow tie.

'Will I do?' he asked amiably.

Before I could reply, a passing infant stopped, stared at him for a moment and then, taking his hand, departed with him down the corridor. 'Come with me,' she said. 'I'll look after you.'

At morning break I asked my colourful colleague from the Red Rose County where he had got to.

'Well,' he said, smiling widely, 'that little girl took me to the school office and told the secretary that she had just found Willy Wonka.'

Growing Pains

Young people nowadays tend to get a bad press. Newspapers often feature articles about the unruly youth of today, the 'hoodies' and the 'yobbos', the football hooligans and lager louts, the rude, the selfish and the aggressive. It is frequently said that if they perform well in their examinations then it's because the exams are easier these days. If they do not perform well then it's an indication of the steady decline in standards. They just can't win. 'It wasn't like that when I was young,' you will hear the older generation say. It is a fact, of course, that young people down the centuries have included those who have kicked over the traces, misbehaved, been unruly and recalcitrant, ignored the advice of their elders and been in want of some good old-fashioned discipline.

What tends to be forgotten is that there are thousands of young people who come from loving, supportive homes, are taught by dedicated and enthusiastic teachers and are a credit to their homes and schools. And some have their crosses to bear, and do so without complaint.

I met Rebecca in a comprehensive school in Sheffield. She was studying for her ten GCSEs and had a Saturday job in a shoe shop, to earn a bit of extra money to supplement the disability allowance her mother received. Rebecca was a carer. She looked after her mother, who was crippled with a debilitating disease, and she washed, cooked, cleaned and dealt with the bills. This bubbly, unself-pitying, good-humoured young woman had little social life and, although her friends were sympathetic, they had stopped inviting her to be part of the activities teenagers enjoy because, invariably, she was unable to join them given her commitments at home.

'You have a challenging and demanding life,' I told her.

She smiled. 'Not half as challenging and demanding as my mother's,' she replied.

Matty was six, and stood out from the rest of the children in his infant class. His skin looked unhealthily pale and his untidy, greasy hair was clearly unwashed. There were milk stains down his jumper and his trainers were grubby. He was one of the sad, fragile children whom I had come across on my travels as a school inspector – children who are neglected, disparaged, damaged and sometimes abused, children who would never know the warmth, encouragement and love of a good home.

'He's such a sad little boy,' explained the head teacher. 'Can you imagine a child of his age having to get himself up in the morning, come to school without any breakfast, unwashed, in the same coat he has had for two years and which is now far too small for him? A child so smelly that none of the other children will sit near him or play with him, a child who watches all the other mummies collect their children from school but who has to walk his lonely way home alone, to a cold, empty house? Poor child hasn't a chance, has he? Is it any wonder he steals and spits and gets into fights? He's never been shown any different. You know, some children come from homes where there is acceptable behaviour and positive attitudes to others, where there's laughter and love and lots of books. And then there are some children, like Matty, who get nothing. Of course, it's the same old story: poverty, inadequate parenting, absentee father, string of stepfathers. There are drugs, of course, and, I suspect, violence.'

On my visit to Matty's school, just before Christmas, I was asked to tell the children the story of the birth of Jesus. Little Matty sat cross-legged and wide-eyed before me, a little apart from the others. There was the unpleasant smell of an unwashed body in the air.

'Baby Jesus was born in a stable, a cattle shed,' I explained, 'and he had a manger for a bed. It wouldn't have been nice and clean and bright, like the crib in shopping centre. The stable in which Baby Jesus was born would have been full of rather smelly, noisy animals, mice and rats and dirty hay. There was no room in the inn, you see, so Mary and Joseph had to stay in the stable and it didn't have lovely furniture and carpets and central heating. Mary had to have her baby in a cold, dark barn,' I continued. 'He had no nice new clothes, no toys and no cot. He came into the world with nothing. He was one of the poor and mean and lowly.'

Matty, who had been watching with eyes like saucers, shook his head slowly and said, quietly but with feeling: 'Poor little bugger.'

Perhaps more than any, he knew what it was to have very little.

I met Mark, aged twelve, at the college for the blind which he attended. He had lost his sight at ten and, amazingly, seemed to take it in his stride. He had a wonderful sense of humour and chatted away as if I were an old friend, explaining that he was very happy at the school, doing well in his work, and he hoped to be a teacher one day. I arrived at Mark's classroom before the children and, as inspectors are wont to do, ensconced myself in the corner as the teacher (who was sighted) nervously shuffled her papers. In came the students. Of course, they were not aware of the figure at the back.

'Miss,' asked Mark, 'will we be having one of these school inspectors in with us this morning?'

'We will indeed,' answered the teacher, glancing in my direction.

'Do you know who it will be, Miss?'

'His name's Mr Phinn.'

'Oh, I met *him* this morning, Miss,' cried the boy. 'He's from Yorkshire and he talks funny. He says, "Eee by gum!" '

'No he doesn't, Mark,' said the embarrassed teacher. 'Now sit down and get out your Brailler.'

'What does he look like, Miss?' persisted the boy.

'All these questions, Mark.'

'I've never met a school inspector before,' he continued, undeterred.

'Well, now's your chance.'

'Go on, Miss, tell me what he looks like. I want to put a face to his voice.'

'Well,' said the teacher, drawing out the word and looking again in my direction, with a mischievous smile on her lips, 'he's young, handsome, elegant, cultivated and very well dressed.'

Mark thought for a moment before replying: 'And he's also in the room, isn't he, Miss?'

Terry was bullied. I met him in the library of an inner-city school where he was leafing through a book on cars.

'They pick on me,' he told me, 'cos I'm little and don't give 'em what they want – money and sweets. I come in the library to get out of their way.'

'I think perhaps you should tell somebody at school,' I said.

'Naw,' he said dismissively. 'What's the use? They never do owt. You just 'ave to put up wi' it.'

'No, you don't,' I said. 'You don't have to put up with it. If you are being bullied you should tell someone you trust. Have you told your parents?'

'I'm fostered out,' he said. 'I've just started at a new place and don't want to cause no trouble.'

'You must never ignore bullying,' I said. 'It won't just go away. Something should be done about it. You should tell your foster parents.'

'Naw, it'd only mek things worse,' he replied.

'No, it wouldn't,' I said.

He looked at me and his face tightened. 'And how would you know? Have you been fostered, lived in a children's home, taken away from your mam, not allowed to see your little brother, always moving around from one place to another, switching schools, having to go to all these meetings when they talk about you? Then you get to this new school and all the teachers know you're in care and then everybody knows and you stand out and kids start to pick on you because you're different. Then they say things about your mam and where you come from and you get into a scrap and sent to the year tutor and you can see it in the teacher's eyes – "These kids are all the same – trouble."'

I listened to his outburst but couldn't reply. I really had no conception of the life this child led. What a sad, angry and troubled child he was.

'Will you promise me you will tell someone?' I said.

He looked up. 'I've told *you*, haven't I?' he said.

In a small primary school, in the heart of the Yorkshire Dales, I found a small boy who was putting the final touches to a written account of his father, and we got to talking. His mother had left when he was small, and he saw little of her. He saw nothing of his maternal grandparents. He felt sad about this and found it difficult to understand, but he was happy living with a father who, he said, was as much a friend as a parent. They did most things together. The account of his father described 'an ordinary-looking sort of man, a bit bald and overweight, the kind of man who wears shiny trousers, baggy cardigans and old slippers', but it went on to tell how special he was and how much he loved him.

'Your account is very honest,' I told him. 'Do you not mind sharing such personal details with other people?'

'Why should I?' he replied. 'It's the truth. I'm not ashamed of it. My father says it is always best to be honest.'

'He sounds a remarkable man, your father.'

'He is.'

There is a stereotype about the one-parent family. It is thought by some that children with only one parent are, inevitably, in some ways deprived, achieve worse at school than their peers and are likely to be more troublesome. Of course, in an ideal world, a child should have a mother and father, but in all relationships there is likely to be friction and discord and it is best sometimes for parents to part. Some children, like this young man, who have just the one parent looking after them, have a warm, loving, supportive and rich life. His father was indeed remarkable and his son was a credit to him.

'And what quality do you admire most in this very special father of yours?' I asked.

The boy thought for a moment, staring at his book and biting his bottom lip. Then he looked up and into my eyes. 'When *he* makes a mistake, my father says he's sorry. Grown-ups don't tend to do that. If my father gets it wrong, he says so. He says it's not being weak to admit you don't always get things right or that you don't know something.'

I thought of the strident television programme about rowdy and disobedient children I had seen recently. Those interviewed, who had little good to say about the younger generation, ought to meet this polite young student, so mature for his age.

'I hope that my children speak about me in the same way as you speak about your father,' I told him.

'That's really down to you, isn't it?' replied the boy, smiling broadly.

'Yes, I suppose it is,' I replied.

No Sort of Childhood

I met Richard McCann at a writers' reception in London. He struck me, at first meeting, as a good-humoured, confident, gregarious and unassuming young man, and we chatted about a number of inconsequential things until I got around to talking about his book, *Just a Boy*.

When I was just a boy I thought that all children had parents like mine: loving, funny, generous and ever-supportive; I thought that all children had mothers who told wild and wonderful tales, fathers who cracked jokes, played tricks and teased them gently. For as long as I could remember, since I was a small boy, I always felt valued and loved.

I discovered that Richard McCann's childhood could not have been different. One cold and misty October morning in 1975, at the age of five years old, he woke up to discoverer that his mother had gone forever. She was the first of the thirteen victims of the notorious 'Yorkshire Ripper', Peter Sutcliffe. Richard was told that his mother had been taken to heaven and he would never see her again. It was only when he was sixteen years old that he discovered where she was buried. His life had changed forever after his mother was murdered, for the tragedy was to trigger years of neglect, deprivation, abuse and pain. It led to drug addiction, a suicide attempt and prison. The child had already been placed on the 'at risk' register, and was sent to a children's home following his mother's death. After some months, he and his siblings were placed with their often cruel and violent father, who found he was unable to cope with four traumatised children. Richard has since forgiven his father for the harsh treatment he received as a child.

'It has been found,' wrote His Holiness The Dalai Lama, in *The Dalai Lama's Book of Love and Compassion*, that 'those children who grow up in homes where there is love and affection have a healthier physical development and study better at school. Conversely, those who lack human affection have more difficulty in developing physically and mentally. These children also find it difficult to show affection when they grow up, which is a great tragedy.' Few would disagree with these words.

What, then, is so remarkable about Richard McCann's inspirational story is that he not only survived a life of terrible deprivation and abuse, but he created for himself a life for which he so yearned – a life of security, compassion and love. He now uses his experiences to help others who have been subjected to neglect, and those who have rock-bottom self-esteem and little expectation from those around them, to show that they can achieve anything in life.

My wife and I recently heard Richard speak to a large group of adolescents in a comprehensive school in Doncaster. I have observed many a lesson as a school inspector but never have I seen young people so engrossed. Several were moved to tears. 'Life is sometimes uncomfortable,' he told them, 'sometimes so painful it becomes almost unbearable, but you must never let those setbacks, however terrible, hold you back. Things in life sometimes don't work out the way you expect but, with self-belief, determination and perseverance, you can overcome.' His unflinching and unself-pitying account of his life should be read by every parent and teacher, and young people in schools should have the opportunity of hearing him tell his inspirational story.

Suffer Little Children

I was once prevailed upon, by an infant school head teacher, to play Father Christmas. Nervously, I donned the bright red costume, cotton-wool beard and Wellington boots, and, after a strong cup of coffee, entered the hall to find row upon row of open-mouthed, wide-eyed children. They squealed in delight when they saw the familiar red coat and white beard. Everything went well until a rather grubby little scrap asked if she could sit on my knee.

'No, Chelsea,' said the head teacher, firmly. 'I don't think . . .' She was too late; the child had already clambered up, and now clung to me like a little monkey. The unpleasant smell of the unwashed emanated from her. She gave me a great big hug.

'I love you, Father Christmas,' she whispered in my ear.

'Come on down, Chelsea,' said the head teacher. 'I don't think Father Christmas wants children on his knee.'

'Now, you be a very good little girl and sit on the floor, Chelsea,' I said, in my jolly voice, 'otherwise all the other children will want to climb up.' Chelsea stayed put and held fast like a limpet. I chuckled uneasily, and left her until the child's teacher managed to prise her off.

Later, in the staff room, the school welfare officer, who had sat at the back of the hall, proffered an opinion. 'I don't think it's a very good idea,' she said, 'to have children on your knee. You have to be so careful these days.'

I feigned ignorance. 'In what way?'

'Pardon?'

'In what way do I have to be careful?'

'Well,' she told me, 'people might get the wrong idea.'

'How could people get the wrong idea?' I asked. 'I was in full view of an entire hall of children, seven members of staff and you.'

'It's just not appropriate any more,' she said.

A newly qualified member of staff told me later that, when she was training, a college tutor strongly advised the students that, when they became teachers, they should avoid cuddling a distressed child. People might get the wrong idea.

I read a newspaper report of two elderly women, Betty and Brenda, who were innocently taking photographs in a park near the paddling pool before being warned not to do so because people might get the wrong idea.

'We don't allow parents to film their children in the school

Nativity play any more,' I was told by one head teacher. 'We've had complaints from some parents. It's all very worrying.'

'Ah yes,' I said, with a degree of sarcasm in my voice. 'People might get the wrong idea.'

I was in church recently, for the christening of my great nephew, Giles William. The priest read from Mark, Chapter 10:

> People were bringing little children to him, for him to touch them.
>
> The disciples turned them away, but when Jesus saw this he was indignant and said to them, 'Let the little children come to me; do not stop them; for it is to such as these that the kingdom of God belongs. I tell you solemnly, anyone who does not welcome the kingdom of God like a little child will never enter it.' Then he put his arms around them, laid his hands on them and gave them his blessing.

Perhaps one of the disciples should have had a quiet word with Jesus later and advised him not to touch the children. After all, people might get the wrong idea.

Miss Reece and the Chicks

I walked down the school corridor in the infant department with Miss Reece, a newly qualified teacher. If she was at all daunted by the presence of the school inspector, she certainly didn't show it.

'I'll tell you this, Mr Phinn,' she told me, in a pronounced Welsh accent, 'if you think my lesson plan bears any resemblance to what I am doing today, then you have another think coming.'

'Really,' I said, rather taken aback.

'I did have a lesson planned for this morning and it was fab'lous but the head teacher says I can't do it because it's illegal.'

'Illegal!' I repeated.

'Yes indeed, illegal,' she informed me. 'He said that, under some new regulation from OFSTED, live creatures cannot be taken into the classroom any more. What with the bird flu and such he thinks it's against the Health and Safety Directive. So, I can't show the children my chicks. They will be so disappointed because I promised the children I would bring them in this morning.'

'Well, it's the first I've heard of such a directive,' I said. 'Were the children going to handle these chicks?' I asked.

'No, they've just hatched out and are in an incubator,' the teacher told me, stopping at the classroom door.

'I should bring the chicks in,' I said. 'I'm sure it's all right. I will have a word with the head teacher.'

'Oh good!' she exclaimed. 'I'll go and get them. Would you let the children in out of the playground? I'll only be a minute.'

The infants had lined up outside the classroom door, ready to be told to enter.

'Right, children,' I said, 'you may go in quickly and quietly.'

'We're not supposed to speak to strangers,' a little girl with great bunches in her hair told me pertly. 'Where's our teacher?'

'She will be here in a minute,' I told the child.

She eyed me suspiciously. 'Well, I hope she is,' she said peevishly.

At that moment, Miss Reece appeared with the chicks.

'Who's this man, Miss?' asked the little girl.

'He's a friend, Bethany,' said the teacher, smiling in my direction. 'He's come to see my chicks.'

Once inside the classroom, the little children gathered around the teacher's desk excitedly. In a small incubator, four tiny yellow chicks cheeped and scratched.

'They look as if they have just hatched out of their eggs, don't they, children?' said Miss Reece. 'All soft and fluffy and golden.'

'I love those little chicks, Miss,' said a small boy with a face as speckled as a hen's egg and bristly ginger hair.

'Could I hold one, Miss?' asked a small girl.

'No, Chloë,' replied the teacher, 'they are very small and delicate and would get very frightened if you were to hold them.'

The small boy stared for a moment at the chicks and then at his teacher. Miss Reece was wearing a fluffy yellow mohair jumper.

'Do you know, Miss,' he said, in that loud, confident voice only possessed by young children, 'you look as if you've just been laid.'

The blush from the teacher's neck rose to her face and the school inspector nearly fell off the chair, laughing.

Reading Without Tears

I was sent a book recently by the eminent Irish educationalist, and wonderfully named, Dr Finian O'Shea. I had mentioned in one of my talks that I collect old reading scheme books and primers, and Dr O'Shea very kindly sent me a copy of *Reading Without Tears or a Pleasant Mode of Learning to Read*. It was published in 1861 by the author of *Peep of Day*, one Mrs Favell Lee Mortimer, the daughter of a wealthy Bristol banker and a woman with great religious fervour.

Winston Churchill learnt to read with the aid of *Reading Without Tears* and, in his memoir, *My Early Life,* noted wryly that, 'it certainly didn't justify its title in my case'. And is it any wonder? This influential and popular work of stark realism certainly does not reflect the intention of the author, who stated in the preface, that, 'great pains have been taken to render this book pleasing to children'. I can only assume that the Victorian nursery-aged children who were given this text were made of pretty strong stuff, for it is full of the most amazingly gruesome accounts of the hazardous injuries and violent deaths of naughty and foolhardy children.

The book begins rather tamely enough, where the early readers are required to read dozens of everyday words and simple sentences such as, 'I had a bun' and 'Nan ran to a log', and are given help in learning the alphabet:

> D is like an old man leaning on a stick.
> E is like a carriage with a little seat for the driver.
> F is like a tree with a seat for a child.
> G is like a monkey eating a cake.

Then we get to meet a singularly nasty little boy called Bill, and a number of accident-prone children:

> Bill hit a pig.
> Bill hit a kid.
> Bill will kill a pig.
>
> Bill is a big lad.
> Bill has a bad dog.
> Get a rod. Hit a dog.
> Jack hit his neck.
> Dick hit his hip.
> Tom got a bad kick in the neck.

The author gets into her stride when it comes to infant mortality. When the wagon gets stuck in the snow, the little sisters freeze to death, and when Jack falls from the high tree, his neck is 'snapped' and 'he is killed on the spot'. A disobedient child drinks poison and dies in agony – 'the poison has destroyed him'. One particularly grisly account involves William, who played with gunpowder with dire results. His father, Mr Morley, rushes up the stairs on hearing a loud noise.

What a sight! All his children lying on the floor burning.
The doctor says, 'The children are blind, they will soon die.'

A century and a half later, material for emergent readers, thank goodness, is very different. These bright, informative and entertaining picture books and early texts enrich life, they take children to places they may never visit and introduce them to characters they may never meet, and the early reader grows to see reading as a pleasurable activity.

In the post with Dr O'Shea's gift came another book, this one produced by the Book Trust. *Treasure, a Book of Ideas* celebrates learning in its broadest sense with advice for parents and teachers on how to give children the very best start in reading: a curiosity about life, an eagerness to learn and a lifelong love of books. Thankfully, *Reading Without Tears* is not a recommended text.

In the Reading Corner

The reading corner in the small Dales school had a hard-backed teacher's chair, a small square of coloured carpet, two large cushions and a bookcase full of assorted books. I had agreed to read a story to the sixteen bright-eyed children, and selected a story from *The Tales of Peter Rabbit*, the children's classic by Beatrix Potter. The selection of this book, I found, was singularly unfortunate, and I came to appreciate just how shrewd, bluntly honest and witty the Dales child can be.

John, a serious little boy of about seven or eight, with a tangled mop of straw-coloured hair, was clearly not very enamoured with the plot. I arrived at that part of the story when poor

Peter Rabbit, to escape the terrifying Mr McGregor, who was searching for him in the vegetable garden, became entangled in the gooseberry net. The frightened little rabbit gave himself up for lost and shed big tears. It was the climax to the story and when I had read this part to my little nephew Jamie and my niece Kirsten, their eyes had widened like saucers and their mouths had fallen open in expectation of the capture of the poor little rabbit by the cruel gardener. But John stared impassively at me, with tight little lips and wide staring eyes.

'What a terrible thing it would be,' I said, 'if poor Peter Rabbit should be caught.'

'Rabbits! Rabbits!' cried the angry-faced little lad, scratching the tangled mop of hair in irritation. 'They're a blasted nuisance, that's what my dad says! Have you seen what rabbits do to a crop?' I answered that I had not. 'Rabbits with little cotton-wool tails and pipe-cleaner whiskers,' he sneered, 'and fur as soft as velvet. Huh! We shoot the buggers! They can eat their way through a crop in a week, can rabbits. Clear nine acres in a month! Millions of pounds' worth of damage when it's a mild winter. No amount of fencing will stop 'em.'

'We don't shoot rabbits on our farm,' announced a little girl of about ten, with round rosy cheeks and closely cropped red hair.

'Don't you?' I asked.

'We gas ours!' she told me. 'That stops 'em, I can tell you.'

'Nay, Marianne,' retorted the boy, curling a small lip, 'gassin' doesn't work.' Then, looking me straight in the eyes, he added: 'Never mind poor old Peter Rabbit. It's Mr McGregor I feel sorry for – trying to grow his vegetables with a lot of 'ungry rabbits all ovver t'place!'

'Perhaps I should read another book,' I suggested feebly.

A Favourite Book

I am frequently asked, by children in the schools I visit, which is my very favourite story. I tell them I have read a good many books in my time but the one story which I love the most, one which brings back such happy memories of my childhood and one which I wish I had written myself, is *The Selfish Giant* by Oscar Wilde. It was my grandmother's favourite story and was read to me when I was small. It is a powerful, poignant and simply written narrative about a mean-minded Giant who forbids the little children to enter his beautiful garden to play.

One Easter time, when visiting a small rural primary school in Nidderdale, North Yorkshire, I read *The Selfish Giant* to a group of eight-year-olds. The children sat in a semi-circle around me on the carpet in the reading corner and listened intently as I recounted the tale.

'My own garden is my own garden,' he tells the children, 'and I will not allow anyone to play in it but myself.' When spring comes, the Giant's garden remains cold and barren and a great white cloak of snow buries everything. The Giant cannot understand why the spring passes his garden by. Summer doesn't come, and neither does autumn, and the garden stays perpetually cold and empty of life. One morning, the Giant sees a most wonderful sight. Through a little hole in the wall, the children have crept into his garden and every tree has a little child sitting in the branches amongst the blossoms. They have brought life back to his garden, and the Giant's heart melts. He creeps into the garden but when the children see him they are frightened and run away. One small boy doesn't see the Giant, for his eyes are full of tears. The Giant steals up behind the child and gently takes his little hand in his. Many years pass and the little boy never comes back to play in the garden. Now very old and feeble, the giant longs to see his first little friend again. One day the small child returns.

Downstairs ran the Giant in great joy and out into the garden. He hastened across the grass, and came near to the child. And when he came quite close his face grew red with anger, and he said, 'Who hath dared to wound thee?' For on the palms of the child's hands were the prints of two nails, and the prints of the two nails were on the little feet.

'Who hath dared to wound thee?' cried the Giant; 'tell me, that I may take my big sword and slay him.'

'Nay!' answered the child: 'but these are the wounds of Love.'

'Who art thou?' said the Giant, and a strange awe fell on him, and he knelt before the little child.

And the child smiled on the Giant, and said to him, 'You let me play once in your garden, today you shall come with me to my garden, which is Paradise.'

And when the children ran in that afternoon, they found the Giant lying dead under the tree, all covered with white blossoms.

At the end, my little listeners were clearly moved, as I was when I first heard the story, and they sat in silence. The teacher dabbed her eyes. Then a small girl sitting at the front declared, 'I'm a Methodist, Mr Phinn, and I'm going to Paradise one day.'

'I am sure you are,' I told her, smiling.

'I'm Church of England,' volunteered another child, 'and I'm going to Paradise as well.'

I nodded. 'Of course.'

A wiry-looking little boy at the back stood up and announced loudly, 'Well, I'm nowt – but I'm gerrin in!'

You will probably be first in the queue, I thought to myself.

Playing Safe

Last autumn, I visited a primary school to read some of my poems to the children, and to open a new block. As I walked across the playground at break, I caught sight of some junior boys playing football with a large foam ball.

'That's not a proper football,' I observed.

'Aye, well,' one replied, wiping his nose on the back of his hand, 'we're not allowed to use a proper one in case someone gets hurt. Last year a lad got hit in the face and bust his nose.' I recalled when I was their age and played football on Herringthorpe Playing Fields, in Rotherham, with a substantial football. I well recall when the heavy, sodden, leather orb arched its way through the air towards me and smacked me on my bare legs. It stung for ages but it was worth it.

'Lasses can't skip, either,' said the other boy, 'in case they fall over.'

'Then t'school could get done,' the first boy told me, 'if somebody gets 'urt and 'as to go to t'ospital.'

'No win, no fee,' said the second boy, nodding sagely.

Earlier that year, I had visited a school in British Columbia, Canada, to speak to teachers and school trustees and work in some of the schools. This school, on the spectacular Victoria Island, was one of the highest achieving in the country; it was bright, cheerful and welcoming, with an outstanding reputation in music, art and poetry. On a glorious day, I sat in the sunshine with a group of elementary school children, outside their classroom, during recess.

Above us circled two magnificent birds with snow white heads, golden beaks and incredibly large wing spans.

'Bald eagles,' said the little girl sitting next to me, shaking her head.

I stared up in amazement. 'I have never seen such huge and beautiful birds,' I said.

'Yeah,' said the girl, in a matter-of-fact voice. 'We get a lot of these around here. They're real nuisances. We have to keep our cat indoors when they are breeding.'

'They take your cats?' I exclaimed.

'Sure do, and anything else they can get. They like the salmon the best but they will eat anything. They're on the lookout now because they've two chicks to feed.'

'I would love to see the chicks,' I said.

'Well, take a walk up the path at the back of the school,' the child told me, 'and turn right at the top and you'll see the eagles' nest high up in the cottonwood tree.'

'I shall do that at lunchtime,' I said.

'Remember to get your bell and pepper spray from the school secretary.'

'Bell and pepper spray?' I repeated.

'In case you come across a black bear up there,' the child told me.

'Black bear,' I mouthed.

'They're breeding at the moment too,' the child informed me, casually. 'It's the brown bears, the grizzlies, that you have to be careful of, but they are up on the mountains and don't usually come down.'

'Grizzly bears,' I whispered.

'The black are mostly harmless unless you get in between the mother and her cub. Then they can be nasty. But if you come across one on the path, look her straight in the eyes, ring your bell really loudly and use the pepper spray, and they soon skedaddle.'

'I see,' I said.

'Keep an eye out for a cougar,' another little girl told me. 'He sometimes likes to rest in the branches of a tree.'

'Don't look a cougar in the eye though,' added the other. 'They feel threatened if you do.'

I sat there in the sunshine and thought for a moment. In some schools in England, the children are not allowed to play football and skip. In Canada there are black bears and cougars in the woods at the back of the schools. Such is life!

A Prickly Customer

It won't be long now before the prickly residents which live in my garden make their appearance. Last October, I set up three boxes by the compost heap for the hedgehogs, so they could settle down for the winter. We have quite a colony in our garden (I believe the correct collective noun for hedgehogs is 'prickle') and, when the children were small, they would wait until dusk and go out onto the lawn to watch these strange, shy and endearing little creatures snuffling about, looking for the dog food we put out for them. Lizzie, my daughter, still loves hedgehogs and, when she was little, her very favourite Beatrix Potter story featured Mrs Tiggywinkle.

I recall visiting a primary school one cold November day, when I was a school inspector. The teacher asked the eight-year-olds to describe anything interesting that they had seen over the weekend. One child informed her that she had seen a hedgehog on the lawn.

'It's very strange,' said the teacher, looking in my direction, 'that a hedgehog has come out at this time of year, isn't it, Mr Phinn?'

'It is,' I agreed.

'They usually have a long sleep in the winter, don't they, Mr Phinn?'

'They do,' I concurred again.

'Did you disturb it, Chardonnay?' asked the teacher.

'No, Miss,' replied the child.

'Well it is strange, isn't it, Mr Phinn?' asked the teacher.

'It is,' I replied, wishing that she would desist from constantly consulting me.

'And did anything happen to you over the weekend, Darren?' asked the teacher of a small frizzy-haired boy with large eyes.

'Some white worms come out of my bottom,' announced the child bluntly.

'Oh dear,' said the teacher, pulling the face of one wearing shoes which were too tight. 'I really do not think we need to hear about that, do we Mr Phinn?'

'No,' I said, smiling.

'They came out of my bottom,' continued the child undeterred, 'and they wriggled about.'

'Darren!' snapped the teacher. 'I really do not think that we want to hear about your white worms, thank you very much. Now, I shall write "hibernate" on the board and we will get back to the hedgehog.'

'We gave it some bread and milk,' said Chardonnay.

'I don't think that is very wise, is it Mr Phinn?' said the teacher. 'I have an idea that bread and milk might be bad for them. Do you know what hedgehogs like to eat, Mr Phinn?'

'Worms,' I replied.

One Sunday, looking through my mother's old cookbooks for a recipe, I came upon *The Practical Cook*, published in 1949. The author was the indomitable Fanny Cradock. I loved to watch Fanny and Johnny on the television in the 1950s. Fanny was self-centred, condescending, insulting, patronising, rude, tactless, offensive and wonderfully prickly but, like many people at the time, I loved her cookery programmes. With that deep, intimidating growl and dressed like a pantomime dame, she carped and cavilled, criticised and cajoled, and it made fascinating viewing.

I have to own that I went off Fanny as I leafed through *The Practical Cook*. One of the recipes is for 'baked hedgehog'. For those who are planning a dinner party and want to serve something a little more unusual, here is her recipe:

Clean the hedgehog and roll in thick moist clay. Stand on a baking sheet and leave in a medium oven until the clay is hard and cracking. Break away the crust and the skin and the prickles will come away cleanly. Place the flesh in a baking tin and continue baking in a medium oven, at Regulo 5, in hot fat, basting frequently until the flesh is tender. Serve with thick brown gravy and small boiled onions.

'I Shall Not Tell You Again!'

Family Life

Being a Parent

Recent research has revealed that one in four parents don't like to tell their children off, and are scared to discipline them. According to a behavioural psychologist, the current culture in an increasing number of homes is for the parent to be the child's friend, and to explain, discuss and negotiate rather than tell him or her what to do. She cited the incident in a supermarket queue, when a toddler, having been told repeatedly by his mother not to put some sweets in the basket, informed her: 'You can't tell me what to do!' There followed a dialogue in which the parent, holding up the queue, tried to explain to the child why he should do as he was told.

Well, when I was small, there was no discussion or negotiation; I was given firm guidelines and clear parameters about how to behave, and the word 'No' was a frequently used word in my parents' vocabulary. I have to say that I have carried on the tradition, and tried to employ the same sort of parenting skills with my own children. When Lizzie, my youngest, was five, I heard her in her bedroom, telling off her dolls. It could have been me speaking, for the words, voice and intonation were mine. 'Now, I've told you once, and I shall not tell you again. Do you follow my drift?'

At the same time as this research appeared, the *Times Educational Supplement* ran an article about what teachers discuss behind the staff room door. In my experience, the conversation predictably turns to children's behaviour and the role of the parent. 'Of course, I blame the parents,' is the usual refrain. 'If they exerted a bit more discipline at home, and supported the school more, then we wouldn't have to deal with these truculent and unruly children.' There is, of course, a great deal of truth in this. It is an old chestnut but certainly rings true in my case.

Parents often come in for criticism from teachers – the pushy one who thinks Tamsin is naturally gifted, the disinterested one who sends the reading book back with the comment that 'it's the teachers job to learn them how to read and not mine', the neurotic one who has seen a television programme and believes his child has every condition under the sun, from dyslexia to irritable bowel syndrome, the bolshy one who takes his child's side on every occasion, the know-it-all who tries to teach the teachers their job, the interfering, the rude and the aggressive. One could add to the list.

'Most of the parents are the salt of the earth,' one head teacher told me. 'They cause me no trouble and, on the whole, they want the best for their children.' Then he rolled his eyes. 'But some . . . I despair!' He then related a catalogue of incidents. 'I have been shouted at by parents, called Hitler and accused of victimisation and child cruelty. But there have been some lighter moments. One young mother with four children – she can't have been much older than eighteen – had real problems filling in the forms when she registered the children to start school. She knew the children's dates of birth, and who the fathers were, but when I asked if all the children were natural born British citizens, she told me that the youngest child was born by Caesarean. When it got to "length of residence", she said it was about fifty feet although she couldn't be sure. I once asked a young lone-parent mother, whose son had a wonderful head of curly ginger hair, if the boy's father was red-headed too. "I don't know," she told me in all seriousness, "he kept his cap on." '

In this day and age, of course, teachers have to be very careful in dealing with parents, and in what they say about the children they teach. How they must look back enviously to the time when teachers were respected, supported, often held in awe and even feared. How head teachers must yearn for the past, when the position they held allowed them to be bluntly honest in dealing with parents, and they could send letters home like this one, from the headmistress of Brampton New National Schools, written to parents in 1871:

You must remember that you have not done all that is required by merely gaining admission for your child into our school. Do not suppose that its education is to be left entirely to the care of the master or mistress, and that you are to do nothing. Unless you labour together with them for your child's welfare, disappointment to all parties will be the result.

Much of the impertinence, bad language, and ill behaviour which so disgrace and degrade the youth of our town, and of which continual complaint is made, is, in too many cases, to be traced to the want of due care in setting a good example and enforcing it at home; and not, as is falsely and wickedly attributed, to the fault of the school.

The Challenge of Childrearing

There's been a lot in the news recently about pushy parents. In a Channel 4 documentary, *Admission Impossible,* viewers were offered a fascinating insight into the efforts of some parents seeking the best education for their offspring. One parent, with what he undoubtedly believed to be in the child's best interests, was determined that his son should gain entry into a desirable and over-subscribed grammar school, so he subjected his son to extensive evening tutoring, combined with a fair amount of parental pressure for the lad to succeed. The father appeared a well-meaning and loving parent, but I question the efficacy of 'hot-housing' children in this manner.

In no way comparable, and far more disturbing, is the tragic story of little JonBenét Ramsey, whose parents' ambitions transformed her into a six-year-old beauty queen. Andrea Peyser, in the *New York Post,* felt little sympathy and no vindication for the parents when she wrote: 'At the age when ordinary girls are learning to walk, this champion baby was taught to sashay like a miniature dime-store tart.'

Dr Madeline Levine, the American psychoanalyst, describes in her new book, *The Price of Privilege,* the depression, anxiety, eating disorders and self-harm endemic in an ever-increasing number of young people from affluent homes, resulting from overly ambitious and fiercely competitive parents who exert unreasonable pressure for their children to succeed.

No doubt such parents believe that they are doing the very best for their children, giving them a head start in life, doing what they think is needed for their children to become successful but, as Dr Levine contends, unreasonable pressure on children can have sad and sometimes tragic consequences. I know this to be a fact. After forty years in the education business, as a teacher, education adviser, school inspector and professor of education, I have witnessed the damage done to children who have parents with overweening ambitions for their offspring.

Let me give a few examples. I was the compère at a young people's music competition. Over a thousand people packed the great hall and, backstage, I was trying to put the young performers at their ease. Damien (not his real name), aged twelve, was understandably nervous. He was to play a difficult piece by Paganini on his violin. I reassured him that he would be fine, that he wouldn't see the audience anyway and that I was as nervous as anyone. During his performance, he lost his way and had to start again. Naturally, the boy was very distressed and received no prize, although the judges were very sympathetic and encouraging. He told me backstage afterwards, clearly in no hurry to see his parents, that his father would be very disappointed. He had set his heart on him winning. I went out front to speak to his parents. Before I could open my mouth, his father, a severe-looking man, clearly very angry with the outcome of the competition, ignored me and approached his son. 'So, what happened?' he demanded. The boy tearfully mumbled some excuse. I introduced myself. 'I know who you are,' he said rudely, and then informed me that his son had practised his piece time and again without so much as a wrong note. 'And now when it comes to the performance, he makes a mess of it.' I shall not forget the devastated look on the boy's face. He looked, and must have felt, a complete failure.

'And do you sometimes not make a mistake when you are playing Paganini?' I asked him.

'Actually, I don't play the violin,' he told me, pompously.

'Neither do I,' I said, 'but your son does, and he plays supremely well.' Did the man not realise what effect his reaction was having on the boy? Shouldn't he have put his arm around him and told him that it didn't really matter, and that he had tried his best, that there was always another competition?

I met Oliver at a prestigious public school. He told me his brother, father and grandfather had all attended the school and had all been captain of house, and that his father hoped he would follow in their footsteps. He was a sad, shy and serious boy who informed me that he was not much good at sports, not particularly bright and that he preferred reading. There was little chance of him maintaining the family tradition. 'Dad keeps on telling me that I ought to make more of an effort,' he told me. I saw in his eyes the distress of a child who felt himself to be a disappointment to his father. I was reminded on that occasion of the film, *Dead Poets' Society*, where Robin Williams played the charismatic English teacher who inspired the student who had aspirations to be an actor. The boy, desperate for his ambitious father's approval that was not forthcoming, and to follow a dream that was never to be, in the end took his own life.

The headmistress of a successful girls' independent school related to me the story of a prospective pupil who came, accompanied by her Svengali of a parent, for the interview prior to being accepted.

'So, what are your interests?' asked the headmistress.

The child delivered her prepared address without faltering. She enjoyed reading (her favourite novelist being Jane Austen), playing the piano ('She has Grade Five,' added the mother), swimming ('She's won cups,' added the mother), was in the Guides ('And has numerous badges,' added the mother) and did ballet ('She took a lead part in this year's pantomime at the Civic Theatre,' added the mother). The child continued to say that she liked theatre and enjoyed writing stories.

'And what television programmes do you like?' asked the headmistress.

'Documentaries,' said the child. She then looked in her mother's direction before asking, 'And what else do I like?'

'I'm a big fan of *Pop Idol*,' said the headmistress. 'Who do you think will win?'

The child suddenly became animated. 'Oh, Gareth is my favourite, much better than Will.'

This headmistress leads and manages a first-rate school. Her prime aim is to provide a cheerful, welcoming, happy and optimistic environment, where the pupils feel secure and valued and where each one is helped to realise her potential. There is no undue pressure, no obsession with league tables and targets, just good quality teaching, effective support, plenty of encouragement and high expectations. Sometimes, she told me, children develop later than others; the seeds take a little while before they become established and the shoots appear, but, with careful and sensitive nurturing, the flowers eventually blossom. She was not, she told me, in the business of producing 'hot-house plants'.

Dr Levine makes the very same point when she writes that: 'We would do well to remember late bloomers like Albert Einstein and John Steinbeck. Sometimes a nudge is helpful, a shove rarely is.'

So let us allow our children to enjoy their childhood, a childhood joyous and carefree, where they are reared in a loving and supportive environment by parents who encourage their efforts and celebrate their successes, but who will always be there with a helping hand if they should stumble, and a reassurance that it is not the end of the world to sometimes fail.

Last week, I read in the paper about the mother of the tennis superstar, Andy Murray, who has beaten Roger Federer, the world number one, in straight sets. On her website, she advises ambitious parents that their offspring's best chance of success is not to heap excessive pressure upon them. She, of all people, should know.

The Simple Pleasures of Life

We had several wonderful family holidays when our children were very young. On one memorable holiday in Ireland, the three little boys and myself would spend many a happy hour walking down the beach, collecting pebbles, bits of coloured glass smoothed and polished by the sea, shells like tiny pink fingernails and little pieces of red coral. We would sit on the end of a jetty on a deserted stretch of shore, fishing for crabs. Each of the boys would be equipped with a piece of string, some strips of bacon rind and a bucket, and they would compete to see which of them could catch the most crabs. Gently, gently, they would pull in the string with the crustacean clinging on, determinedly.

One morning we were joined by two youths.

'What are yous doing?' one asked.

I explained we were fishing for crabs.

He peered into the buckets and looked bemused. 'Why, sure you can't be eatin' those!'

'We're not going to eat them,' I told him. 'We're just catching crabs for the fun of it. Then we throw them back. Have you never fished for crabs when you were young?'

'Never,' he replied.

'Would you like a go?' I asked.

'Sure, I would,' he replied.

'Could I have a go too?' asked the other young man.

Half an hour later, they were well into the competition until, with fading light, we called it a day.

The following afternoon the two youths appeared again, as my sons and I were attempting to stem the oncoming tide from destroying our sandcastle. We had built a barricade, which continued to be breached, and we shovelled sand frantically to try and hold back the sea.

The two young men joined us in our endeavours and then, when our futile attempts failed, we all watched as the great ocean devoured our sandy fortress.

'Sure, that was great craik,' said one of the youths.

They shook my hand, thanked me and waved goodbye.

'You don't want to be encouraging those two,' the landlady told me later. She had observed us from the window of the boarding house. 'They're always in trouble. Real tearaways they are. Always up to no good.'

Research says that many youngsters these days spend up to thirty hours a week inside the house in front of a screen, watching television or playing games on the computer. Many, it is said, have television sets and DVD players in their bedrooms, and spend an increasing amount of time texting their friends. They are bought more and more expensive and sophisticated toys and gadgets, and have little experience of the simple pleasures enjoyed by youngsters of the past. How many these days, one wonders, go fishing for sticklebacks and minnows, collect frogspawn, build dens, play football on a piece of waste ground, cycle into the country, visit the swimming baths, catch a bus into town, run errands, play marbles, compete at conkers and pick blackberries?

Perhaps I am turning into a grumpy old man and it has been ever thus that the older generation looks back, through rose-tinted spectacles, to a halcyon time when life for the young was less complicated and more enjoyable. Certainly, back in 1824, the great philosopher, J J Rousseau, writing in *Emile: Or Treatise on Education*, had a deal to say about the simple pleasures of life which seemed, even in his age, to have sadly disappeared:

We no longer know how to be simple in anything, not even in our dealings with children. Gold or silver bells, coral, elaborate crystals, toys of all kinds and prices – what useless and pernicious furniture! Nothing of all this. No bells, no toys. Little branches with their fruits and flowers, a poppy-head on which the seeds are heard to rattle, a stick of liquorice which he can suck and chew, will amuse him just as much as these gorgeous trinkets and will not have the disadvantage of accustoming him to luxury from the day of his birth.

Do You Speak French?

Another of our holidays was a camping trip to France. Each year I would drive down to the south coast in the early morning, and we would take the ferry to St Malo. Then I drove to the campsite at La Tranche, in the Vendée, where a friendly courier from Eurocamp would be there to greet us and show us to our tent.

There was always a get-together on the first evening, when the courier introduced all the happy campers to each other, described the facilities on offer and took us through a few golden rules. My wife and I were both teachers at the time, but never revealed this. I did once, and then I had to listen to a diatribe from one red-faced parent in khaki shorts, about his son's failing school, sympathise with another whose daughter was dyslexic and try and give some advice to a mother whose son was being bullied by his classmates. After this experience, I told people I was a systems analyst with British Fuels and thankfully was left alone.

One summer, our tent was sandwiched between a miserable know-it-all and his ever-complaining wife on one side, and a very pleasant and good-humoured couple and their teenage daughter on the other. The girl, Melanie, a very capable and articulate young woman, was only too happy to baby-sit for us on a few evenings, and we got to know her quite well.

One morning, Melanie rushed over to our tent, beaming widely.

'I've just got my GCSE results,' she told us, excitedly. 'I can't believe it. I've got five As, three Bs and an A star in French.'

'Congratulations!' I said. 'Very well done. That's brilliant.'

When the girl had gone, the miserable know-it-all in the next tent, who had been eavesdropping, shared with me his considered opinion. 'Hardly brilliant,' he commented. 'Exams these days aren't anywhere near as hard as they were in the past. A monkey could pass some of them.'

'Oh,' I said, 'you work in education, do you?'

'No,' he replied.

'You mark examination papers then?'

'No, I fit double glazing,' he told me. 'I'm just saying that standards in school have declined and that the exams are easier. Kids these days don't know half as much as what we did at school.'

The following day I came across the 'educational expert' in the supermarket.

'Do you speak the lingo?' he asked me.

'Pardon?'

'French. Do you speak French?'

'A little,' I replied.

'Well, the wife wants to know the name of this cheese we've been eating. She wants to see if they have it back home. Can you come and ask the fellow at the charcuterie what it's called?'

I accompanied him to the counter to find 'the wife' was pointing and nodding and mouthing something volubly, in a sort of pigeon English.

'May I help?' I asked.

'No, thank you,' she said, 'I can manage.'

'If you would like me to ask—' I started.

'No, thank you,' she interrupted sharply. 'I said I can manage.'

At the checkout the couple were ahead of me.

'Did you discover what sort of cheese it was?' I asked.

'Oh yes,' said the man, holding up a large wedge in greaseproof paper. The wife's going to ask for it back home at Sainsbury's. It's called *fromage*.'

'Actually I think it's called Roquefort,' I ventured.

The woman gave me a sort of sympathetic smile. 'I'm sure the man on the cheese counter knows a little bit more about cheese than you do,' she told me.

Bon Appetit!

On another French holiday, my wife took the three little boys and me on a nostalgic journey. As part of her training as a modern language teacher, Christine spent a year as an *assistante* in the beautiful French town of Arcachon on the River Garonne, famous for the *Pyla Dunes*, the highest sand dunes in Europe. One evening, my wife, keen to introduce our children to French cuisine, took us to a restaurant she had frequented when a student, and ordered a typically French meal. When I saw the plate of oysters, *langoustines*, *lapin en aspic*, *escargots*, *cuisses de grenouilles*, *bifteck saignant*, *moules marinières* and *calamar*, I recalled my first visit to a French restaurant as a boy of fifteen, with my mother and her friend.

It was a smart restaurant in Montmartre, a sumptuous place with white tablecloths, shining silver cutlery and great glittering chandeliers. A rather arrogant waiter, attired in a black apron which very nearly touched the ground, presented us with the menus – huge, square, fancy-looking folders with all the dishes written inside in French. None of us could speak a word of the language and we stared for an inordinate amount of time until my mother's friend, taking the initiative, called the waiter over, and, pointing to the set menu, placed the order. The waiter returned to the table some time later carrying a bowl of cut lemons in small glass dishes, a large bottle containing a liquid which looked

a lot like vinegar and a huge plate of oysters, open and sparkling in the bright lights, and resting on a bed of brown shiny seaweed. Then the snails arrived, on a special china plate with small hollows to accommodate the little shelled creatures. I stared in horror as the waiter placed the small fork before me, to enable me to extract the garlicky-smelling gastropods, and said, smirking, '*Bon Appetit!*'

We were cautious eaters in our house back in Rotherham, and tended to look with great suspicion upon the rare occasions when we were faced with food with which we were unfamiliar. We never ate spaghetti (unless from a tin and soaked in tomato sauce), any cheese (other than Cheddar); we never touched garlic, mayonnaise (we ate salad cream from a bottle), veal, shrimps, yoghurt, noodles, brown bread, sweet potatoes, pâté, any spices other than salt and pepper or anything else deemed 'foreign'. Fish was invariably cod, and came perfectly rectangular in shape and smothered in bright orange breadcrumbs. When the fish arrived that evening – head, skin, tail, fins, eyes and all – I lost my appetite. The third course – cubes of white meat suspended in a pale yellow jelly – made me feel sick.

Some say that memories, even the most precious ones, fade surprisingly quickly with time. Well, the recollection of my mother's face, when she saw the oysters, the snails and the fish with the popping eyes, will never fade. Her mouth dropped open. The three of us must have appeared a comical trio as we sat upright and motionless, staring at the untouched food with expressions of distaste. My mother called for the bill, which she paid hurriedly, and we left, I am sure, much to the amusement of the waiter and the other diners. The whole meal remained untouched.

In the restaurant in Arcachon, my three sons surveyed the repast before them with eyes like chapel hat pegs. Christine explained that the meal comprised of rabbit in jelly, snails, frogs' legs, steak, mussels and octopus. Richard and Matthew pulled faces and, reaching for the *baguettes*, announced they would settle for the bread. Dominic, the youngest, licked his lips and tucked in with gusto. He tried everything, much to the disgust of his brothers and the amusement of the waiter and the other diners. Henceforth, he became known as Dominique, *la poubelle*, an appellation he delights in to this day.

Parents' Evening

Just before my first child, Richard, started school, I completed a three-year research degree in reading development and put my findings into a book. I was also appointed as a school inspector. The day before the first parents' consultation evening, my wife Christine gave me a stern warning.

'And don't go telling Richard's teacher what you do. She's only in her first year and will be nervous enough without you telling her you're a school inspector and putting the fear of God in her.'

'I won't,' I replied.

'And don't go on and on about all that research on reading you've been doing.'

'I won't,' I said again.

Miss Smith, my young son's teacher, smiled warmly when we sat down in front of her. If she was nervous she certainly was not showing it.

'Richard is doing very nicely,' she said confidently, scanning her mark book. 'He's a well-behaved child and has settled in well.' Before we could reply, she continued: 'Now, reading is perhaps the most important skill he needs to learn in these early years.' My wife gave me a sideways glance. I smiled smugly but remained silent. Miss Smith continued enthusiastically. 'It is fundamental to learning and we must work together, not only to get Richard to read clearly and fluently, but also to help him become a lifelong reader.' This young woman was very impressive, I thought. She continued: 'So let me explain about early reading development and the reading scheme we are using, and give you a little advice on how you, as Richard's parents and most important teachers, can help him at home.'

I said nothing but felt my wife tapping my foot under the table. After five minutes listening to Miss Smith, Christine, a former infant teacher herself, felt she ought to say something.

'Actually, Miss Smith, my husband and I know a little about reading development and the various schemes,' she said amiably.

Miss Smith smiled a sympathetic smile, the sort of resigned expression of a teacher responding to a child's willing but incorrect answer. 'A lot of parents think they do, Mrs Phinn, but they often get the wrong end of the stick.' So we sat it out.

Next morning, Miss Smith told Richard how she had enjoyed her conversation with his daddy and mummy, and asked what they did for a living.

'Daddy goes out in the morning with a big black bag and comes in late with his big black bag.' I must have sounded like Jack the Ripper.

'Ah,' sighed the teacher, 'your daddy is a doctor?'

Like all infants, Richard was bluntly honest. 'Oh no, my daddy's a school inspector who has just written a book about reading, and my mummy used to teach infants – just like you.'

That afternoon, Richard came home with a brown envelope addressed to Richard's parents. Inside, on a sheet of coloured paper, four words were printed in bold lettering: 'Ha, ha, bloody, ha!'

Something on My Plate

There is something about auctions that brings out the worst in people. I suppose it's the fiercely competitive nature of the business: people bidding in public against each other for a desired object, sometimes going way over the value of the item, just so they can have the satisfaction of having done the other person down. But I have to admit I do love auctions. Many a Sunday morning I have spent at the local auction room with the best of the bargain hunters, rooting through cardboard boxes crammed with cracked plates and chipped jugs, garish glassware and old bottles, pot lids and costume jewellery, and flicking through dusty tomes and stamp albums, folders of carefully mounted cigarette cards and old photographs. Like all the other bidders, I hope to come across an undiscovered and priceless Canaletto or an unrecognised piece of unique Clarice Cliff pottery.

Before we were married, Christine collected Willow Pattern plates. When we were courting, I thought I would surprise her on her birthday with a fine specimen I had seen displayed in the auction house window. Unfortunately, on the day of the sale, the auctioneer rattled through the lots like a Gatling gun and, by accident, I bought another plate. It was without doubt the ugliest piece of pottery I had ever set my eyes upon. It was a large plate depicting three stiff Chinese figures walking across a crudely painted bridge. The picture looked like one executed by a small child. Worst of all, there was a long hairline crack right across the centre.

Christine was aghast when she saw it and even more aghast when I told her how much I had paid for it.

'It's horrendous!' she cried. 'I wouldn't eat my fish and chips off it.'

The plate was consigned to the back of the cupboard, where it stayed for many years. It saw the light of day one afternoon when Christine decided to attend a social event at our children's school. The head teacher had prevailed upon another parent, a local antique dealer, to talk about and value small items brought in by the parents and teachers.

Christine took in a very old and delicately carved Japanese ivory figure, given to her by a great aunt, and a delicate and beautifully hand-painted porcelain bowl, a Phinn heirloom, given to her by my mother. After some coaxing, I persuaded her to take in the plate.

The antique dealer examined the objects displayed on the tables before him with a world-weary expression. His comments were cursory and deeply disappointing for the owners of the objects: 'damaged', 'of little real value', 'cheap copy', 'poor quality', 'rather ugly'. He was not impressed with the Japanese figure. 'It's bone,' he said, placing the Japanese ivory figure to his cheek. 'It's a way of telling ivory from cheap objects like this,' he explained. The beautiful hand-painted porcelain bowl, he informed her, was mass-produced and of little interest or value. Then he spied the plate and went weak at the knees. 'I could swoon!' he gasped, stroking the rough textured pottery. 'It's magnificent! This is Delft, circa 1680, an extremely rare example of Lowestoft ware.' He pleaded with Christine to sell it to him.

My wife politely declined and, on returning home, told me of the plate's provenance as she placed it in pride of place on the dresser.

'Shall I fetch some fish and chips?' I asked her.

Losing Your Marbles

I was in the Casualty Department at Doncaster Royal Infirmary again recently. Christine, while snipping bits off the Virginia Creeper which covers the front our house, snipped off a bit of her finger. She was reluctant to let me accompany her to the hospital after the last time, when she fell off a ladder and broke an ankle while pruning the roses. As she hobbled in to see the doctor a nosy patient had enquired: 'What's wrong with her then?' I replied, in hushed tones, that it is always unwise to drink too much when line dancing. On the way home, I had to explain to my wife why she had received so many strange looks when she emerged from the examination room.

Over the years, I've been a regular visitor to Casualty. With four lively children, and a wife who enjoys climbing and balancing, pruning and digging, I guess it is not surprising that I have been something of a fixture at the DRI. Dominic was particularly prone to accidents as a child: popcorn up nose, wax crayon in ear, assorted broken bones, stubbed toe, trapped finger, splinter down nail, cracked head, grit in eye. He was a walking pathological dictionary.

One Monday evening, I was all dressed up in dinner jacket, bow tie and fancy shirt, about to set off to speak at an after-dinner event, when young Dominic, aged eight at the time, flew down the stairs to kiss me goodbye. He tripped, hit a sharp corner of the bannister and split open his forehead. I have never seen such blood. Christine drove to hospital with me cradling our distressed child on the back seat, a flannel pressed to his head. My wife parked the car as I rushed through the door of Casualty with Dominic, the front of my dress shirt liberally spattered with blood. There were audible 'Aaahs' and 'Ohhhs' and 'Good Gods' and 'Bloody hells' from the waiting patients as they caught sight of me, looking like some gunshot victim out of a James Bond film. I was grabbed by a nurse and pushed towards a trolley.

'It's not my dad!' shouted Dominic. 'It's me.' Then he removed the flannel and announced, 'It's stopped now.' A couple of stitches later, Dominic climbed into the car and asked, with a great smile, if we could go bowling.

The following Friday, Dominic came in from the garden. 'I've swallowed a marble,' he told me glumly.

'How did you manage to do that?' I asked

'I just popped it in my mouth,' he explained. 'I was pretending it was a sweet.'

Back at Casualty, the receptionist remarked, as she signed us in, 'You know, I've never come across the spelling of Phinn like this before but this week we had another person with that name in Casualty.' I didn't enlighten her.

It was the same doctor who had stitched Dominic's head. 'You're keeping me busy, young man,' he told my son. 'Don't look so worried. You'll get your marble back. What goes in one way usually comes out the other. It's a matter of waiting. Ask your dad to buy you some prunes.'

The following morning, Dominic proclaimed he was ready to perform. Christine and I kept vigil outside the bathroom door.

'Anything?' I asked.

A moment later, there was a clunk and a cry. 'Dad, Dad! I've got my marble back.'

Trust Me, I'm a Doctor

Half way through her finals at Leeds University, my daughter Elizabeth was rushed to hospital with a suspected ruptured appendix. It was a worrying time but she came through it with flying colours. She had the operation and, when I phoned through to the hospital, she sounded as lively and cheerful as ever and said the doctors and nurses were splendid. She shared a small ward with two other women, both of whom were recovering from their operations. The elderly woman in the next bed, Elizabeth told me, was chatty and amusing and never complained; the woman opposite could not have been more different. For her, the tea was too weak, the food too cold, the doctors too young and inexperienced and the nurses not very helpful and too busy to be bothered. She delighted in complaint. It was no wonder, Lizzie told me, that her visitors curtailed their visits.

By chance, I was to give a lecture to the post-graduate education students at Leeds University the day following my daughter's operation, so I could give my talk and then walk the short distance to the hospital to visit. My lecture was in the morning and visiting hours in the afternoon, but the very accommodating ward sister said I could call in during the morning before the doctor made her rounds.

I duly arrived at the small ward straight from the lecture, carrying my notes on a clipboard. I was dressed formally in grey suit, maroon waistcoat with my father's watch chain dangling across my stomach, white shirt and college tie, and sporting a pair of half-moon, gold-rimmed spectacles. I guess I looked every inch the specialist as I entered the ward. The university had produced a large lapel badge for me on which the name DR GERVASE PHINN was emblazoned in bold black capitals, and which I still wore.

Conscious of the eagle eyes and the finely tuned hearing of the woman opposite Elizabeth, I pulled the screens half around my daughter's bed for some privacy, and spent a good ten minutes in conversation. I then kissed her goodbye, removed the screens and, on my way out, exchanged a few words with the elderly woman in the next bed.

'And how are you feeling?' I asked her.

'Mustn't grumble,' she replied.

'A replacement hip, I hear,' I said. 'Is it very painful?'

'Oh not that bad,' she said, and then added pointedly for the eavesdropper opposite, 'and everyone here has been wonderful.'

'You'll be back line dancing before you know it,' I told her.

As I headed for the door, the woman in the opposite bed called after me. 'Excuse me. Can I have a word?'

'Yes, of course,' I replied, approaching her.

'I've not seen anyone this morning.' She pursed her lips as if sucking a lemon.

'Pardon?'

'I said I've not been seen by anyone, Doctor.' She had obviously caught sight of the badge. 'The young woman in the corner bed has seen two nurses and a doctor already today and the woman next to her saw her specialist this morning. I've not been seen.'

'I'm sorry about that,' I said.

'Are they private patients?' she asked. 'Because if they are, it's preferential treatment.'

Before I could enlighten her as to my position in the world, she continued: 'I might as well be invisible, Doctor, for all the attention I get.'

'Are you not feeling too well?' I enquired solicitously.

'No, not really.'

'Are you eating?'

'Yes, but the food in here's not good,' she complained.

'And are you regular?' I asked mischievously.

'Yes, I'm all right in that department.'

'Well, I'm very glad to hear it,' I said, smiling warmly. I turned to go.

'Is that it?' she demanded.

'I beg your pardon?'

'Aren't you going to examine me?' she asked sharply.

'No, I'm afraid not.'

'Well, you are a doctor, aren't you?' she asked.

'Yes indeed,' I replied, 'but I'm a doctor of letters, not of medicine. Good morning.'

I left an acutely embarrassed daughter, a chuckling elderly patient with a replaced hip and the woman in question open-mouthed and, for once in her life, lost for words.

A Present for Christmas

'Bah! Humbug!' exclaimed Dominic, when I informed him that I would not want any presents on a recent Christmas. It is not that I am a Christmas killjoy; I love the festive season and most of the things it brings with it, but I honestly do not need any presents.

'Buy a cow for Africa,' I told my son, 'or make a donation to the donkey sanctuary.'

You see, I have all I need. I want for nothing. I certainly do not require any more socks or scarves, shirts or cardigans, ties or underpants. I prefer to buy such items myself and do so in the January sales when everything is half the price. Invariably, any Christmas offerings of this kind which I receive end up in an Oxfam shop in the New Year.

At one time, I did like to receive a bottle of single malt for Christmas but my daughter put a stop to that. Elizabeth is a research psychologist at Newcastle University, looking into effects of alcohol on intelligence. She used to talk to her father but now she tends to observe me as if I am a case study. A week after her taking up the post I found bottles of wine had mysteriously disappeared. Lizzie watches me eagle-eyed if I so much as look in the direction of a decanter.

I only buy one Christmas present – for my wife. The children are quite content with cheques. Each year, I ask Christine what she would like. Each year, it is the same response: 'Surprise me.' I once considered jumping out from behind the Christmas tree, wearing only a fake leopardskin thong and with 'LOVE' and 'HATE' tattooed on my knuckles. That would have surprised her and no mistake. In the past, Christine has received bags she never uses, CDs she never plays, chocolates she never consumes and jewellery she never wears. She is very gracious on opening the presents, and declares with great enthusiasm that the gift is lovely and one she really wanted. Then it is returned to the box and doesn't see the light of day again.

One year, I did surprise her – and every member of the assembled family as well. A colleague in the office at Harrogate enquired what I had bought for my wife that Christmas.

'A very nice rope of pearls,' I informed him

'Pearls!' he snorted. 'Pearls! That's what old women wear.' Then the expert on the psychology of women informed me that: 'When women get older they still want to feel attractive and desirable. You need to get her a bottle of expensive perfume, an emerald ring, an outrageous bouquet of winter roses or a sexy negligee.'

I was prevailed upon to accompany this colleague to an exclusive ladies' shop in Harrogate, and to buy some skimpy red silk underwear.

On Christmas morning, with all the family gathered in the lounge, Christine opened her present and held up the contents. It was as if she had been poked with a cattle prod. Our four children turned the colour of the underwear.

My sainted mother, sitting in the armchair by the fire, shook her head, sighed wearily and told my wife: 'Put them away, Christine. His father went through that stage.'

This year I settled for a flat-screen television set.

Backward Reader

I was once asked, by a large educational supplier, to compile a book catalogue for schools, to recommend a wide range of reading material for teachers to use with infants. I was to write a short paragraph on each text. Over six months, I had the most wonderful time, reading more than 500 picture books and early readers. During the summer, while my wife Christine took Maeve Binchy and Sebastian Faulks, Dick Francis and Deric Longden on holiday to Majorca with her to read, I packed fifty or so large, bright picture books.

I would get up early – so early that I was always the first to the sun beds – take a glass of orange with me and relax around the hotel pool before anyone else had stirred, reviewing the early readers. Each morning Jose, the pool cleaner, would pass me as I read *Stories for the Very Young* or *Early Nursery Rhymes*, and greet me with 'Ola!' to which I would reply 'Ola.' He was not at all interested in my reading matter.

At about seven-thirty, a large, bleary-eyed individual in a white towelling dressing gown would flip-flop past me and reserve the four sun beds next to mine with towels, magazines, parasols, sun-tan lotions, cold creams, lilos and an inflatable dinghy, and then he would disappear until a couple of hours later, when he would re-emerge with his wife, his sullen-faced daughter, let's call her Tracey-Jo, and a large, aggressive-looking son, who we'll call Duane. There was the whole of the poolside to choose from but he picked the spot next to me. He would recline there for the day, gradually taking on the colour of a boiled lobster.

On the fifth day, he spoke to me. I was at that time reading a delightful book all parents of young children should read. The cover depicts a large happy rabbit bouncing across the page and has the title *Read to your Bunny*.

''Appen you'll get onto t'big books one day, then,' he said, grinning inanely.

'I'm sorry?' I said, looking up.

He gestured at the picture book with a fleshy hand. 'I said, 'appen you'll get onto t'big books one day.'

'I have problems with my reading,' I informed him seriously.

The smile disappeared and was replaced by an expression of some discomfort.

'Oh, I see,' he said. Clearly embarrassed, he rose from the sun bed and flip-flopped off to have a swim.

'I don't know why you do that,' said Christine, looking up from her novel and shaking her head. 'People will start believing you.'

'Well, if I had got problems with my reading,' I replied, 'the last thing I would want would be to hear that sort of comment.'

Later that morning, Duane approached. He was a large young man embellished with various silver studs and rings. He clutched a pint of lager, which he then placed in front of me.

'Mi dad's sent this,' he said, articulating every word. I felt awful. 'He says he's sorry for what he said.' I felt worse. Christine sighed and tut-tutted. Then the lad turned to my wife, adding in a theatrical whisper of a voice and nodding in my direction: 'Mi dad didn't know he was backward.'

A Message for Mums and Dads

Teach me compassion.

Help to keep an open mind and respect the views of others.

Expect a lot of me.

Allow me some space.

Don't tell me my dreams are wild and my fears are foolish.

Offer advice now and again, but please don't nag.

Listen to what I have to say.

Encourage me and please don't criticise me in front of others.

Support me and realise that – once in a while – I can be difficult.

Cope with my moods and try to be a bit more patient.

Enjoy my successes but please don't be disappointed in my shortcomings.

Never make promises you can never keep.

Take no notice when I say hurtful things, I don't mean them.

'God's Own Country'

Yorkshire

Discovering Yorkshire

Young people these days are much more widely travelled than was the case in the past. They see much more of the country than I did when I was young, and many have had a Spanish holiday or visited the Disney theme parks in Paris or Florida. Growing up in Rotherham in the 1950s, the child of parents with modest incomes, I saw little of the country outside South Yorkshire, and my first trip abroad was to Paris for a weekend when I was fifteen.

Most summers, when the steelworks had 'shut-down week', the family had a fortnight in Blackpool. Apart from Christmas, the holiday fortnight held the greatest thrill for me. Most families like mine had neither the money nor the opportunity to travel and see the world, and therefore spent the holidays at one of

Britain's seaside resorts. Rotherham is about as far as you can get from the sea so, apart from the day trips to Scarborough, Filey and Bridlington and the school trips to the Isle of Man, I saw little of the coast. There was, therefore, an extraordinary feeling of excitement and anticipation when the summer holiday came around.

It was only when I was in the sixth form, studying for my 'A' levels, that I discovered North Yorkshire, where I was later to spend much of my working life as a school inspector. On the field study trips, organised by my geography master, the inimitable J Alan Taylor, I came across the Yorkshire Dales and the North York Moors for the first time, and the experience was unforgettable.

One memorable field trip was to Malham Cove. We had read about 'clints' and 'grykes', limestone pavements and caverns, potholes and subterranean rivers in our physical geography text-book, but I was not prepared for what I was to see. We approached by a footpath from the south, and this immense bow-shaped cove came into view like some great walled cathedral. It was breathtaking. I had never seen anything quite as bleak and rugged. Mr Taylor had us stand beneath the towering cove and not say anything at all – just take it in for a moment. Then he explained that it was formed millions of years ago, when the earth's crust cracked, fracturing the rock so that it dropped vertically. 'It's over two hundred feet high,' he told us, 'a thousand feet wide and, once, a crashing waterfall cascaded over the vertical cliff, creating a fall higher than the Niagara Falls. Now, can your small minds take that in?'

Another time, we stayed in a youth hostel set in the North York Moors. This part of England, a silent, bleak world with its great tracts of heather and bracken, fascinated me. We explored the incredible landscape, visited great abbeys like Byland and Rievaulx, ate our sandwiches in the shadow of lofty castles at

Helmsley and Pickering, and sat in the sunshine outside local inns, in villages untouched by modern life. One weekend, Mr Taylor led us deep within the moors towards the coast at Ravenscar. The journey followed the old Viking route known as the 'Lyke Wake'. Legend has it that the Vikings carried the 'lyke' or corpse across the forty boggy miles to the sea, where the body was given up to the waves. With the coming of Christianity, the practice was continued, but it took on a deeper meaning and the walk came to symbolise the journey of the soul towards heaven. I had never seen such magnificent scenery in my life. Beneath a shining blue sky, there stretched a landscape of every conceivable colour: brilliant greens, swathes of red and yellow gorse, which blazed like a bonfire, dark hedgerows speckled in pinks and whites, twisted black stumps, striding walls and the grey snake of the road curling upwards to the hills in the far distance. Light, the colour of melted butter, danced amongst the new leaves of early summer.

Now, as I reach pensionable age, and have visited many parts of Britain and a goodly number of foreign places over the years, it is the dales and the moors of North Yorkshire which still hold for me an enduring fascination.

A Language of its Own

When I sent the manuscript of my memoir to my London editor, she returned it with several words ringed. She had written in the margins: 'What does this word mean?' I assumed that everyone knew what 'mardy' meant, despite the fact that it does not feature in the computer thesaurus. It is such an expressive word for that sort of whining, sulky, spoilt child ('with a face like a smacked bottom,' as my grandmother would say) and was so well used when I was a youngster that I assumed everyone knows and uses it. 'The sight of the steam train on its journey from Settle to

Carlisle, clickerty clacking down the line,' I wrote, 'puthering sulphurous smoke and smut and sounding the shrieking whistle reminds me of the heady childhood days.' Here was my editor again with her pencil. 'Puthering?' Then she got to 'crozzled' and 'sprag' and 'wammy'.

Yorkshire dialect is full of the most vivid and unusual words, intriguing examples of how English continues to be the most quirky language in the world. Three colourful examples are 'stridewallop', a term for a tall and awkward woman, 'shot clod', which describes a drinking companion only tolerated because he pays for the drinks, and 'crambazzled', used to describe someone who is prematurely aged through drink and a dissolute life. I had never come across the words 'fornale' (to spend one's money before it has been earned), 'cagg' (a solemn vow to abstain from strong liquor for a period of time) and 'petrichor' (the agreeable smell in the air after a rain shower) until I met the professor of linguistics who introduced me at a conference. He had heard of all three, and many more. He was a self confessed 'bowerbird' – someone who accumulates an amazing collection of quite useless objects.

When, as a school inspector, I visited Upper Nidderdale High School for the first time, I sat with a young man, looking through his work. It was wonderfully descriptive and entertaining, but I stopped at a word he had used and I had never come across before. I asked him what he meant. A slight smile came to the boy's lips and his expression took on that of the expert in the presence of an ignoramus – a sort of patient, sympathetic, tolerant look. He had written in his account that his father, a farmer, had arrived home on the Friday night, after a really tough week, thoroughly exhausted. He used another colourful word for 'thoroughly exhausted' which I will not repeat, but I am sure it is one with which you are familiar. However, the boy had written: 'My dad came in from the fields, flopped on the settee and said, "I'm fair riggwelted."' He explained: 'It's a word which describes a yow when she's heavily pregnant, so heavy you see, she falls over on her back and just can't move, she's helpless. Sticks her legs in the air and just can't shift. It's called "rigged", proper word is "riggwelted".'

Some weeks later, I was speaking at the North of England Conference in York. A Minister of Education enquired of me how the teachers were coping with the recent changes in the National Curriculum. I smiled and just could not resist. 'They are feeling "fair riggwelted",' I replied.

Afternoon Tea

An American friend of mine stayed with me for a couple of days over the summer. I met Bill when I was lecturing in Vancouver at an international education conference, and invited him to stay should he ever visit these shores, stressing that the place to see in England was not London but Yorkshire.

Bill was *en route* from the capital to a conference on contemporary English literature in Durham, so broke his journey in God's own country. He was very keen to see something that was typically British, and had heard about the tradition of afternoon tea. There was only one place to take him: Bettys Tea Rooms in Harrogate.

To say my colleague was impressed by the interior was something of an understatement. He stood and stared at the opulence of the surroundings: light brown leather banquettes, burnished brass handrails, elegant easy chairs and carefully arranged centrepieces on each sparkling table. The café was very busy, but Bill espied a couple of vacant seats. Before I could stop him, he approached two elegant elderly ladies, let's call them Myriam and Joyce, taking afternoon tea in a quiet corner. One was considering the selection of dainty finger sandwiches and miniature cakes displayed on the tiered stand, the other pouring tea from a silver-plated pot into a Royal Doulton china teacup.

'May we join you?' asked Bill, amiably.

The women gave him looks that would curdle milk.

'Certainly not!' they snapped in unison.

'One has one's own table at Bettys,' the more formidable of the two informed him, frostily.

'And you have to wait to be seated,' added the other, screwing up her mouth.

A moment later, a smiling young waitress, in a pristine white blouse with the Bettys logo emblazoned in red on the front, escorted us to the adjacent table.

It was then that I lost my colleague, who eavesdropped on the conversation between the two ladies. 'Tell me, Gervase,' he whispered after a while, 'is this rehearsed?' I listened in too. I had to admit it was fascinating.

'Do you know, Myriam,' said the formidable one, who bore a remarkable resemblance to, and sounded very much like, Dame Edith Evans playing Lady Bracknell, 'I was up and down those steps like a shuttlecock.' I guess she meant yo-yo. 'If I vomited once, I vomited five times.' Her companion nodded and made a little sympathetic noise but she didn't interrupt the monologue. 'Of course, Sidney would insist on coming back via Cherbourg. He's that stubborn. We always come back via St Malo but, oh no, he thought best and we set off from Cherbourg, against my better judgement I might add. The sea was mountainous, the ship rolling and rollicking. Up and down, up and down it went, like a fiddler's elbow. I was closeted in the ladies' lavatory, heaving and splashing, the sea was outside, heaving and splashing, and where was Sidney?' I was tempted to ask where he was too. 'I'll tell you where he was,' continued the woman, now well into her stride, 'he was in the restaurant with a French bap, a lump of Camembert and a half a bottle of red wine. Static. If he'd have been on the *Titanic* he wouldn't have shifted his backside. "Bit on the rough side," he says to me, when he did finally emerge. I could have crowned him. It was horrendous.' She paused to select a sandwich before adding: 'I've never been so glad in my life to get my feet back on terra cotta.'

'Gervase,' asked Bill, after the women had departed, 'does your Alan Bennett come here for his material?'

The Great Yorkshire Eccentric

On a recent visit to South America, Christine and I took an aerial tram through the rain forest and saw the most amazing variety of vegetation and animal life: towering trees which grow five metres a year, blood-red tree frogs, shimmering blue butterflies, sloths and snakes and strange reptiles. The guide, a professor of ecology, asked me where in England I came from. When I told him Yorkshire, his eyes lit up.

'Yorkshire!' he cried. 'The home of the great Charles Waterton.'

I was then informed that Waterton inspired Charles Darwin and many other scientists, and was England's first eco-campaigner, an outspoken pioneer and conservationist, a passionate man who despised the destruction of the natural environment, especially when wilfully done. He is considered a visionary to environmentalists throughout the world.

Embarrassed, I had to admit that I had never heard of the said gentleman.

Back home, I undertook a little research. Born at Walton Hall in Wakefield, in 1782, 'Squire' Waterton travelled widely, exploring remote areas in the world and recording his observations and discoveries in wonderful detail. In 1825, he published a travelogue, *Wanderings in South America*, which became an instant bestseller. His love of animals, and of the natural beauty of the tropical rainforest, fills every page.

It was Charles Waterton who created England's first wildfowl and nature reserve, erecting a nine-foot-high wall around three miles of his estate at a cost of £6,000, which was a considerable sum of money in those days. He fought a long-running and ultimately successful case against the owners of a soapworks. The factory, built close to his estate, exuded toxic chemicals, causing widespread pollution.

In his lifetime, Waterton was on the edge of social exclusion; he was an odd character, one of the world's great eccentrics, of striking appearance and with an anarchic sense of humour. He had his hair cut short when the fashion was to have a full head of hair, he devised a new method of preserving animals, using them to create unusual tableaux, he climbed St Peter's in Rome and left his gloves on the top of the lightning conductor and he jumped on the back of a cayman and rode it like a horse. Waterton didn't care what others thought of him or how crackpot they thought his opinions. Edith Sitwell, a biographer of English eccentrics, concluded he was an extremely happy man. 'Few of us,' she wrote, 'are so full of life, love, curiosity and plain joy.' I guess he would have made a splendid teacher.

I have to admit that when I visited schools as an inspector, I always had a soft spot for the teacher who was a little bit out of the ordinary. Some, of course, would say that there is no room in education for the eccentric teacher. I would disagree. Thinking of my own schooldays, it was the teachers who were idiosyncratic, and who did not always follow the various directives, who made the greatest impression upon me. In a rather gloomy and violent world, there is room for the Charles Watertons, for eccentrics, in my experience, brighten our lives; they are less inhibited and more imaginative and are often disarmingly childlike in their approach to life than we 'ordinary' folk. And, after all, there is a pantheon of men and women – Isaac Newton, Mary Ward, Elizabeth Fry, Isambard Kingdom Brunel, William Blake, Charles

Darwin, Winston Churchill, Barnes Wallis, Lewis Carroll and many more – who were labelled outspoken, non-conformist and eccentric during their lifetimes, and who have gone on to be viewed by later generations as monumental people, gifted with originality and vision.

Drama Off-Stage

My wife and I are regulars at the theatre; we enjoy the variety of events staged there, love the intimate atmosphere and like watching the reactions of other playgoers.

One memorable performance at the Crucible Theatre in Sheffield was of *Edward II*, Christopher Marlowe's greatest tragedy. Christine and I had just settled down comfortably, in the middle of row B, when an elderly man informed us that we were in the wrong seats. We compared tickets to discover that he and his companion (a diminutive woman, who observed proceedings from the aisle with a tragic expression on her face) were in the row behind. There was no apology, just a sort of snort from the man and an impatient tut-tut from the woman.

I knew, when the couple who were now directly behind me, started discussing what they were about to see, that I was destined for an 'interesting' evening.

'What's it about?' asked the woman of her companion, who, I guessed, judging by the noise of pages turning, was flicking though the programme.

'It's historical,' he told her without further elaboration.

'Is it a musical?'

'No.'

'I thought it was a musical.'

'It's like Shakespeare,' the man told her.

'I thought it was a musical about Edward and Mrs Simpson.'

'No, that's another Edward.'

'I shan't like it.'

'Well, we're not paying for t'seats are we, and it were a pity to let 'em go to waste,' he told her in true Yorkshire fashion. 'We can always leave at t'interval if we don't like it.'

'I shan't like it,' repeated the woman.

'Shurrup moaning,' he told her.

Then the conversation turned to other, rather more mundane, matters. First, it was the sweets they had bought.

'Do you want an Opal Fruit,' asked the woman, 'or a Werther's Original?'

'I'll have an Opal Fruit,' said the man.

'What flavour?'

'Lemon.'

There was a rustling of a bag, accompanied a moment later by a variety of sucking sounds.

'Did you put the cat out?' asked the woman.

'Yes.'

'And lock the back gate?'

'Yes.'

And so it went on, until the play began.

Edward II has some pretty brutal parts in it, the most violent and shocking being the murder of the king when a red-hot poker is inserted in a rather intimate part of his anatomy. Screams and shrieks filled the theatre as the king writhed and flailed under his murderers' hands. This was followed by a deathly silence as his body flopped back dead.

The voice of the woman behind me could be heard quite distinctly.

'And I only hope the dog's not been sick in the car.'

How Much?

I have heard it said that the Yorkshireman's war-cry is: 'How much?' On our recent holiday in France, I used this well-worn phrase so many times that Christine, my long-suffering wife, started to total them up. It started at East Midlands Airport. The flight to Nice on easyJet was a reasonable £152.78 for the both of us. When we checked in at the airport we were told that it would cost a further £64 for the two small cases we were taking.

'How much?' I exclaimed.

'And,' added the smiling young woman at the check-in counter, 'just to let you know, all refreshments on the plane must be paid for.'

Then we got to France. We took a taxi from Nice to Vence, where we were staying, which is some fifteen miles away.

'*Soixante euros,*' said the lugubrious-looking taxi driver, when we arrived at our destination.

'*C'est combien?*' I exclaimed.

He shrugged. '*Service non compris,*' he added.

'Sixty euros and a tip on top!' I cried. 'We'll be going back on the bus.'

In the *pâtisserie* the next day, I peered into the display cabinet at the delicious-looking pastries and flans. The apple tart cost 22 euros.

'*C'est combien?*' I exclaimed again.

The assistant shrugged.

'Well, I'll tell you this, Christine,' I said, 'we'll not be eating cakes.'

'I wish you would enter the holiday spirit,' chided my wife later, as we wandered around the supermarket.

'What, with these prices?' I grumbled, pointing to a shelf. 'Even the wine is dearer than in England.'

'Not everything's dearer,' the English woman behind me vouchsafed. 'Cotton buds are cheaper in France.'

It is not that Yorkshire folk are parsimonious. It is just that we like value for our money. We are thrifty, prudent, economical people and there is no way we would pay £20 for an apple pie.

A friend told me the story (clearly a tall tale, but worth repeating) of the Yorkshireman who went to place an 'In memoriam' notice in the *Yorkshire Post*, following the death of his wife. The couple had been happily married for fifty years.

When informed of the cost by the woman at the desk, the man uttered, in true Yorkshire fashion: 'How much?'

Shaking his head, he reluctantly produced his wallet. 'I want summat simple,' he explained. 'My Gladys was a plain, good-hearted and hard-working Yorkshire lass, but she wunt 'ave wanted owt swanky.'

'Perhaps a small poem,' suggested the woman at the desk.

'Nay,' said the man, 'she wunt 'ave wanted anything la-di-da. Just put in: "Gladys Braithwaite's died".'

'You need to say when,' he was told by the receptionist taking his order.

'Do I? Well, put "died 17th March, 2008". That'll do.'

'It is usual for the bereaved to add some meaningful phrase,' said the woman. 'Something tender and heartfelt about the dearly departed.'

The man considered for a moment. 'Well, put in "Sadly missed". That'll do,' he said.

'You can have another four words,' the woman at the desk explained.

'No, no!' cried the man. 'She wouldn't 'ave wanted me to splash out.'

'The words are included in the price,' the woman informed him.

'Are they?' The man raised an eyebrow. 'You mean I've paid for 'em.'

'Yes, indeed,' replied the woman.

'Well, if I've paid for 'em,' exclaimed the man, 'I'm 'avin' 'em!'

The obituary was duly printed:

'God's Own Country'

Gladys Braithwaite. Died 17th March, 2008.
Sadly missed. Also tractor for sale.

Christine and I didn't bring much back from France: a couple of bottles of wine, a wedge of Camembert, some ground coffee and a mug. We did, however, stock up on enough cotton buds to last us for the next forty years.

Conversation in the Country Inn

I don't spend a great deal of time in country inns but, some years ago, I had a memorable evening listening to a Dales' farmer in The Black Bull entertaining his two companions. I was inspecting a school near Settle that week and, having finished my report that evening, went down for a well-deserved pint.

In the corner of the inn, three figures sat around a small round table, two of them listening to the third, who was entertaining them with a story. The speaker was a small wiry individual with rosy red cheeks and large jug ears. His companions were a particularly striking-looking figure with brown leathery farmers' hands, mustard colouring and grey watery eyes sunken in a sepulchral face, and a large woman with an abundant bosom and beehive hair-do.

Like all writers, I am a magpie, a collector of stories and an inveterate eavesdropper and, as I raised the beer to my lips, I took a professional interest in the entertaining conversation. The speaker had the animated voice and timing of a professional comedian.

'Now, mi Uncle Stan were a character and no mistake,' said the small man. 'Wa'n't 'e, Beryl?'

'Aye, 'e were,' replied the woman.

'Once mi Uncle Stan goes and buys this tup from t'market. Lovely-looking creature it were. Texel. Square as a box, four solid legs, beautiful fleece. Anyroad, he puts it in t'field wi' yows and sits back to watch 'im do what nature intended 'im to do, if you follow mi drift. Well, nowt 'appens. Tup just stands theer, then does a bit a walking, a bit o' grazin', but he's not interested in any o' yows. They stand theer waiting for 'im to mek a move but 'e's just not interested. Well, mi uncle scratches 'is 'ead and dunt know what's up. 'E's nivver seen the like afoor. So, he sends for t'vet. T'vet's puzzled an all. "I shall tell thee what I'll do, Mester Bannister," he says, "I've got this 'ere Dutch medicine which might just do the trick. Just come on t'market." And he tells mi Uncle Stan to give t'tup one o' these pills in t'mornin'. Vet gus back on t'Thursday and 'e asks how things are goin'. "Champion," says mi Uncle Stan. "I've nivver seen the like. Them theer pills certainly did t'trick. Tup's gone mad. Chasing anything that moves. Sex mad 'e is. Nothing's safe in t'field wi' 'im." We were talking about it in t'pub later that day and I says to mi Uncle Stan, I says, "I wonder what was in them theer pills what t'vet give t'tup." "I don't know," says 'e, "but they taste of peppermint."' The speaker threw his head back and roared with laughter, and his female companion chuckled. 'It's a good un, that one, in't it?' he asked.

'Aye, it is,' said the man with the mustard colouring, his face still as solemn as ever. Then he added, 'I can't say I'm all that partial to peppermint, tha knaas.'

Man's Best Friend

I was at the Broughton Show last June. This always proves to be a superb day out and, on this occasion, it was held on a beautifully sunny day and was packed with families. At this traditional country show there is a range of activities, displays, events, talks and commentaries: acrobatics, clay shoots, pipe and brass band performances, eagle flying, a flat cap whanging competition, ferret racing, stunt teams, fly tying, lure coursing and dressage. The hilarious Birdman Challenge is not to be missed. There is a cask of ale for the one who can achieve the farthest non-powered flight across the river at Broughton Hall. Competitors fly across the river in the most inventive outfits and on a range of incredible contraptions.

Actually, I managed to see very little of the events for I spent most of the day outside the Dalesman Tent, signing one or two books. Not many people stopped, so I sat in the shade with a pint of traditional Yorkshire Dark Horse Brewery Ale, people watching, an activity I love to do.

At this vantage point, I was able to see the most incredible variety of dogs. There were spaniels and setters, retrievers and terriers, pointers and foxhounds, and some other breeds of the most remarkable appearance. I have never seen such creatures in my life and, as owners passed by with their canine companions, I would stop them and enquire: 'Tell me, what sort of dog is that?'

Proud owners would be only too pleased to give me details of the dog's breed and provenance.

'He's a Tibetan Mastiff,' said a large man with a shaven head, tight-fitting vest and sporting an assortment of tattoos. The Hound of the Baskervilles eyed me and growled. 'Soft as a brush,' he added, before tugging the beast away.

'Old English Bulldog,' said another man, who bore a remarkable resemblance to his 'pet'. 'He'll let anyone in the house, won't you Buster, but just let them try and get out.' The dog looked up at me with grey button eyes, showed a set of bottom teeth like tank traps and strained at the leash. It emitted a deep rumbling growl. 'Once he gets hold of anything,' the man told me, 'his teeth lock on and he won't let go.' I crossed my legs.

'It's a Dandie Dinmont Terrier,' a small lady, wearing a turban and coloured smock, informed me. 'I did have a Shih Tzu.'

'Really?' I said.

One of the highlights of the show was the terrier race. A strip of fur was pulled at great speed across the arena, and the terriers were let loose and went in frantic chase. Another popular event was the all-breed race, when any dog could take part. This proved to be absolute mayhem, as great lumbering beasts of every conceivable shape, colour and size galloped around the field, accompanied by hairy little creatures yapping madly at their heels.

My mother was a health visitor and regularly had to visit houses in the poorer parts of Rotherham. At one house, there lived a huge black mongrel called Major and, rumour had it, the creature had been trained by the owner to attack anyone in uniform. Police officers, postmen and rent collectors consequently never made it down the garden path. My mother had to visit the house to look at a baby whom neighbours claimed was undernourished and they thought might be neglected. She was accompanied by a social worker and warned him about the dangerous dog, suggesting he rattle the gate to see if the beast was about before venturing down the path.

'No need, nurse,' said the man casually. 'I can handle dogs.'

As she walked nervously behind him as he sauntered up the path, Major appeared from around the back.

'Be careful,' my mother warned her companion, ready to swing her bag, 'that dog's vicious.'

'Don't worry, nurse,' he replied, nonchalantly, 'I have come across many dogs in my time.'

The creature, the size of a small bear, bounded towards them, teeth bared, tail in the air and ears back. The social worker, whom my mother described as a small, insignificant-looking man with a bald head and large ears, remained perfectly motionless until the dog leapt up. He then promptly punched it on the right hinge of its jaw, knocking the beast out cold. 'You have to know how to handle dogs,' he told her calmly. 'I was featherweight boxing champion in the army.' After that, Major was as gentle as a lamb.

A Country Parish

A curate friend of mine has just secured a living as vicar in a small rural parish in North Yorkshire. He is moving from a vibrant parish in the industrial south of the county to an idyllic spot in the Dales and, although much looking forward to the move, he is a little apprehensive. Having spent ten years travelling around the schools in that part of the country, and meeting many a cleric on my travels, I warned my friend that he will find life very different in rural Yorkshire and will need to adjust to the dry wit and the bluntness of his new congregation.

At a charity dinner in Settle, at which I had been asked to speak, I was entertained with the following story of a grizzled farmer.

'My mother nivver missed a service at t'church,' he told me. 'Come rain or shine she'd walk all t'way from t'farm up to t'village. One winter, it were thick wi' snow, drifts up to ten foot deep, rooads like icing rinks, wind that 'ud cut thee like a sharpened scythe, but she made it up t'church. Cooarse, vicar were not expectin' anybody and then mi mother turns up. Only one theer, she were, sitting in t'front pew as large as life. Anyroad, vicar asks 'er if 'e should carry on wi' service like, seeing as she were t'only one in t'church. "Look 'ere, vicar," she tells 'im, "I can't tell thee what tha should do, but if I went out of a morning to feed t'cows and only one on 'em 'ad tekken trouble to turn up, I'd feed it." He were nonplussed at this, was t'vicar. "Do you know," he says, "yer right." And he went ahead with t'service and give one of these long sermons just for mi mother's benefit. He were pretty pleased wi' hissen afterwards. "I hope you felt it were worth the walk through all that snow, Missis Bannister," he tells 'er. "Look 'ere, vicar," she replies, "I don't reckon I know all that much about sermons and the like, but if I went out of a mornin' to feed t'cows and only one 'ad tekken trouble to show up, I'd not be likely to give it t'whole lot of feed."'

The vicar in the rural community often plays a vital part of the life of the people, not just by being there for the momentous events, like births, marriages and deaths ('hatches, matches and despatches'), but by taking an active role in a whole range of activities. This frequently includes chairing the governing body at the local school, and taking the assemblies.

One new vicar had started his assembly in the primary school by telling the children how he had walked to the school that morning through the churchyard.

'And do you know, children,' he told them, 'I had a big, big surprise this morning as I passed the big oak tree near the church gate. I saw something watching me with large black shiny eyes. There it was, perched in the branches of the tree, grey in colour and with a great bushy tail. And what do you think I'm talking about?' he had asked.

A large boy, with very fair hair and a round red face, replied, 'I know it's Jesus, vicar, but it sounds like a squirrel to me!'

Of course, vicars' feet are kept firmly on the ground by their wives or husbands, who play important roles in the community too. I recall a certain head teacher of a school near Ripon, married to a vicar, telling me that her husband had a tendency to get rather carried away in the pulpit, and his sermons were sometimes over-long. She found a good way of telling him it was time to wind up. She informed him that when he smelt the Yorkshire pudding it was time for him to stop.

In a Manner of Speaking

A study commissioned by the Paramount Comedy Channel claims that the funniest accents in the UK, in rank order, are:

Birmingham 20.8%
Liverpudlian 15.8%
Geordie 14.5%
Welsh 10%
Yorkshire 9.3%
Cockney 8.4%
Belfast 8%
South West 6.6%
Glaswegian 3.4%
Mancunian 2.1%
Received Pronunciation 1.1%

Researchers led by Dr Lesley Harbridge, of the University of Aberdeen, asked 4,000 people to listen to the same joke in eleven regions, and found that those with a pronounced northern accent got the greatest laughs. Here is the joke:

Workmen are eating sandwiches, balancing on a girder miles above the ground.

'You ever get that urge, Frank? It begins with looking down from forty storeys up, thinking something about the meaninglessness of life, listening to dark voices deep inside you and you think, should I? Should I? Should I push someone off?'

Dr Harbridge also found that those with the 'funniest' accents were also deemed to be the least intelligent. In my own career, I have found a correlation between accent and people's perception of who is, or who is not, intelligent.

Despite the fact that, at university and in later life as a teacher and inspector, some of my colleagues found my way of speaking and turn of phrase amusing, I am proud of my Yorkshire accent and do not intend to change it.

'Could I ask you to speak a little more slowly when you speak to the students, Mr Phinn?' asked the headmistress of the girls' grammar school. I was there in the south of the country with two inspector colleagues. 'It's just that some of the gels,' she continued, 'might hev a little difficulty with your Yorkshire accent.'

I have to admit that I do pronounce the word 'bath' and not 'barth', 'buck' and not 'boook' and 'house' rather than 'hice', but I assumed that my accent was comprehensible.

'Actually,' continued the headmistress, 'I do so like to hear that wonderful Barnsley burr. You remind me so much of the character in the television programme *Heartbeat*.'

'Lord Ashfordly?' I ventured.

'No no, the amusing character who squints.'

'Claude Greengrass?' I suggested, thinking of the tramp-like figure played by Bill Maynard.

'That's the one,' she said.

With my two colleagues, I joined the headmistress on the school stage at the assembly, to be introduced to the staff and pupils. The three of us stood to the side, like the Beverley Sisters waiting to break into song.

'It will not have escaped your notice, gels,' started the headmistress, 'that we hev with us this morning three distinguished visitors.' She waved a hand in our direction. 'These gentlemen are school inspectors.'

All eyes focused on the three of us.

'They are here to spend a few days with us and should they ask you a question, answer them in your usual clear, cogent and enthusiastic way.' She looked in our direction. 'And should they

look lost, I am sure you will be able to tell them where to go.'
She gave a small self-satisfied smile. 'You may sit.'

Everyone in the hall sat down, but we three remained standing.
I managed to catch the headmistress's eye.

'Oh, I'm sorry,' she said. 'Could we have three chairs for the
school inspectors?'

Her request was followed immediately by three hearty cheers
of 'Hip, hip, hooray!'

A Yorkshire 'Amlet

When I visited Grassington Primary School some years ago, I
was told by the head teacher about a unique theatrical enterprise
which took place in the town in the early nineteenth century.
The village postmaster, Tom Airey, born in Grassington in
1771, having seen a performance in Skipton by the celebrated
Shakespearean actor, Edmund Kean, founded his own theatre
company, using a spacious barn on Garrs Lane. Most of
the leading performers of the day, including Miss Harriet
Mellon (later the Duchess of St Albans) and Edmund Kean
himself, took to the stage in this unlikely venue. Tom's own
performances of the Bard in a rich Yorkshire dialect were
much appreciated in the locality, although often derided by
purists and off-comed-uns. The theatre ran for many years
before closing in the 1830s. Tom's granddaughter recalled
that: 'He was himself a grand actor and stirred others with his
enthusiasm.' One Edmond Bogg captured his verse speaking
for posterity:

'A hoss, a hoss, wh'ull hev me kindum fur a hoss?'

'Ye damons o'deeth, cum sattle mi swured.'

'Wat pump, wat paggyantry is thare heer?'

My thoughts were of Tom Airey when, some months later, I
witnessed a wonderful Yorkshire version of Hamlet performed in

a school in Sheffield, by the senior students. As an introduction to the play, the teacher had transposed the original into Yorkshire dialect.

Two boys ambled towards each other at the front of the room, hands thrust deep in their pockets.

'Hey up, 'Amlet.'

'Hey up, 'Oratio, what's tha doin' 'ere?'

'Nowt much. 'Ow abaat thee then, 'Amlet? I ant seen thee for a bit.'

'Nay, I'm not that champion, 'Oratio, if t'truth be towld.'

'Whay, 'Amlet, what's oop?'

'Mi dad's deead, mi mam's married mi uncle and mi girl friend does nowt but nag, nag, nag. I tell thee 'Oratio, I'm weary wi' it.'

'Aye, tha's not far wrong theer, 'Amlet, She's gor a reight gob on 'er, that Hophilia. Teks after 'er owld man.'

The highlight of the performance was following the most famous of Shakespeare's soliloquies:

'To be or not to be, that's t'question.

Whether 'tis nobbler in t'mind

To suffer t'slings and 'arras of outrageeous fowtune

Or to tek harms agin a sea of troubles.

And by opposin', end 'em.'

So the tradition of performing Shakespeare in dialect lives on. Tom Airey, resting now in Linton churchyard, would no doubt have been proud of those youngsters, sithee.

The Surprise

John lived on a farm way out across the moors. It was a hard but happy life he led. He was expected, like most children from farming families, to help around the farm – feed the chickens, stack wood, muck out and undertake a host of other necessary jobs, and all that before he started his homework. He was a shrewd, good-natured, blunt-speaking little boy, with a host of stories to tell about farm life. When he was little, his teacher told me, he had been awakened by his father one night and taken into the byre to see the birth of a black Angus calf.

'Now look, young man,' the vet said, 'tonight you are going to see a miracle. You must be very very quiet and watch. Can you do that?'

The child nodded, and his father lifted him onto a bale of hay to watch proceedings.

'When I was your age,' the vet continued, 'I saw what you are about to see for the first time, and knew then that I wanted to be a vet. It's very special and you will never forget it.'

The black Angus cow was led onto the byre and, in the half light, she strained to deliver her calf. The small, wet, furry bundle soon arrived and the vet, wet with perspiration and with a triumphant look on his face, had gently wiped the calf's mouth and then held up the new-born creature for the little boy to see. John had stared, wide-eyed.

'And what do you think of that?' the vet had asked him. 'Isn't that a wonderful sight?'

John had thought for a moment before replying. 'How did it swallow the dog in the first place?' he had asked.

Knowing Your Sheep

My first experience of straight-speaking and knowledgeable country children was in a grey stone primary school in the heart of the Yorkshire Dales. I was the visiting school inspector, there to test the reading standards, and was asking a number of children in the infant class to read to me. I chose a bright picture book about a brave old ram that went off into the deep, snow-packed valley to look for a lost lamb. I decided that a story about sheep, which were clearly very popular in this part of the world, would be very appropriate. Graham, a six-year-old, began reading the story with great gusto. 'Ronald was an old, old grey ram who lived in a wide, wide green valley near a big, big farm.' At this point, he promptly stopped reading and stared intently at the picture of the ram for a moment. It had a great smiling mouth, short horns, a fat body and shining eyes like black marbles.

'What breed is that then?' Graham asked.

'Breed?' I repeated.

'Aye,' said the child. 'What breed is he?'

'I don't know,' I answered in a rather pathetic tone of voice.

'Don't you know your sheep then?'

'No, I don't,' I replied.

'Miss,' shouted the child, 'could Tony come over here a minute? I want to know what breed of sheep this is.'

We were joined by Tony, another stocky little six-year-old with red cheeks and a runny nose. 'Let's have a look at t'picture then,' he said. I turned the picture book to face him. The large white sheep with black patches and a mouth full of shining teeth smiled from the page.

'Is it a Masham or a Swaledale?' he asked me.

'I don't know,' I answered, in the same pathetic tone of voice.

Another child joined the discussion. 'It looks like a blue-faced Leicester to me. What do you reckon?'

'I have no idea,' I replied.

'Don't you know your sheep, then?' I was asked again and once more replied that I did not. By this time, a small crowd of interested onlookers had joined me in the reading corner.

'They're not Leicesters,' ventured Tony.

'Is it a Texel?' ventured a plump girl, peering at the picture. Then she glanced in the direction of the ignoramus. 'That's a Dutch breed.'

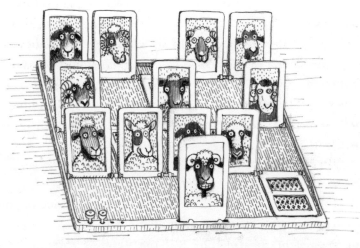

'Texels have white faces, not black,' Graham commented.

Very soon, the whole class was concentrating on the breed of the picture-book sheep.

'Well,' smiled the teacher, 'you are causing quite a stir in the reading corner, Mr Phinn. In order to solve the mystery, will you pop next door, Tony, and ask Mrs Brown if we could borrow Marianne for a moment. Say we have a little problem she can help us solve.' Tony scampered off into the next room. 'Marianne has eight breeds on her farm,' explained the teacher, 'and her grandfather's prize ram won a blue ribbon at the Yorkshire Show.'

'She knows her sheep, does Marianne,' I was told by a serious-looking girl with dark plaits. The children nodded in agreement. Marianne strode confidently into the classroom from the juniors.

'Is it sheep?' she asked.

'What breed of sheep are these, do you reckon, Marianne?' asked Tony, stabbing the page on the picture book that I was holding.

Marianne scrutinised the illustrations, shook her head, sucked in her breath. All eyes were on her, everyone was waiting for the definitive answer.

'I reckon they're Bleu de Main or Rouge de l'Ouest,' she suggested. Then she turned to the dunce holding the book, and looked me straight in the eyes. 'What do you reckon?'

Before I could answer, Tony, shaking his head like a little old man, remarked, 'It's no good askin' 'im. He knows nowt abaat owt!'

Hail Caesar!

One of the most unusual venues at which I have appeared on my recent theatre tour was the Skipton Auction Mart. During the day, livestock is auctioned and the place is crammed with would-be buyers and sellers, inspecting, comparing, conversing and bidding. In the evening, the space is converted into a makeshift theatre with tiered seating, and a stage, good acoustics and excellent lighting. It is such a clever, innovative concept and brings comedians, folk groups, pop bands, one-man shows and actors to the market town, and they perform in an intimate atmospheric arena redolent of animals, earth and hay.

It was to the Skipton Auction Mart that I made a special journey, to see a Belgian Blue bull being auctioned. It was a magnificent beast, like a huge box on legs, pale brown and white in colour with a massively thick neck, mighty horns and great muscles. Here was the Schwarzenegger of bulls.

I had seen my first Belgian Blue when, as a school inspector, I visited a school in the Yorkshire Dales. In a nearby field I had come across this striking-looking creature of impressive girth and incredible muscles, staring impassively over a gate. Approaching him, I could smell his grassy breath, and felt a tingle of fear as he scraped the compacted earth with a massive hoof. He was, indeed, a remarkable creature. I was told by the head teacher of the school I later visited that the bull was called Caesar and was owned by her neighbour, Mr Purvis, a man of few words and strong views.

'He's a great, fat, pompous creature,' the head teacher told me. 'The bull that is, not Mr Purvis. He keeps Caesar only for breeding purposes and the bull looks like the emperor himself, the way he struts round the field until he's called upon to "do his duty", as one might say. But he has a really vicious streak, has Caesar, and many's the time Old Mr Purvis has stamped back to the farmhouse, cursing and swearing, and black and blue with bruises. The bull broke his arm a couple of times when he was trying to get hold of him. Anyway, when Jacob, his grandson, was about eleven, as the story goes, he rushed into the farmhouse kitchen one morning, shouting blue murder. "Grandfather! Grandfather!" he cried. "Caesar's gone! He's not in his field! Somebody's stolen Caesar!" His grandfather didn't bat an eyelid but carried on drinking his tea. Then he nodded in the direction of the window. In the field beyond was poor old Caesar, yoked to a plough, pulling away down the furrows, with two of the farmhands flicking his haunches with sharp switches. Caesar snorted and bellowed and puffed and heaved and looked very hard done by. "I'll show him that there's more to life than love-making!" said Mr Purvis.' The head teacher chuckled loudly, her body heaving and her eyes filling with tears of pleasure.

Farmers often struggle to make a living. Their life is hard, wearisome and often with little reward. They are also guardians of the country, and preserve its beauty. It is important for them to have a sense of humour. Another story concerning Mr Purvis and his young grandson was about their visit to the Auction Mart. On their way out of Skipton, in the Land Rover with attached trailer, which had several recently purchased sheep in the back, the old man asked Jacob. ''As tha put t'cooats in?''

'Yes, Granddad,' replied the boy.

'And t'tools?'

'They're under t'seat.'

'And t'bran?'

'It's in t'back.'

'I'm sure there's summat we've forgotten,' said Mr Purvis, shaking his head.

'Where's Grandma?' asked the boy.

A Dalesman to His Son

Well lad,
I'll tell thee summat:
Life for me aint been no easy road to walk.
It's been a long hard journey –
Mostly uphill all the way.
At times it's been a hot and dusty trail,
Wi' potholes and sharp stones beneath mi feet
And a sweltering sun burning the back o' mi neck.
Sometimes it's been knee-deep wi' mud
And thick wi' snow and blocked wi' fallen trees,
With an icy wind blowing full in mi face.
There were times when it's been dark and dangerous
And I've been lonely and afraid and felt like turning back.
But all the time lad,
I've kept plodding on,
And climbing stiles,
And scaling walls,
And seeing signposts,
And reaching milestones,
And making headway.
So lad, don't you turn round,

Don't go back on the road
For I'm still walking,
I'm still walking,
And life for me aint been no easy road to walk.

'The Slippery Snake'

Troublesome Language

Places Out of the Ordinary

Following the publication of my book, *The Other Side of the Dale*, I received a letter from a disgruntled reader. 'Not being a native of Yorkshire, but reading all about the county in your book,' she wrote, 'I decided to have a week in the Yorkshire Dales, hoping that while I was there I might visit some of the quaint villages – such as Scarthorpe, Barton Moor and Hawksrill – which you mention. I was very disappointed to discover that they do not exist.'

It is true, I made them up. Being a somewhat cautious person, I felt it politic not to mention actual place names in my books, in case it gave offence to the residents or attracted unwanted visitors to their villages. So thorough was I in making certain the names I invented did not in fact exist, that I checked in *The*

Dictionary of Place Names, written by Adrian Groom. I should never have opened the pages of this book. Devoted to the origins of the names of towns, villages and other spots throughout the country, it is a fascinating and comprehensive compendium. The reader learns about the oldest and newest, longest and shortest, most obscure and just plain silly, places throughout the British Isles. I just could not put it down, and now carry it with me as I tour the country on book signings and theatre tours, enlightening any companion brave enough to travel with me, with the origins of our destinations.

There is a village called Lover, just outside Salisbury in Wiltshire, that attracts hundreds of die-hard romantics each year, but this is not the only place where 'love' appears in the British landscape. There is Truelove in Devon, Heart's Delight in Kent and Cupid's Hill in Monmouthshire. Couples can kiss in Valentine's Park in London, find Red Roses in Carmarthenshire, cuddle in the shadows of Love's Hill in Peterborough and say Isle of Ewe off the coast of Scotland.

Amongst the strangely named places to be featured in the dictionary are: Beer in Devon, Wyre Piddle in Worcestershire, Little Snoring in Norfolk, Spital in Lincolnshire, Rest and Be Thankful in Argyll, Barton in the Beans in Leicestershire, Bonkle in Lancashire, Pease Pottage in Sussex, Loose in Kent, Pennycomequick near Plymouth, Matching Tye in Essex, Dirt Pot in Northumberland, Pity Me near Durham, Great Cockup, Robin Hood's Butts, Pratt's Bottom and Puttock End. There's a wonderfully expressive place called Old Sodbury, in Gloucestershire, which sounds like the wrinkled retainer in a P G Wodehouse novel, and Shitterton in Dorset, the name deriving from 'the village on the stream used as an open sewer' (but you probably knew that anyway).

My editor was slightly dubious about some of the more imaginative places I invented in my books – Backwatersthwaite,

Ugglemattersby, High Ruston-cum-Riddleswade, and others, until I pointed out that Yorkshire is famed for its bizarre place names. 'God's own country' is particularly rich in imaginative and wonderfully expressive names: Sexhow, Booze, The Land of Nod, Land of Green Ginger (near Hull), Bedlam, Idle (near Bradford, and home of the famous Idle Working Men's Club), Bugthorpe, Slack (near Halifax), Jump (near Barnsley), Wetwang, Giggleswick, Blubberhouses, Studley Roger, Thwing, Ugglebarnaby and Fartown. At the Rock and Heifer Inn at Thornton, near Bradford, is a signpost pointing the ways to Moscow, Jerusalem, Egypt, Jericho and World's End, all of which are a couple of miles away. Also near Bradford is a Greenland and Cape of Good Hope, and, at East Ardsley, near Wakefield, is an area known as 'Who Could Have Thought It', which was the scene of a tragic mining accident in 1809.

The story goes that William Hague, on becoming the MP for Richmond, telephoned a constituent but dialled the wrong number.

'Is this a Hawes number?' he enquired cheerfully.

'Certainly not!' came the sharp reply, before the receiver was slammed down. 'There is no sort of woman like that here.'

Just Words

I love this rich, poetic, tricky, troublesome, inconsistent language of ours. Since an early age, I have written down words in my notebook which have unusual spellings, ones which I have never come across before and those which simply appeal to me. I have lists of them.

Here are some of my favourites: hobbledehoy, ragamuffin, brouhaha, autochthonous, esurient, lucubration, prescience, swashbuckling, dandified, deracinated, troublous, inspissated, monody, propinquity, nonchalance, haecceity, ptarmigan, viscosity, weasel, pontificate, avuncular, contrapuntal, expostulatory, harridan and gewgaws.

Shakespeare was the first recorded user of about two thousand words, of which nearly half have now, sadly, fallen out of use. We continue to use 'abhorred', 'abstemious' and 'accessible', but we have lost some wonderful words like 'adoptious', 'abidance', 'allayment' and 'annexment'. He was a great one for inventing words too, was the Bard of Avon. Like Shakespeare, some people still love to create new words and expressions, words that don't exist in the language but the inventor thinks they ought to. There was a wonderful office cleaner who was greatly adept at this. 'Mr Phinn,' she once said to me, 'you're so artificated.' On another occasion, she saw a colleague waving at me madly from across the office, and pointing to the ringing telephone. 'Mr Smith's testiculating,' she told me.

I met Hilary Murphy on a cruise ship. She was in the front row for one of my lectures on English spelling – always a hot potato – and was willing, with some in the audience (but not all), to have a go at a spelling test. 'Anyone who gets them all right,' I said, confident in the knowledge that none would, 'I will give to him or her a signed, first edition copy of my latest book.' I have given this spelling test numerous times before, to parents, teachers, head teachers and academics, and no one got them all right. Hilary, however, not only spelt the thirty words correctly but gave me a list of other tricky words. I was amazed by her knowledge, and then discovered that it is she who sets the questions on the television programme, *Who Wants to Be a Millionaire?* I am indebted to Hilary for these wonderfully expressive words and their meanings:

ALEATORY – depending on the throw of the dice
BIBULOUS – addicted to alcohol
BORBORYGMUS – rumbling of gas in the intestine
CICATRIZATION – healed by the forming of a scar
DEFENESTRATION – throwing a person out of a window
ERGOPHOBIA – dread of work
EXCORIATE – peel off, strip, remove skin by abrasion
GALLIMOUFRY – jumble, medley
GLABROUS – bald, completely smooth
GNOMON – the rod of a sundial
PICAYUNE – insignificant thing or person
STEATOPYGIC – having excess fat on the buttocks
TERATOGENIC – producing monsters

Being a nosy sort of person, I asked Hilary what was the most memorable moment on that popular quiz show. A contestant, she told me, was asked the question: 'The Archbishop of Canterbury is known as a . . . ?' There were four options: 'primate', 'marsupial', 'mammal' and 'rodent'. The contestant opted to go 'fifty-fifty', and was given two choices, of 'primate' or 'marsupial'. 'I'll phone a friend,' said the contestant. The friend, yes, you have guessed, opted for 'marsupial'. Whenever I see the warm bearded face and shining eyes of Dr Williams on the television screen, I cannot think of him as being anything other than 'The Marsupial of All England'.

A Tricky Language

Robert McClosky, a State Department spokesman, once said:

> I know you believe that you understand what you think I said, but I'm not sure that you recognise that what you heard is not necessarily what I meant.

How true. What we say and write can lead to a great deal of misunderstanding and unintentional mirth. 'Better to trip with the feet than with the tongue,' said Zeno, 300 years before the birth of Jesus Christ. Shakespeare, that master wordsmith, shows us in his plays that words can be delightful and amusing, but also can be cruel, cutting and dangerous in their seduction.

I have just returned from a week in Tenerife. Whenever abroad, I am always interested in the ways in which foreigners try and get their heads around this tricky and troublesome language of ours. In the toilet at the hotel in which we stayed was a large notice which read: 'In the event of fire evacuate immediately and leave the premise.'

Over the years, on my travels abroad, I have collected a fair number of amusing, inventive and ambiguous instructions and notices. Here are a few:

Would you like to ride on your own ass? (Egypt)
Special today – No ice-cream (Venice)
We take your bags and we send them in all directions
    (Sweden)
It is forbidden to enter a woman even a foreigner if dressed as
    a man (Bangkok temple)
A special cocktail for ladies with nuts (Tokyo)
If this is your first visit to Moscow you are welcome to it
    (Russia)
Specialist in women and other diseases (Rome)
English well talking (Majorca)
You are invited to take advantage of the chambermaid
    (France)
Our wines leave you nothing to hope for (Lisbon)
Drop your trousers here for best results (Nanjing cleaners)
Ladies have a fit upstairs (Hong Kong tailors)

You are welcome to visit the cemetery where famous
    Russian and Soviet composers, artists and writers are
    buried daily except Thursdays (Moscow monastery)

Of course, we indigenous speakers of English have a few
problems with our own language:

PLEASE LEAVE HEATHER FOR ALL TO ENJOY (Peak
    District)
Bargain Basement upstairs (Harrogate shop)
Children may not skate on the frozen water unless passed by
    the head teacher (on school staff notice board)
The management is looking for a mature person to cook
    (Doncaster café)
Tek Care! Lams ont road (Wensleydale)
Labrador for sale. Eats anything, fond of children (newspaper
    advertisement)
Toilet for sitting down customers only (Sheffield café)
Playground fine for littering (children's playground in Halifax)
Lions, please stay in the car (safari park)
Guillotine wanted for playgroup (newspaper advertisement)
Do not use as a hair dryer (instruction on heat gun)
Wearing this item does not enable you to fly (on child's
    Superman costume)
Caution! Water on road when wet (A1)
For sale Braille dictionary. Must be seen to appreciate
    (newspaper advertisement)

The last words must go to our American cousins. Oscar Wilde
once said that 'we share everything with the Americans except
the language'. Here is President George W Bush, on proposed
education reforms: 'You teach a child to read and he or her will
be able to pass a literacy test.'

But my very favourite are the words reputedly spoken by David Edwards, head of the Joint National Committee on Language in the United States, answering a question about the necessity for a commercial nation to be multilingual.

'If English was good enough for Jesus Christ,' he allegedly stated, 'then it's good enough for me.'

Nicknames

I met a colleague of my father-in-law recently.

'How is Legs these days?' he asked.

My father-in-law has been known by the nickname 'Legs' Bentley since the war, when, as a sprinter in the RAF, he won many a trophy.

'Do you know,' continued the friend, 'in all the years I have known Legs, I never did find out what his real name is.'

'Walburga,' I told him mischievously.

A nickname might be no more than a contraction of a given name: 'Holloway' becomes 'Ollo', 'Docherty' becomes 'Docko', 'Montgomery' becomes 'Monty', 'Patterson' becomes 'Pat', 'Godfrey' becomes 'Goff'. My friend, Richard Fairclough, is called by all who know him (and that includes his wife and daughter) 'Fairy', a nickname given to him when he was a pupil at Silcoates School. I should imagine when he was playing rugby, the call down the bar of 'Oi, Fairy!' raised a few eyebrows.

A nickname might be based on an association with a famous (or infamous) character or television personality. I remember a boy at school called Craddock, who was burdened with the nickname 'Fanny' (after the celebrity chef, Fanny Cradock), and another called 'Percy' (after the television gardener, Percy Thrower). I never did discover what the first name was of a boy whose surname was Moss. We all knew him as Stirling, after the racing driver Stirling Moss. My eldest son, Richard, attended the first formal dinner at Durham University in a new grey tight-fitting suit with small lapels. Thereafter he was known as 'Reg' (after one of the notorious Kray brothers).

Nicknames are thrust upon us by colleagues, friends and family, and sometimes represent us as others see us. They can serve as thumbnail sketches or short illustrations of quirks of personality, reflecting our physical and social endowments such as bodily shape and skin colour, accent and manners. Nicknames can be closely bound up with our sense of identity. A nickname is not always just a label or a mere neutral referential device, it can be rich in connections and the effect of the name may last a lifetime.

Some nicknames given by pupils to their teachers are very inventive. A teacher called Gardener was known as 'Weed', a Mr Canning as 'Tin' and Mr Nelson as 'Horatio'. A head teacher, Mr Arrowsmith, was know as 'Twang', another, a Mr Lancaster, was known as 'Bomber' and a third, Dr Nottingham, as 'Sheriff'. Many a head teacher, swirling down the corridor in his black academic gown, is known as 'Batman'. Such nicknames are rather affectionate but others, based upon some physical characteristic, are particularly unkind and hated by the recipients. Children can be delightful but also corrosively cruel in labelling others. I have come across children in schools referred to as 'Dumbo', 'Beaky', 'Hippo', 'Blobby', 'Barrel', 'Squeaker', 'Snorter', 'Rabbit', 'Ape', 'Porky', 'Goggle-eyes', 'Acne' and 'Bandy'. I could go on. When I once discussed, with a teacher, the use of a derisive nickname given to a boy by his peers, the reply surprised and saddened me.

'It's all part of growing up,' he told me. 'It's not meant to be hurtful, and children, in my experience, learn to cope with it.'

I wondered if he would have taken it in good part had he been given the nickname 'Snot' or 'Scab' by his pupils. Those unfortunate children labelled with pejorative nicknames realise only too well that such labels make them objects of derision, and are in themselves stigmas, primed for joking and taunting.

On a more light-hearted note, I was told this anecdote by the eminent vulcanologist, Professor Bill McGuire, whom I met at the Dartington Literary Festival. He was asked to visit Eton College to talk to the boys and, following his lecture, was approached by a polite and good-humoured young man who wished to ask him a question. He informed the professor that he was known in the college as 'Prog', a nickname based on his initials.

'Ah,' said Professor McGuire, 'you have rather a long name, do you? Peter Robert Oliver Gordon, or something like that?'

'No, no, sir,' replied the young man. 'Prince Richard of Gloucester.'

What's in a Name?

I was speaking to teachers on the themes in some of Shakespeare's plays in the town of Shrewsbury.

'It's a pleasure to be here in Shrewsbury,' I told my audience.

'It's pronounced Shrowsberry!' chorused the audience.

'Thank you for that,' I said, and continued: 'I shall be considering in my talk one or two of Shakespeare's plays, including *The Taming of the Shrow*.'

How foreigners cope with some of our English place names, I have no idea. Well, I do actually – many of them don't.

I was walking through Harrogate one day, at a time when I worked in that beautiful spa town, and was approached by an American tourist.

'Excuse me, sir,' he said, 'could you possibly tell me where Wet Herbie is please?'

'I've never heard of him,' I said, thinking this may be the lead singer in the latest chart-topping pop group – 'Wet Herbie and the Evergreens'.

'No,' he said, 'the town near to here called Wet Herbie.'

It then dawned upon me that he was referring to Wetherby.

A colleague in the Harrogate office related to me how he had been asked, by a young man with two small children in tow, if the theme park – Flaming Go Land – was near the town. He meant Flamingo Land.

My brother, Alec, who lives in Galway, overheard a conversation in the Keys Inn in that magnificent city, between two American tourists who were poring over a small guidebook.

'Do you think we'll see any of these Lepreecians?' asked one.

I guess he meant leprechauns.

In my time, I have been approached by a number of our Atlantic cousins at stations, asking for directions to Logboroo (Loughborough), Stratford Youponovon (Stratford-Upon-Avon) and Scarboruff (Scarborough).

George W Bush was often held up to ridicule for his misuse of language. One laugh at his expense has been the discovery that he has a phoneticist (or, if you prefer, a phonetist), who helps him pronounce difficult words. On the president's autocue are names like Mugabe (Mu-GAA-bee) and Harare (Haa-RAA-ree), displayed to help him. I must say that I feel a certain sympathy with the former president because there, but for the grace of God, go many of us. Until we are told how to pronounce a place name, we have to make a stab at it and then, when we get it wrong, we are barracked by people in the know who make us feel something of an idiot. I was speaking at the village hall in Chopgate, in North Yorkshire, and raised a laugh with my pronunciation.

'We say Chopyat up 'ere, love,' I was told by a woman in the front row.

So let's show a little tolerance to those of us who get it wrong. I mean, how many people, unless they have heard a local pronounce it, would be able to get right first time such towns and villages as Leominster, Bicester, Bacup, Lewes, Towcester,

Rawstonstall, Towton, Todwick, Warwick, Alnwich, Bohuntine and Blenheim. How many, I wonder, would guess that Mousehole in Cornwall is pronounced Muzzle, Mytholmroyde in Lancashire is pronounced Mythemroyd, Slaithwaite in Lancashire is pronounced Slowitt or sometimes Slathwaite, Lympre in Kent is pronounced Lim and Woolfarisworthy in Devon is pronounced Woozy? And that's before we go north of the border to Kircaldy (Kircoddy), and into the Principality, with places an English person has little chance of pronouncing correctly.

In 'Shrowsberry', the vote of thanks was given by a Mrs Cholmondley, who informed me that the name was pronounced Chumley. Now, there's another thing – the way people pronounce their names: Sidebottom, Onions, Cockburn, Denziel . . .

Getting it Write

Last year, a family friend died. His widow, a former teaching colleague and close friend of my wife's, was understandably devastated, and viewed arranging the funeral and the reception with great trepidation. I agreed to read at the funeral, and for Christine, my wife, to arrange the reception to be held at our house. The deceased had been a well-loved man and there was a large turn-out at the crematorium and at the reception.

One man arrived at my house and his first words were: 'I've read your book and did you know there was a mistake on page 69?' I felt like escorting him to the door but, since it was a solemn occasion, I merely smiled (not a pleasant smile I might add) and thanked him so very much for pointing it out to me. John Humphrys, in his excellent book, *Lost for Words*, writes:

> Pedants are the people who can't pick up a copy of *The Times* without wanting to write about some solecism they spotted on page 17. They think there is only one thing that matters:

observing the rules. Every transgression is an outrage. They will avoid a split infinitive however convoluted the resulting sentence may sound. They will cling to the rules until their fingertips bleed and believe that any other approach will lead to anarchy. They cannot see a dangling participle without wanting to hang it in the right place. Solecisms are scars on their backs.'

Humphrys defines good English: 'Clear, simple, plain and unambiguous. Those are the essentials. It should be easy to read and to listen to.' None would argue with this, but the fact is that English is a tricky and troublesome business and we all of us, at times, come a cropper.

One reader of the *Yorkshire Post* took exception to my misuse of the word 'aggravate'. He informed the newspaper in his letter that the correct word I should have used was 'irritate', since you can only 'aggravate' a disease, condition or situation and not a person. The *Collins* dictionary states that 'aggravate' is often used informally to mean 'to annoy, exasperate, especially a persistent goading'. *The Oxford English Dictionary* states that the word 'aggravate', which dates back to the seventeenth century and comes from the Latin word *aggravat* – 'to make heavy' – is in widespread use in modern English to mean 'annoy' but that it is still regarded as incorrect by some traditionalists.

Professor Lisa Jardine is one of the country's leading academics. Her writing is provocative and inspirational, and she makes every subject she writes about interesting, informative and accessible. In *Points of View*, she states:

I want to use the moment as a springboard for some big ideas.
I want to stimulate and challenge the reader and seduce them into thinking differently.

Does it really matter that she breaks the rule on agreement in a sentence? We all know what she means and, after all, some of the greatest users of English break the rules on occasion.

Sweet Bassanio, my ships have all miscarried, my creditors grow cruel, my estate is very low, my bond to the Jew is forfeit; and since, in paying it, it is impossible I should live, all debts are clear'd between you and I . . .

Wonderful writing, but did the great Shakespeare really write 'you and I'? And what about Dickens, in the opening of his masterpiece, *Bleak House*?

London. Michaelmas term lately over, and the Lord Chancellor sitting in Lincoln's Inn Hall. Implacable November weather.

Was one of the world's greatest novelists not aware that the rules require sentences to contain proper main verbs?

My former English master, Ken Pike, quite rightly taught us the rules of spelling and grammar because such knowledge, he argued, helped the user to write clear and effective English. He also pointed out that, sometimes, rules do not apply. This was most clearly illustrated when I observed a lesson in which the English teacher taught his class that a double negative always equals a positive. To illustrate his point, he wrote on the blackboard: 'I can't not go to the dance.' 'This means,' he said, 'that you would be going to the dance.' He continued, 'There is no occasion in the English language where a double positive equals a negative.' One bright spark at the back murmured, 'Yea, right!'

The Use of English

The comedian who spoke after me at an after-dinner event 'entertained' the audience with the usual stories about the thick Irishman. I smiled, not because I thought this material was in the slightest bit amusing, but because it seemed to me ironic that this asinine individual had perhaps never read a book in his life, and had clearly never heard of Brendan Behan, W B Yeats, Sean O'Casey, George Bernard Shaw, James Joyce, Dean Swift, J M Synge, Oscar Wilde, Oliver Goldsmith, Frank O'Hara and the many other distinguished Irish writers.

I am a regular visitor to Ireland – North and South – and am fascinated by the way these immensely hospitable people have such a wonderful command of the English language. Ireland is a paradise for the connoisseur of the colloquial, where the idiom has qualities no less striking than those which characterise our own great county of Yorkshire. There is a unique quality of speech in Ireland – lively, colourful and expressive. My Grandma Mullarkey was a great user of the most imaginative phrases and comparisons. Here are a few examples:

'She's so good she bites the altar rails.'

'Sue, he hadn't a leg to stand on when they found the arms on him.'

'Could you lend me a wee colour of milk?'

'He'll not last long, so he won't, for there's the smell of clay on him.'

'She has a tongue that would clip tin.'

'You should get down on your knees and thank God you're on your feet.'

'He's so quiet he comes into the house like a drop of soot.'

'He has a mouth on him like a torn pocket.'

'She has a smile like last year's rhubarb.'

'Sure didn't I know a fella with exactly the same complaint as you –

God rest his soul.'

On a visit to a small school in Galway some years ago, I met little Bernie. The child, aged six or seven, approached the head teacher and me. 'It's still there, Mrs Callaghan,' she informed the head teacher. 'In the girls' toilets.'

'Is it, Bernadette?' replied the head teacher calmly.

'It is so, and it's got bigger.'

'Well, I shouldn't worry about it too much. It won't hurt you.'

'But it's got great curved claws and gigantic jagged jaws and it's turned a mouldy green.'

Mrs Callaghan smiled. 'It can't harm you, Bernadette.'

'But, Miss, it puts the very fear of God into me every time I looks at it.'

'Well, don't look at it then.'

'Sure aren't your eyes just drawn to it?'

I could not restrain myself. 'What is it?' I asked, fascinated by this exchange.

'Sure isn't it a monster, a great, dark, green, frightening monster with popping eyes and sharp teeth,' said the girl, without seeming to draw breath.

'A monster!' I exclaimed.

'In the girls' toilets,' she added.

'A monster in the toilets?' I repeated.

She patted my arm. 'Sure it's not a real monster,' she chuckled. 'It's a great dark stain from water leaking through the roof, but it gives me the shivers right enough just to look at it.'

The head teacher explained that the flat roof always leaked after heavy rain, and that the water had left an ugly stain on the walls of the girls' toilets. It had grown in size.

'Is it a very bad leak?' I asked the child.

Before Mrs Callaghan could respond, the small girl piped up: 'A bad leak? Sure it'd baptise you!'

Spelling it Out

The chairman of governors tut-tutted as he looked through the applications at the interview for the headship of the school.

'It's a great pity, Mr Phinn,' he said, 'that the standards of spelling have declined so much since I was at school.' He pointed to a letter of application in which the word 'liaison' had been spelt incorrectly. 'Even head teachers can't spell these days,' he bemoaned.

'"Liaison" is a difficult word,' I said, in the applicant's defence, 'and I think you will agree that we all have problems with certain words at one time or another.'

I was recalling the time when I got my new laptop and sent a letter to a school which should have begun, 'Dear Headmaster', but inadvertently went out beginning, 'Dear Headamster'. Fortunately, the recipient had a wry sense of humour and replied, 'Dear Gerbil'.

'Mr Phinn,' said the chairman of governors, pompously, 'I don't have any difficulty. I pride myself on being a very good speller. I have no problem with spelling.'

Well, bully for him, I thought, but I bet he does. He, like many I have met who think they are excellent spellers, suffered from something of a delusion. None of us is a perfect speller and occasionally even the best of us has a problem. I was tempted to give him my 'little test' of thirty commonly used words, which I have set on my English courses to teachers to demonstrate the loveable lunacies of the English spelling system. Should that be 'loveable', 'lovable', or can it be both? You see what I mean.

If every word in English were spelt (or should that be 'spelled', or can it be both?) the way it sounds, it would be so much easier, but this is not the case. One in ten words is not spelt the way it sounds, and many of the non-phonic words are amongst those most frequently used in the language – words like 'the', 'of',

'one', 'two', 'could', 'shall', 'ought', 'woman', 'women', 'write' and 'people'. One could never solve the spelling of 'could' by trying to relate its letters to its sounds. I recall a clever child once asking me, 'So why is the word "phonics" not spelt the way it sounds?'

Once, in an infant school, I came across a most inventive little speller who had written 'EGOG' at the top of the page.

'What does this say?' I enquired (or should that be 'inquired', or can it be both?)

'Can't you read?' she asked.

'I can,' I replied, 'but I am not sure about this word.'

She sighed. ''Edgehog,' I was told.

G B Shaw famously demonstrated the wild phonetic inconsistency of English by pointing out that if English spelling were phonetically consistent, then the spelling of 'fish' might be 'ghoti': 'gh' as in 'laugh', 'o' as in 'women' and 'ti' as in 'station'.

English is a rich and poetic language but is more complex, irregular and eccentric than most other written languages and is arguably the most difficult European language to read and write. This is what makes it so fascinating.

Now, I guess you are wondering which thirty tricky and troublesome words make up my 'little test'. Well, here they are. You might like to try them out on family and friends, but be warned – the exercise is likely to cause some argument, so have a dictionary handy.

Asinine, liquefy, purify, rarefy, pavilion, vermilion, moccasin, inoculate, impresario, resuscitate, supersede, rococo, mayonnaise, cemetery, titillate, desiccate, sacrilegious, impostor, consensus, minuscule, bureaucracy, canister, predilection, tranquillity, psittacosis, harass, unforeseen, linchpin.

Changing the Canary's Water

I once visited a convent high school. Before leaving I enquired of the headmistress, a small bright-eyed little nun, if I might wash my hands. She directed me to a room with nothing more than a row of hooks and a small washbasin in it.

I returned to her study. 'Actually, Sister,' I said, rather embarrassed, 'I was wanting the toilet.'

'Why didn't you say you needed the lavatory, Mr Phinn?' she said, with a wry smile. I am certain she knew what I meant in the first place but was just being mischievous.

There must be hundreds of euphemistic descriptions for the toilet: 'the little boys' room', the place where one 'spends a penny', 'powders one's nose', 'sees a man about a dog'. It's called the 'convenience', 'comfort station', 'rest room', 'cloakroom', 'smallest room in the house', 'facility', 'loo', 'necessary'. When I was in America, I heard it frequently referred to as 'the john' and the 'WC' and once, interestingly, as 'the honey bucket'. I am reliably informed that, when members of the royal family wish 'to pay a visit', they inform their hosts that they 'wish to retire'. Mark, my editor at the *Dalesman*, tells me that in Spain a customary phrase is: '*Me voy a cambiar del aqua al canario*' ('I am going to change the canary's water'). Perhaps the most elegant of euphemisms for visiting the lavatory is, surprisingly, a naval one. The officer would excuse himself from the table with the phrase: 'I am going to shed a tear for Nelson.'

The most interesting euphemistic description was told to me by Nigel Rees, who devised and chairs the Radio 4 programme, *Quote . . . Unquote*. We were speaking at the *Yorkshire Post* Literary Lunch last year, and he amused the audience with the story of the rather precious woman, who, when she wished to visit the said place, would tell her companions that she was 'going to turn the vicar's bike around'.

I was once inspecting a primary school in Harrogate, and the formidable infant head teacher, a woman of great expertise and long experience, informed me that she had once been approached by a mother of two children in the school who was the very mistress of the euphemism. The parent in question had been in to see her, complaining that her daughter had told her there was only tracing paper in the girls' toilets. It was, in fact, the good old-fashioned shiny IZAL paper that I remember well as a child. Her daughter, explained the mother, liked the 'soft tissue variety'. When the girl's small brother started in the infants, the parent had appeared again.

'Excuse me, Mrs Smith,' the parent said. 'Could I have a word?' She explained that sometimes, when her small son went 'for a little tinkle', he 'got his little nipper caught in his little zipper'. The teacher arched an eyebrow. 'So I was wondering,' continued the parent, 'if you could oversee his "performance".' The teacher explained that were she to 'oversee' all the children's 'performances' when they went 'for a little tinkle', she would be there all day and suggested that the child be sent to school in trousers without a zip.

'I hope you don't mind me mentioning it,' went on the parent undeterred. 'My husband said it was a bit embarrassing to bring it up with you, but as I said to him, Mrs Smith must have had a lot of them through her hands in her time.'

Watch Your Language

I reckon I got a grade B in 'A' level Geography, and not the predicted grade A, because of the wretched question on cotton. Mr Taylor was adept at predicting what might come up on the papers. One topic he reckoned we should revise thoroughly was concerned with the cotton industry in the southern states of the USA. Mr Taylor looked pretty pleased when we came out of the examination room, and announced: 'I had an idea that cotton would come up.'

'Where?' I asked, holding up the paper. I had searched for the question but never found it.

The examiner, rather than simply asking the candidates to discuss the reasons for the decline in the cotton industry in the southern states of the USA, phrased the question thus: 'King Cotton is dead! Discuss.' I was unfamiliar with this expression; the only Cotton I had heard of with the capital 'C' was Billy Cotton, who had a variety programme on the television. Perhaps this King Cotton, I thought, was some rich American industrialist. Anyway, I had never heard of him so opted for another question.

When examiners fail to use words and phrases which are not part of the students' everyday language and are not likely to be encountered in a school situation – language which is complex, formal and metaphorical – problems arise. Sometimes, the wording of the question on a paper causes difficulties in a totally unexpected way, in that it comes between the examiner's intent and the candidates' perception of that intent: those sitting the paper think they understand what is required but they get it wrong. In the following statement: 'Sugar is a mixed blessing', the candidate thought 'mixed blessing' was a kind of dessert like Angel Delight. Another candidate tackling the question: 'Which lochs afford deep water berthage?' wrote: 'The ones near the richest towns and cities.'

When candidates misunderstand the questions, there can be amusing results. Many answers of this type are published annually as 'howlers'. You know the sort of thing:

What is a seizure?
A Roman emperor.

Under what circumstances are steroids used?
They keep carpets from slipping on the stairs.

Explain what you understand by the term 'artificial insemination'.
It's when the farmer does it to the cow instead of the bull.

What is a 'Caesarean Section'?
It's a district of Rome.

In a democratic society how important is it, do you think, to have elections?
Because if men didn't have them they couldn't have sex and produce children.

What was Hitler's secret weapon?
He used the dreaded Gaspacho.

What is a terminal illness?
It's when you are sick at the airport.

It is important to remember that the students are usually not trying to amuse; their answers are honest attempts to make sense of the questions. Of course, sometimes the candidate deliberately tries to make the examiner smile. One boy, required to write the essay, 'Imagine you are a new-born baby and describe your first week in the world', wrote a side of: 'Glug, glug, glug, glug.' Another, asked to discuss the disastrous effects of global warming, wrote: 'Am I bovvered?'

The guidelines for those setting GCSE papers are clear in stating that 'the language used in question papers (both rubric and questions) must be clear, precise and intelligible to candidates'. Perhaps someone should have a word with the examiner who set the question, 'Trace the events leading up to the birth of Henry VIII' and the one who informed candidates at the top of the examination paper that: 'This option is compulsory.'

It's the Way I Say it

I still recall with great pleasure the occasions when, as a small child, I stood with my father at the kitchen sink as we washed and dried the dishes (which we called the 'pots'). He would launch into a funny poem or a monologue; I thought my father made them up.

The following week, after hearing a particular monologue – which I discovered later was the famous *The Lion and Albert* by Marriott Edgar – I was listening with the other children to Miss Wilkinson, headmistress of Broom Valley Infant School, telling us in the assembly to sit up smartly and rub the sleep out of our eyes.

'You are a lot of sleepyheads this morning,' she told the six-year-olds sitting cross-legged before her on the hall floor. Then she asked: 'Does anyone know another word for "sleepy"?' I imagine she was looking for a word like 'tired', but I raised my hand.

'Yes, Gervase?' she asked.

'Somyoolent,' I replied, with all the precocious confidence of an infant. This was a word used in the monologue to describe the 'posture' of the sleepy old lion, Wallace.

It was years later, after many recitations of the monologue, that someone pointed out to me that the word was actually pronounced 'somnolent'. I have to admit, I still have problems with the word.

It is a fact that many of us have trouble getting our tongues around bothersome words. I had an education lecturer at college who got in a great tangle trying to pronounce 'pedagogy' (ped-a-go-gee), 'ethnicity' (eth-nis-i-tee), 'phenomenon' (fi-nom-uh-non) and 'philosophical' (fil-uh-sof-i-kuhl). At an interview for a teaching post, a candidate asked what the 'remuneration' (which he pronounced 're-noo-mer-a-shun') would be, and, in a recent message from a call centre, a young woman said a representative would be in the area in February (which she pronounced 'Feb-yoo-ary'). I was tempted to correct the mispronunciations – 'ri-myoo-nuh-reyshun' and 'Feb-roo-er-ee) – but resisted. There but for the grace of God . . .

Research on pronunciation was recently undertaken by Spinvox (a voicemail-to-text-message system, which corrects the inaccurate pronunciation of words). It was discovered that there are a surprising number of commonly used words that we get wrong, words like 'anaesthetist', 'statistics', 'provocatively', 'anonymous', 'thesaurus', 'regularly' and 'aluminium'. Mispronunciation, of course, is no laughing matter, for when we get it wrong it is deeply embarrassing, particularly if some helpful person points it out.

My friend Alban, who farms near Whitby and is a plain-speaking Yorkshireman with a wry sense of humour, tells the story of when he was at school.

'I'll tell thee what,' said his brother, 'I just can't get mi 'ead round all this stuff abaat speykin' proper. We say "path", and t'teacher says "paath", we say "grass" and she says "graas", we say "luck" and she says "loook", we say "buck" and she says "boook". It's reight confusin'.'

'Tha dooan't wants to tek no notice,' his brother told him.

'Nay, we've got to practise it for t'next week. Dust thy know then, dust tha say "eether" or dust tha say "ayether"?'

His elder brother thought for a moment before replying. 'Dun't mek no difference 'ow tha says it. Tha can say owther on 'em.'

Words to Make You Wince

The *Sunday Times* conducted a survey to discover what people thought were the most beautiful words in the English language. The top ten words were: Melody/velvet, gossamer/crystal, autumn, peace, tranquil, twilight, murmur, caress, mellifluous and whisper. After this was published, I asked readers of my own newspaper column for their favourite words, and those words which they thought to be the ugliest. I received quite a post bag about the latter. I guess it was the unpleasant connotations which were the reasons for the appearance of words like 'gizzard', 'slop', 'carbuncle', 'scrawny', 'ganglion', 'insipid', 'tyrannical', 'incarcerate', 'haemorrhaging', 'bulbous', 'slimy', 'snot', 'clot' and 'prig'.

It is understandable that words that bring on nausea like 'vomit', 'gobbet', 'sputum' and 'scum' were high on the list, but there were some idiosyncratic and sometimes surprising offerings. These included 'gusset', 'hubby', 'panties', 'poppet' and (predictably from the two teachers who wrote) the acronym OFSTED.

Poets at the Ledbury Literary Festival were asked which word they thought was the ugliest in the language. Geraldine Monk disliked the word 'redacted' (to have written out in literary form or edited for publication), a word I have to admit I had never come across. 'It's a brutish sounding word,' she said. 'It doesn't flow, it prods at you in a nasty manner.' Philip Wells had an intense dislike of the word 'pulchritude' (which paradoxically means 'beautiful'). Wells was vehement in his aversion to the word. 'It violates all the magical impulses of balanced onomatopoeic language,' he said, 'being stuffed to the brim with a brutally Latinate cudgel of barbaric consonants.' Wow! That's a bit strong. Actually, I quite like saying the word. It's from the Middle English and has fallen out of use. I think it should be more commonly used, particularly the adjectival form of 'pulchritudinous'.

My pet dislikes are the jargon words and phrases that have crept invidiously into the language. I wince, when listening to a lecture on management, when the speaker employs the latest buzzwords and phrases. I particularly bristle when I am exhorted to 'run that extra mile', 'give it 110 per cent', 'get on board', 'suck it and see', 'bounce ideas around', 'throw it into the ring', 'pull in the same direction' or 'give it my best shot'. I dislike having things 'flagged up' for me and I don't feel inclined to 'get up to speed', 'think outside the box', 'climb aboard', 'have a thought shower', 'push the envelope' and 'find a window in my diary'. I don't want to 'touch base', 'run it up the flagpole', 'square the circle' or engage in 'blue-sky thinking'. I do not like 'no-brainers' and 'bullet points' and I don't want to 'chill out' or 'have a comfort break'. Buzzwords reveal nothing that couldn't be more effectively communicated using simple language. There are ample words in English to express one's feelings clearly and accurately without resorting to this gobbledegook. Of course, buzzwords are designed to make the speaker (sorry, 'facilitator') sound go-ahead, up-to-date and something of a specialist.

One word I do find rather ugly is 'galimatias'. It sounds like a disease of a very personal nature or a species of parasitical plant. However, it is a word which those who use that management terminology which infects the language like bacilli should know. It means a style of writing which is confused and full of somewhat meaningless jargon.

So There!

Our English teacher Mr Smart
Says writing English is an art,
That we should always take great care
When spelling words like *wear* and *where*,
Witch and *which* and *fair* and *fare*,
Key and *quay* and *air* and *heir*,
Whet and *wet* and *flair* and *flare*,
Wring and *ring* and *stair* and *stare*,
Him and *hymn* and *their* and *there*,
Whine and *wine* and *pear* and *pare*,
Check and *cheque* and *tare* and *tear*,
Crews and *cruise* and *hare* and *hair*,
Meet and *meat* and *bear* and *bare*,
Knot and *not* and *layer* and *lair*,
Loot and *lute* and *mayor* and *mare*.

Well frankly, I just couldn't care!
So there!

'Are You Anybody?'

Becoming Famous

Do You Know Who I Am?

I was once asked by a self-important councillor with whom I had crossed swords: 'Do you know who I am?' I wish I had summoned up the courage to reply, 'No, and frankly, I couldn't care less who you are,' but I bit my lip and merely replied that I did not.

I really have to smile when I hear that ridiculous question. A Mr Don Mudd of Nantwich was waiting patiently in the queue at the check-in counter at Auckland Airport. The single attendant was attempting to deal with a long line of exasperated passengers when one loud and angry man pushed his way to the front, slapped his ticket on the counter and informed her, haughtily, that he was in first class and insisted on being dealt with before the rest. The attendant explained that there was a queue of people before him and asked if he would mind waiting his turn. Undeterred, he shouted at her: 'Do you know who I am?' Without hesitating, the young woman picked up the public address system microphone and announced: 'May I have your attention please. We have a passenger who does not know who he is. If anyone can identify him, could they please come to Check-in 14?'

There's the story of Margaret Thatcher who, when Prime Minister and at the height of her power, visited Yorkshire with Bernard Ingham and a handbag. She was touring a residential home for the elderly and, of course, the residents were keen to meet her. There was one exception; one lady continued reading her book, apparently oblivious of all the fuss.

The Prime Minister, intrigued, approached her. 'Hello,' she said.

'Hello,' replied the woman.

'And how are you?'

'I'm all right. How are you?'

'I'm fine,' replied the Prime Minister. 'And are you enjoying it here?'

'Mustn't grumble,' came the reply.

'And have you any children?'

'Two – a boy and a girl. Grown up now, of course. Have you?'

'Have I? asked Mrs Thatcher, rather startled.

'Children,' repeated the woman. 'Have you any children?'

'Yes I do,' said the PM. 'I too have a son and a daughter.'

'And what are they called?' enquired the elderly lady.

'Mark and Carol. Tell me dear,' said Mrs Thatcher, looking the woman in the eyes, and asking, with a sympathetic smile on her lips: 'Do you know who I am?'

'No love,' replied the old lady, 'but Matron will tell you.'

As a visiting professor of education, I lecture at various universities. At one university, when the examination period came around, lecturers were told to be extra vigilant and keep a keen eye out for any cheating or 'flouting of the rubric'. One of my colleagues, invigilating an examination, explained to the students sitting their finals that, when he told them to stop writing, they must put down their pens immediately. One young man continued writing after the order had been given and, when he came to hand in his paper, the invigilator refused to accept it.

'You were still writing,' he told the student, as he collected together a huge pile of papers.

'I was merely writing my name,' explained the student.

'Nevertheless, you were writing and your paper will have to go to the Dean of the Faculty for his decision.'

'Do you know who I am?' demanded the student angrily.

'No, I do not,' replied the invigilator.

'Take a closer look,' said the student. 'Do you know to whom you are speaking?'

'No!' snapped the invigilator. 'I do not know who you are!'

'Thank goodness for that,' said the student, and pushed his paper into the middle of the pile.

Celebrity Status

I was recording my fourth Dales book in Bath, and booked into the hotel near the studio where the readers usually stayed. Behind the reception desk, signed photographs of famous actors and celebrities who had stayed there were displayed, each with various complimentary comments scrawled across them.

'You have a studio booking?' the pleasant young receptionist enquired.

'Yes I do,' I replied.

'And you'll be at the recording studio all day tomorrow?'

'That's right.'

'Could I ask you a favour?'

'Yes, of course.'

She gestured behind her, to the hall of fame. 'It's just that we usually have signed photographs of the famous people who read at the studio displayed on the wall.' Above her were signed photographs of distinguished actors and politicians, broadcasters and television stars.

'I should be delighted—' I began.

She cut me short. 'We've got Greg Wise staying at the hotel.'

'Who?' I asked.

'You know, Greg Wise, the actor. He's married to Emma Thompson.'

'Yes, of course,' I said, recalling the dashing, darkly handsome Mr John Willoughby in the film version of *Sense and Sensibility*, the man who rescues Marianne Dashwood (Kate Winslet) when she gets caught in the rainstorm and sprains her ankle. He turns out to be a bit of a cad and later deserts her to marry for money.

'Well,' continued the receptionist, 'he's staying here and he's recording at the same studio tomorrow. Could you ask him if we could have a photograph? I just went weak at the knees when he booked in. I was lost for words.'

'I'll see what I can do,' I replied. It was clear that there was little chance of my photograph joining the great and good on the wall behind reception.

Greg Wise was a most charming and unassuming man, and readily agreed to the request to have his photograph taken. In fact, he was extremely courteous when people approached him for his autograph or to tell him how much they enjoyed the films and television programmes in which he had appeared.

'I suppose it's part of having an easily recognisable face,' he confided in me. 'A little tiresome at times when you want to get about your business and people keep on coming up to you. But I don't mind really.'

One evening, as we ate a meal in the hotel restaurant, I was conscious of people staring, pointing and discussing him and, as we got up to go, several approached him for his autograph.

'Are you his agent?' one man asked me.

'No, I'm not,' I replied, rather peevishly, 'and I'm not his father either.'

It was the last day of recording and we were setting off for the studio when two elderly women caught sight of us crossing the small square to the front of the hotel. I saw one of them point at us and another scrabble in her handbag for a pen.

'Here we go again,' said Greg. 'I'm really sorry about this.'

The elderly couple approached, but looked past my companion and straight at me.

'It's Gervase Phinn, isn't it?' said one of the women.

'It is,' I replied.

'I thought it was you. I said to my friend, that's Gervase Phinn.'

'We heard you speak at the Women's Institute AGM last year,' said her companion.

'And we've read all your books,' added the other. 'Do you think we could have your autograph?'

I turned to Greg Wise. 'Ah, what it is to be famous,' I said smugly.

Didn't They Do Well?

I was greeted at the entrance of the exclusive Simpson's in the Strand by a member of staff, a young woman in a smart grey suit.

'Mr Phinn?' she enquired.

'Yes,' I replied, surprised to be recognised.

'The manager would like to see you in his office, sir, if you would like to follow me.'

I was at this sumptuous hotel to speak at the '*Oldie* Luncheon' for Richard Ingram, along with Barry Cryer and John Julius Norwich, and could not for the life of me think what the manager wanted.

'Me?' I asked. 'He wants to see me?'

'Yes sir,' she said.

'Do you know what it is about?'

'No sir. He just said it was important that you see him.'

In his plush office, the manager rose from his chair and smiled warmly. He was elegantly dressed in a dark jacket, pin-stripe trousers, crisp white shirt and grey silk tie.

'Mr Phinn,' he said, holding out a hand. 'How very good to see you.'

'Thank you,' I said, intrigued.

'Do sit down,' said the manager. He smiled. 'You don't remember me, do you?' he continued.

'No,' I said. 'I'm afraid I don't.'

'Stephen Busby. You used to teach me.'

'Stephen Busby,' I sighed. I saw in the man's face the child I taught some thirty or so years before – that small, bright-eyed, good-natured little boy who sat at the front desk. It's a cliché, I know, but I knew he would go far.

'I always enjoyed your lessons,' he told me. 'My sister Ann is coming down later this morning to see you. You taught her as well.'

I remembered Ann, my star pupil, whose work was imaginative, beautifully neat and accurate. She went on to get top grades in her examinations.

'She works for the BBC World Service now,' my former pupil told me. 'She's really looking forward to seeing you again.'

Teachers always feel that small tingle of pride when meeting former pupils who have done well in life. They feel perhaps they have had some small part in their successes. I have to admit that I guess I have not had such a positive influence on some of my other former pupils.

Some weeks later, I was shopping in Rotherham when I was approached by a bear of man with a tangle of curls and a great bushy beard, sporting a selection of aggressively colourful tattoos on his arms. He was holding the hand of a small boy of about eight or nine.

'Hey up, Mester Phinn,' he said. 'Does tha remember me?'

I remembered this former pupil only too well. He was often in trouble for fighting, answering teachers back, failing to do his homework, truanting and being generally a real nuisance. Teachers tend to recall the difficult and demanding youngsters and I certainly recalled this particular wayward and disobedient young man.

'I do, it's Johno, isn't it?'

'Aye, that's reight. Does tha remember when I answered thee back and I got caned?'

Oh dear, I thought, this might get ugly. 'I don't,' I said, feebly.

'Aye, well I do, and it bloody well hurt.'

'Well, you see—' I began to try and explain.

'I deserved it, reight enough,' he interrupted. 'Oh aye, I deserved it, all reight. I were allus in trouble for one thing or t'other and I'll tell thee what, Mester Phinn, if teachers today were like t'ones I 'ad when I were at school, stricter like, then we wunt 'ave all this yobbish behaviour. It never did me no 'arm.'

'Perhaps you're right,' I agreed. I was not inclined to argue with the giant. 'And who is this young man?' I asked, smiling at the glum-faced little boy staring up at me with large wide eyes.

'Him? This is our Kyle,' I was told. 'Mi grandson.'

'Grandson?' I repeated.

'Aye, I've got eight.'

'Eight,' I mouthed. I suddenly felt very old.

Digging the Garden

I was positioned at the very entrance to a massive bookshop, sitting at a small table, surrounded by towers of books and feeling not a little embarrassed. People passed and glanced in my direction but not a soul stopped to talk to me or to buy. Then an elderly couple approached. They observed me for an inordinate amount of time, as if I were some rather strange specimen in a museum case.

'Are you anybody?' asked the woman eventually. She was dressed in a thick black coat with a multicoloured headscarf wrapped around her head and tied in an enormous knot under her chin.

'I beg your pardon?' I asked pleasantly.

'Are you anybody? 'Ave you been on anything?'

'No,' I replied simply.

'Do you know who he is, Ron?' the woman enquired of her companion, a small man in a flat cap with the face the colour and texture of a mouldering russet apple.

'No, I don't,' he replied.

'What's it about?' asked the woman, picking up my book and flicking through the pages.

'It's about my life as a school inspector in the Yorkshire Dales.' She screwed up her face. 'It's a humorous account of the children and teachers I have met – sort of gentle, life affirming, observational writing. There's no sex and violence and bad language,' I added.

'Doesn't sound my cup of tea,' remarked the woman, putting down the book.

'Cookery books sell,' the man told me.

'And gardening books,' added the woman. 'Person they 'ad 'ere last time wrote one of them gardening books and there was a queue right out the door and round the corner.'

'Mind you,' said the man, 'it were somebody.'

'Really,' I sighed. 'Who was that then?'

'Charlie Dimmock,' the woman told me.

'And what's he got that I haven't?' I asked, mischievously.

The woman shook her head. 'It's a woman,' she told me.

'And she digs the garden without a bra,' added the man.

'So do I,' I said.

The man threw back his head and laughed. 'Aye, but you 'aven't got what Charlie Dimmock's got.'

My mother always advised me never to try and be clever with people. It never pays off. I should have heeded her advice.

'So, is that the main criterion for writing a book then?' I enquired.

'What?' asked the woman.

'Digging a garden without a bra?'

She thought for a moment before sharing her thoughts. 'It might not be, love,' she told me with a small smile playing on her lips, 'but I reckon she sold more books than you're ever going to sell. Come on Ron.'

And with that they departed, leaving me sitting by my lonely self amidst the piles of unsold books.

The Curse

When my first Dales book, *The Other Side of the Dale,* was published I was understandably very excited to see it in the shops and to read the reviews in the papers. Christine and I were staying at a hotel in the Yorkshire Dales and were joined for dinner that evening by my editor, Jenny Dereham, and the writer and broadcaster, Mike Harding, and his wife. In the corner of the lounge sat an elderly woman, engrossed in reading the very book.

'Why don't you tell her you've written it,' urged my dinner companions. 'I'm sure she'll be thrilled to meet the author.'

I took little persuading and approached the woman.

'Excuse me,' I said pleasantly. 'You perhaps aren't aware but that is my book that you are reading.'

'I think not,' said the woman tartly. 'I borrowed it from my sister. And if you do find your copy I wouldn't bother reading it – it's not up to much.'

Borrowed books are a sensitive subject for me.

My brother-in-law, Keith, is something of a bibliomaniac – his nose is forever in a novel or a biography and his house has wall-to-wall shelving in virtually every room, all crammed with books. He has one golden rule when it comes to his treasured books: never ever lend them to anyone. 'Invariably,' he says, 'those who do never see them again and if the books are returned they are stained with sun-tan lotion or coffee or have the corners of the pages turned down or the spines hanging off.'

I do wish my dear wife Christine would take a leaf out of Keith's book, if you will excuse the metaphor. I have a study at home which has its fair share of tomes but time and time again I will be searching the shelves for a particular book and, having been unsuccessful and enquiring of Christine if she has seen it, my dear wife will say: 'Oh, I lent *The Kite Runner* to Margaret', or: 'If you're looking for the Basil Hume biography, Mum's got it', or: 'I let Anne borrow the Michael Dobbs.'

'Christine,' I say with exasperation in my voice, 'will you please, please ask me first when you lend people my books, and if you feel compelled to loan them out will you ask for them to be returned?' Of course, the books rarely are returned and I have to go out and buy another copy, which, being a thrifty Yorkshireman, does not go down well at all.

The pasting of a bookplate at the front of my books, with EX LIBRIS printed in red and, just for good measure, stating that the book is the property of Gervase Phinn and could it please be returned, I am afraid has had little effect. I have now resorted to placing in each loaned book a copy of the splendid Spanish *Curse on Book Thieves*, discovered in the library of the monastery of San Pedro in Barcelona, and I have to say that now my books are returned pretty promptly.

For him that stealeth or borroweth and returneth not
This book from its owner,
Let it change into a venomous serpent in his hand and rend
    him.
Let him be struck down with palsy and all his members
    blasted.
Let him languish in pain, crying aloud for mercy
And let there be no surcease to this agony 'til he sing in
    dissolution.
Let bookworms gnaw his entrails
And when at last he goeth to his last punishment,
Let the flames of hell consume him forever.

A Character of Fiction

'We've been having a little *contretemps* about you,' said the very elegant elderly woman at a literary luncheon. She turned to her equally elegant companion. 'Have we not, Patricia?'

'Indeed,' agreed her friend.

'Could you settle our difference of opinion?' she continued, resting a heavily bejewelled hand on my sleeve.

'If I can,' I replied.

'Where did you acquire your *soubriquet*?'

'My what?'

'Your cognomen, your pen-name, your *nom de plume*?'

'Obviously, Gervase Phinn is clearly not your real name,' added her companion.

'It's so very literary, like a character from Dickens. I said to Doris that I think it comes from Trollope – Phineas Finn – but my friend here thinks you acquired it from Edmund Crispin's novel, *Love Lies Bleeding*, in which the main protagonist is the sleuth, Professor Gervase Fen.'

'It's my real name,' I told them, smiling.

Doris arched an eyebrow. 'How very singular,' she said.

'However did you manage, growing up in Rotherham?' enquired her friend.

I was relating this conversation to another speaker at the luncheon. My fellow writer gave a wry smile. 'Well, can you imagine what I had to put up with?' replied David Nobbs.

Gervase is a name which appears quite frequently in historical romantic fiction, but he surfaces as a thoroughly bad lot. The name is usually given to aberrant aristocrats, narcissistic, dandified poseurs and devious, upper-crust and well-connected villains. Rather than the Regency buck, with his coal black curls, swarthy skin, dark smouldering eyes and tight-fitting britches, the Gervase of literature inevitably turns out to be a bloated, raddled old roué with quivering jowls, a wet handshake and extremely questionable habits.

In *Slightly Tempted* (a story of 'sparkling courtship, scandalous passion and all-consuming love') by Mary Balogh, Lord Gervase Ashford is the notorious rake, intent on ravishing the beautiful Lady Morgan Bedwyn. In *The Faun's Folly* by Sandra Heath, Lord Gervase Mowbray, Duke of Wroxham, is only marginally better. Georgette Heyer, in *The Quiet Gentleman*, had a central character called Gervase, Earl of St Erith and, in *The Queen's Man*, by Sharon Kay, Gervase Fitz Randolph is no better than he should be. In *Mistress Wilding*, by Rafael Sabatini, portly Sir Gervase Scoresby is not someone to be trifled with and, in *Mr Castonel*, the eponymous hero is Mr Gervase Castonel: 'It was a prepossessing face; it was silent, pale and unfathomable with grey impenetrable eyes that disliked the look of you; and dark hair.' Mary Jo Putney, in her romantic saga, *Dearly Beloved*, paints a picture of a cold and brittle man who prefers his own company to that of others:

> In spite of their physical closeness, Gervase was remote from her, his expression harsh and withdrawn. Diana leaned across the narrow gap for a light kiss, asking softly, 'Is something wrong?'
>
> His eyes were shadowed and he was silent for too long.

So, I think I have made my point: the Gervases in literature are well connected, but not very nice.

When I met the third speaker at the literary luncheon, the bestselling novelist Margaret Dickinson, author of such cracking reads as *Wish Me Luck*, *The Miller's Daughter* and *Chaff Upon the Wind*, I suggested rather facetiously that she might like to name the hero of her next novel, *Suffragette Girl*, a Gervase, and use my second name, Richard, as his surname. To my surprise and delight, she agreed. True to her word, the novel features a young, dashing military hero called Gervase Richards.

The Critic

'I think Mr Phinn will agree with me that his books won't win a Booker or a Pulitzer prize for literature, but if you want a light-hearted, entertaining, easy holiday read you need go no further.'

That was the introduction to my talk at a recent literary festival. Damned with faint praise, I thought. I know none of my books will ever rank amongst the great works of literature or become set texts for 'A' level, but the comments did, I have to say, rankle a little.

Those who write books, however, have to accept that some critics will be less than generous in their opinions and should not get too upset about it. If you present your work for public scrutiny, you have to take the rough with the smooth. Authors and poets should follow the advice of Lord Byron, in his clever and amusing *English Bards and Scotch Reviewers:*

> 'To spurn the rod a scribbler bids me kiss,
> Nor care if courts and crowds applaud or hiss.'

Of course, authors sometimes entertain wicked thoughts about their critics but to enter into a slanging match with a mean-minded reviewer can do a deal of harm to that writer's reputation. If I receive a letter criticising some aspect of my work, I never reply. It will irritate the sender to think that their efforts have been wasted and their opinions ignored.

Recently, the philosopher Alain de Botton became apoplectic when he read the review of his book, *The Pleasures and Sorrows of Work,* by the critic, Caleb Crain. He accused Crain of being 'driven by an almost manic desire to badmouth and perversely depreciate anything of value'. He went on to wish his critic 'nothing but ill will in every career move you make,' and to declare, 'I will hate you till the day I die!' He really was upset.

Nicci Gerrard, writing about the novelist Jeanette Winterson, wrote somewhat cruelly that: 'She has come a long way from playing tambourine in a missionary tent in Lancashire; she's the ultimate self-made woman – self-taught, self-improved, self-produced, self-invented and oh-so self-confident.' Miss Winterson was so angry she turned up one evening on Gerrard's doorstep and confronted the critic with the words: 'Never come near me or my writing again, do you hear?'

In reviewing Piers Morgan's book, *God Bless America*, Giles Hattersley, rather than focusing on the content of the book became rather personal in his attack when he wrote that 'being Piers Morgan these days sounds exhausting – naff parties, D-list squabbles and pictures of your wobbling moobs splashed across tabloids'. Morgan's retort to Hattersley was equally personal, branding his reviewer as 'a Norton-esquely camp, pint-sized toe rag.' Let us hope they don't meet each other at one of the 'naff parties'.

If writers must respond to critical reviewers it is best done with humour. I was speaking at another literary lunch with a very popular and successful author of romantic fiction. There is a great deal of critical and patronising clap-trap about what are dismissed as 'pot-boilers', that the characters are shallow and the plots predictable and far fetched, but those who write these massively popular stories know their audience, research their subjects and produce entertaining reads. Those quick to criticise should have a go at writing one of the novels. I asked the author at the literary lunch if she felt upset and angry with the critical reviews of her work.

She smiled. 'I sell more books than any Booker prizewinner,' she told me, 'and laugh at my critics – all the way to the bank.' Then she added, 'And after all, critics are like eunuchs, aren't they? They like to tell you how to do it but are incapable of doing it themselves.'

The Campbells Are Coming

I was asked to speak at the Scottish Education Conference in Glasgow. There was a stipulation: tartans will be worn.

I was recommended 'Scotland's Premier Kiltmaker' in Glasgow, and duly paid the shop a visit to get kitted out.

The delightfully friendly and somewhat mature lady enquired of my clan. I explained that my paternal grandmother was Margaret Helen Macdonald, a fearsome and zealous matriarch who hailed from South Uist. My grandmother maintained she was a direct descendent of the famous Ranald Macdonald, who fought for Bonnie Prince Charlie. I guess many have laid claim to this but, if my turn comes to be on the television programme which traces ancestry, I will know one way or the other.

'I'm minded to have a pair of trews rather than a kilt,' I told the proprietor.

'Turn roond,' she said, and proceeded to examine my nether regions. 'Aach no!' she exclaimed. 'Yev no the buttocks for the trews. They have to be small and well formed – like two duck's eggs in a handkerchief. You see, the short Bonnie Prince Charlie jacket exposes everything at the rear. Yours are far too big and flabby.' She was nothing if not blunt. 'Better a kilt to cover things up.' When I tried on a kilt she was rather more complimentary. 'Aye, that's better. You've the legs for a kilt.'

My Granny Macdonald married an Irishman, John Finn, but, wanting to retain her proud Scottish name, and being a bit of Patricia Routledge's Mrs Bucket aka Bouquet, changed the name to Phinn, and styled herself, rather grandly, Mrs Macdonald-Phinn. Like many a Macdonald, she had little time for anyone bearing the perfidious name Campbell. It was they, she reminded anyone inclined to listen, who massacred the poor

defenceless members of her clan at Glencoe. She would never countenance anything in her house with the word 'Campbell' on – cans of soup and meatballs bearing the dreaded name were banned.

I guess Granny Macdonald spun in her grave when I went to work for a head teacher called Mr Campbell. One February morning I arrived at school wearing a black and white tartan tie of the Menzies Clan. Sister Brendan, a teaching colleague, commented how nice it looked.

'I don't wear this to look nice, Sister,' I said mischievously, 'I wear it on this day in memory of those who died at Glencoe, those members of my grandmother's clan who were massacred by the Campbells.'

'Good gracious,' said the nun, visibly shocked, 'whenever was this?'

'The thirteenth of February, 1692,' I told her.

'That was a terrible long time ago, Gervase.'

'It was, Sister,' I said, 'but we have long memories and when Mr Campbell, the head teacher, sees this tie, he will feel suitably ashamed of what his clan did.'

'Surely it's time to forgive and forget,' she said.

After assembly that morning, Mr Campbell approached me about some inconsequential matter. Sister Brendan watched with interest.

'What did he say?' she asked in hushed tones as I headed for my classroom.

'He apologised,' I said loftily.

An Interpretation

'I hope you don't mind,' said the Director of Education, 'but we have some foreign visitors with us this evening.'

I was the after-dinner speaker at a large education conference entitled: 'Education: Where are we going from here?' Frankly, when I saw the foreign visitors, a pretty large delegation of Eastern-looking principals, education officers and university lecturers, I felt like going home.

'They do speak English, don't they?' I asked, trying to reassure myself.

'Very few of them,' said the Director of Education, smiling.

'I am afraid they won't understand a deal of what I say,' I ventured.

'They won't understand a bloody word,' said the helpful head teacher on my right, 'not if you start talking about all those Yorkshire children and the things they say. I have difficulty with some of your material myself and I'm from Lancashire.'

That's understandable, I thought to myself, but I didn't say anything.

'Don't worry,' said the Director of Education, 'there's an interpreter. He will translate what you say.' I felt my heart begin to sink. 'I've told them you are a very amusing speaker and that they are in for a most entertaining evening.' My heart had now sunk into my shoes.

I joined a group of head teachers at one of the tables. 'Do you speak Japanese then?' asked one, a large bearded individual who would have looked at home as a bouncer outside a club.

'No, I don't,' I replied.

'I'm going to enjoy this,' he said, 'watching their expressions when you get going. Their faces will be a picture.'

'I don't think your material will easily translate into Japanese,' another Job's comforter told me.

'And the Japanese sense of humour is very different from our own,' added another.

I can't say that my address was a resounding success. The foreign visitors sat politely, with bemused expressions on their faces, while the interpreter struggled valiantly to translate my anecdotes. After the first five minutes, he threw in the towel and joined his colleagues in observing me with the same inscrutable expression on his face.

After twenty minutes or so, I too threw in the towel and decided the poor Japanese visitors had endured quite enough of me rattling on about children and schools in Yorkshire.

'Most enjoyable,' said the Director of Education, in a rather lukewarm tone of voice, as I prepared to make a hasty exit. 'Do come and say hello to our foreign visitors. I am sure they would like to meet you.'

'My son Matthew lives in Japan,' I told a most distinguished-looking man in thin gold-rimmed spectacles.

The interpreter informed him what I had said with an expressionless face.

'He loves Japan,' I continued, 'the people, the culture, the scenery, the food.'

The interpreter translated.

'Matthew has been there for five years now, in Hiroshima. He's an artist in residence there.'

The interpreter translated.

'He has fallen in love with your country.' I was now getting rather effusive.

The translator gave a small sympathetic smile. 'We are from China,' he told me.

'Aah . . . so,' I said, smiling weakly. 'China?' I hoped that the floor would open and swallow me up. All eyes were focused upon me. 'My son Dominic lives in China, you know,' I said cheerfully. 'He is the General Manager at the European Chamber of Commerce in Nanjing. He loves your country, the people, the culture, the scenery, the food . . .'

After the Brigadier

I like Rotarians. They are invariably friendly, good-humoured and kindly people with a great sense of fun and, after the Women's Institute and the Townswomen's Guild, they are my best audience.

One bright Sunday morning, I was in Bournemouth to speak, at the District Governor's autumn conference, to over a thousand Rotarians and their wives or partners. I was greeted warmly at the entrance of the venue by the Sergeant-at-Arms, a jolly red-faced man dressed in a striped blazer and straw boater, and sporting a large yellow sash.

'You're speaking after the Brigadier,' he told me.

'Really,' I said cheerfully.

'Have you heard the Brigadier speak before?' he asked.

'No,' I replied, 'I haven't.'

'You are in for a real treat. I've been coming to these conferences for years and I've never yet heard a better speaker – amusing, informative and challenging and not a note in sight.'

My heart sank.

'I wouldn't like to be in your shoes,' he vouchsafed.

I was taken to meet the District Governor, a distinguished-looking, heavily bemedalled individual.

'You are speaking after the Brigadier,' he told me.

'So I believe.'

'Have you heard the Brigadier before?'

'No, I haven't,' I said.

'The Brigadier was speaking at our conference a couple of years ago, and is back by popular demand. Quite a brilliant presentation.'

My heart was now thumping away in my chest and my stomach was doing kangaroo jumps.

I have followed many distinguished, charismatic and amusing speakers in my time – Simon Weston, Barry Cryer, Sir John Mills, Lord Snowdon, George Galloway, P D James, David Mellor, Andy McNab and others – and it is a frightening experience because the audience feels so let down if you are not as good, which invariably you are not. Now here I was, speaking after the British Army's answer to a cross between Oscar Wilde and Winston Churchill.

Backstage, the sound technician, fiddling with my lapel microphone, whispered, 'Have you heard the Brigadier before?'

'No, I have not!' I snapped irritably. 'And before you tell me, I do know what a brilliant speaker he is.'

My outburst was overheard by an attractive woman, a little younger than myself, dressed in an elegant grey suit and pristine white blouse. She was standing in the wings.

'Good morning,' she said, giving me a disarming smile.

'Morning,' I muttered.

'Are you one of the speakers?' she asked.

'Yes I am,' I told her.

'You must be the school inspector.'

'That's right. I'm following this bloody Brigadier when he deigns to show up.'

The woman smiled even wider. 'I'm the bloody Brigadier,' she said.

Him Off the Telly

It is you, isn't it?

Him off the telly?

I thought it was.

I said to my friend

Look, I said, there's that man off the telly,

The one with the hair and the fancy ties.

The comedian,

The one who makes people laugh.

I just knew it was you.

I said to my friend,

I said, it's him all right,

I recognise him,

Him off the telly,

The one with the jokes and the cheeky smile,

The comedian.

The one who makes people laugh.

I'll pop over, I said

And have a word.

No don't, she said.

I am, I said.

I said, he'll be used to people

Pointing him out and going up to him.

'Are You Anybody?'

It's part of being a celebrity,
Of being on the telly.
Anyway, I just thought I'd have a word.
And tell you –
That *I* don't think you're all that funny.

'It's a Funny Old World'

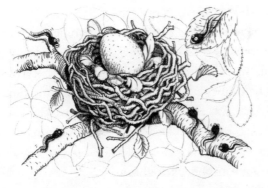

Health, Life and Death

The Facts of Life

The cleaner at York Teachers' Centre was pulling a face when I arrived to direct a poetry course.

'They've got someone talking to the teachers on sex education in Room 4 this morning,' she told me, shaking her head. 'Why in the world do children need to know about that? It will give them ideas. There's too much sex on television as it is. I mean, when we were young we knew nothing about that sort of thing.'

'No, we didn't,' I agreed, recalling that 'the facts of life' when I was growing up in Rotherham was something of a soiled phrase. 'No one ever talked about it.' Perhaps they should have, I thought.

'I mean,' continued the cleaner, 'I didn't know what a homosexual was until I married my husband.'

The Government is now bringing in guidelines on sex education which all schools will be required to include on the already crowded curriculum. England has one of the highest rates of unwanted pregnancies in Europe, and this initiative is to warn youngsters of the dangers of unprotected sex and the looming menace of HIV.

Of course, ideally it should be the parents who take on the responsibility of explaining things to their offspring. Christine and I tried, but with little success.

When Dominic was seven he asked the question we were expecting. He was always a very inquisitive child so when he asked casually, one day, 'Daddy, where do I come from?' I was not surprised.

'I'll get your mother,' I told him.

Christine and I sat him down between us on the settee.

'You know, Dominic, that Daddy loves Mummy,' I told him.

'Yes,' he replied, his little brow furrowing.

'And that Mummy loves Daddy?'

'Yes.'

'Well, you are here because we love each other.'

'How do you mean?'

'Over to you Christine,' I said.

'No,' replied my wife, 'you are doing very nicely.'

I took a breath. 'Well, Dominic, inside Mummy's tummy is an egg.'

'An egg!' he exclaimed.

'It's not a big egg. In fact it's a tiny little egg and you can't see it.'

'I've got more than one,' interrupted Christine.

'You have a go,' I told her.

'And down there,' said Christine, vaguely gesturing to my nether regions, 'Daddy has a sort of little tadpole.'

'I have 400 million,' I told her.

Dominic's eyes widened. 'Wow!'

'And when Mummy and Daddy have a very close cuddle,' continued Christine, and the little tadpole meets the little egg, then a little baby forms.'

We continued with our explanation until I finally asked our wide-eyed son: 'So does that explain where you come from?'

'No,' replied Dominic simply. 'I just wanted to know where I come from. David comes from Halifax.'

When I was a school inspector, I observed a lesson where a young woman teacher was explaining the facts of life to a group of eleven-year-olds. She had informed me, prior to the lesson, that she found the task daunting, and predicted that one notoriously naughty boy would no doubt embarrass her by asking a tricky question at the end. She pointed out the said child: a frizzy-haired boy with a face full of freckles and a cheeky expression.

Sure enough, after the lesson the boy waved his hand in the air like a daffodil in a strong wind.

The teacher sighed. 'Yes Duane,' she said. Her expression betrayed the fact that she expected that, of all the children, he would be the one to ask a question. 'What is it?'

'Can I ask you something, Miss?' he said.

'If you must,' replied the teacher, giving me a knowing look.

'Will we be having rounders this afternoon?'

Getting up My Nose

I was once invited to contribute to a radio phone-in on the topic: 'What are the things that really wind you up?'

'Gervase,' asked the producer, 'are there any things that really annoy you?'

'Where shall I start?' I asked.

I will disclose what my irritants are a little later on but shall now reveal what the many listeners who phoned in found really annoying.

The show had a quite exceptional response from grumpy old men and women who vented their fury on, amongst other things, litter louts, unhelpful shop assistants, chewing gum on streets and seats, automated greetings on customer care lines, slow drivers, spitting, queue jumpers, dawdlers and ditherers, cyclists and begging on streets. Other pet hates included speed cameras, loud personal stereos on public transport, white van drivers, IKEA, backpackers on trains and shoppers who fumble for money at the checkout. One of the most unusual complaints was from an elderly woman who complained about men and their 'genital adjustments in public places'.

I added to the list. Dog mess on the streets really really gets up my nose. Let me rephrase that – it makes my blood boil. Many dog owners are responsible, of course, and take the mess home in a plastic bag, which is the thing to do. But then there are the others. John, a neighbour of mine, was astounded to see a small hairy dog performing directly in front of his gate while the owner looked on. By the time he had put on his shoes to confront the offender, man and dog had set off down the street. Not to be deterred, my neighbour scooped up the deposit with a spade and followed the culprit until he caught up.

'I think this is yours,' he said, holding the spade at arm's length.

Just as well the dog wasn't a Doberman.

The other people who get my goat are loud mobile phone users on trains. The whole of the carriage is privy to the most personal conversations, delivered at maximum volume.

On one London to Newcastle train, a businessman, who had commandeered the table with his Filofax, laptop, folder and briefcase, was holding forth on his mobile phone opposite a woman passenger who was clearly irritated.

'Yes, darling!' he shouted down the phone, 'I'll be back in Doncaster at eight. Yes, darling, the meeting went fine. No, darling, Raymond never made it. Really darling? Well, bring the Range Rover to the station. Yes, I know you're not used to driving it, darling. Well, get Robert to reverse it out for you, darling. Yes, darling.'

The woman had had quite enough and, snatching the phone from his hands, said into it in a loud and alluring voice, 'Come back to bed, darling.'

Keeping Calm

So the story goes, Oscar Wilde was dining at the Café Royal with a group of friends and admirers. Through the elegant restaurant strode the irascible and boorish Marquess of Queensbury, the father of Wilde's lover, Lord Alfred Douglas. Queensbury was carrying a rotten cabbage, which he presented to Wilde with the words, delivered loudly enough for all to hear: 'This, sir, is what I think of you!' There was an expectant hush amongst the diners, and all eyes looked at the celebrated wit and playwright to see his reaction. Oscar Wilde smiled, nodded and held the foul-smelling vegetable to his nose. He sniffed it dramatically.

'Thank you, my lord,' he replied serenely. 'Whenever I smell a stinking cabbage, I shall always think of you.'

I have a great admiration for people who can keep calm and collected in the face of a furious outburst from a rude and angry person, and manage to make a witty riposte.

I took Christine out for a meal on her birthday to an exclusive restaurant. Everything about the evening was superb – the meal, the presentation, the ambience and the attention we received from the friendly waiters – until the man on the next table, a large, loud, red-faced and voluble individual came to settle his bill.

'I hope you enjoyed your meal, sir?' enquired the owner.

'No,' replied the man, 'I can't say as I have. It were far too fancy for me. I likes plain food not this *nouveau riche* stuff. It were not my cup of tea at all. And I have to say it were very pricey for what it was. I don't want to get into an argument about it, but since you asked, I can't say as how I enjoyed it.'

'Get into an argument?' repeated the owner, smiling. 'No sir, neither do I, but were I to challenge you to a duel, I should select the English language as my weapon.'

It amazes me how shop assistants, waiters, police officers, receptionists and traffic wardens (yes, traffic wardens have a job to do) manage to keep unruffled when faced with such people.

Last year, I was signing books in a delightful bookshop in Cumbria. It was a veritable treasure chest, with friendly staff, superb displays and a wonderful selection of fiction, poetry and reference books.

Into the shop came a stony-faced woman with a narrow bony face and an equally mardy-looking child in tow.

'Where are the bestsellers?' she demanded. There was no 'please'.

The owner smiled and showed her to the appropriate part of the shop.

The woman plucked a tome from the shelf and sniffed noisily. 'This is half price in Tesco's,' she clucked disapprovingly, before sticking it back.

'Perhaps you might like to purchase it from Tesco's, then, madam,' replied the owner.

'I don't like this writer anyway,' she told him, sniffing again. 'Your books ought to be alphabeticalised,' she told him.

The owner's face signalled that he was getting rather irritated but he retained the forced smile.

The ill-tempered customer bought a guidebook, which was placed in a small brown paper bag. Then she departed. A moment later, she returned with the whinging child.

'He wants a book,' she said. 'Where's the children's section?'

The owner took a deep breath and showed her to the shelf.

She selected a book.

'May I put it in with your other book, madam?' asked the owner. 'It would save using another bag.'

The woman exploded. 'Of course I want a bag!' She said, outraged that the owner should suggest otherwise.

The owner produced the largest brown paper bag he could find.

'That's far too big!' she snapped.

'Please take it, madam,' he told her.

'I said it is too big,' she repeated angrily.

'Please, I insist,' said the owner.

'I said it's too big!' snapped the woman.

'It's not for the book, madam,' the owner told her. 'It's for your head.'

Take Care with Your Writing

I was delighted to learn that one of my picture books, *Our Cat Cuddles*, was to be published across the Atlantic. I was told, however, that there had to be certain minor alterations to suit the American market: 'Mum' would become 'Mom', the 'RSPCA' would become 'Animal Shelter' and the reference to giving the kitten milk needed to be changed. They wanted to change milk? It was Oscar Wilde who observed that we British share everything with the Americans except the language, but I was intrigued, and asked my editor, somewhat naively: 'Don't they have milk in America?'

'Children are taught in schools that it's very bad to give cats milk,' I was told. 'You'll also upset the powerful cat lobby.' It was then pointed out to me that, when Hillary Clinton dumped the White House cat, Socks, on Betty Currie, her husband's PA, when Bill's term as president expired, she came in for a deal of criticism, and her abandonment of the pet could hinder her ambition to return to the White House as the first woman president.

The same week, I received a sharp letter from a head teacher who had heard me speak at a conference. She informed me, in a high-handed manner, that the term 'brainstorming', which I had used, was inadvisable. She pointed out that 'people who have brainstorms would feel singled out and upset, and the acceptable term to use now is "thought shower" or "cloudburst".' She continued to inform me that the term 'nitty-gritty', another term I used, was 'racist' and that 'it refers to the nits which covered the holds in slave ships and is deeply offensive to black people'. Then she mentioned that the bully in one of my Royston Knapper children's stories was 'a fat boy' and discriminated against overweight people. As my father would have said: 'Well, I'll go to the bottom of our stairs!'

I have to say that I get a bit hot under the collar when the 'language police' start flexing their muscles. I certainly do not wish to upset or offend anyone, but sometimes I do feel we go a tad too far with this creeping censorship of what we should or should not say.

Well, I earnestly hope that we do not go down the road of our American cousins. According to Diane Ravitch, an educational historian and former US government official, some of the censorship imposed on books and on teachers in America is often trivial, sometimes ludicrous and, on occasion, breathtakingly stupid. In her book, *The Language Police: How Pressure Groups Restrict What Students Learn*, she reveals that a story entitled *The Friendly Dolphin* was rejected by one school committee because it discriminated against students who did not live near the sea. Another story, *The Silly Old Woman*, was barred because it contained the stereotype of an elderly woman. Other banned words and topics included 'blind as a bat' (handicapist), 'henpecked husband' (sexist), 'past one's prime' (ageist), 'mother cleaning the house' (sexist), 'bookworm' (offensive to hard workers) and so the list goes on. One school board objected to a picture book about an old lady with too many cats. It was deemed a sexual stereotype.

Ah me, I have an idea my little picture book, *Our Cat Cuddles*, has little chance of seeing the light of day across the Atlantic, and my book on dinosaurs hasn't a cat in hell's chance. You see, all books on dinosaurs are banned by several school committees in the southern states because they imply the theory of evolution, which is not universally accepted.

Customers Are Not Always Right

I took my brother-in-law and my sister out recently, to celebrate a significant birthday. We sat in the glorious sunshine outside the Cliffemount Hotel at Runswick Bay, overlooking one of Yorkshire's most magnificent vistas: a crescent of pale yellow sand, great looming rock faces, small stone cottages with pantile roofs clinging to the cliff and tiny boats bobbing on a smooth and glassy sea. It was idyllic.

'What a wonderful view,' I said, sighing and turning to the glum-faced couple on the next table.

'It's a bit too chocolate-boxy for my liking,' observed the woman. This reminded me of an anecdote recorded in the *Countryman* magazine when a Sheffield couple was asked: 'Did you enjoy your holiday in the Lake District?'

'There were nowt but watter and scenery,' was the blunt reply.

I related the story to the proprietor of the Cliffemount when we went in for lunch.

'There's no pleasing some people,' she said. 'I have had guests who seem to make a career of complaining. One resident grumbled that the sunshine was too bright in his room, another that the toilet was too noisy and a third that the birds sang too shrilly in the morning and woke her up.' Short of arranging an eclipse, inventing a silent flush and shooting all the seagulls, there wasn't much the proprietor could do.

The report on holidaymakers' genuine complaints, by the travel agency Thomas Cook, makes amusing reading. There are complaints about the beach being too sandy, the local store in Spain that didn't sell proper biscuits like custard creams and ginger nuts, and the sea being a different colour from that in the brochure. One traveller complained that the flight from Jamaica to England took nine hours but it only took the Americans three to get home. Perhaps you can guess which country *this* next tourist had visited: 'There were too many Spanish people. The receptionist spoke Spanish. The food was Spanish and there were too many foreigners.'

There was the sightseer on honeymoon with his new wife, at a game park in Africa, who spotted a very amorous and visibly aroused elephant and complained that the beast made him feel inadequate. A guest at a Novotel hotel in Australia grumbled that his soup was too thick and strong, only to be informed that he was eating the gravy. 'My fiancé and I booked a twin-bedded room,' complained another holidaymaker, 'but we were placed in a double-bedded room. We now hold you responsible for the fact that I find myself pregnant. This would not have happened if you had put us in the room we had booked.'

At the Cliffemount Hotel, we had a magnificent meal of fresh Whitby fish, sitting at a table overlooking the bay and served by a smiling and friendly waitress. The chef emerged from the kitchen to ask if we had enjoyed his efforts and, when settling the bill, I was asked by the proprietor if everything was satisfactory.

'How could it be otherwise?' I asked. 'It was splendid.'

She smiled. 'You would be surprised. One guest remarked that she felt the place had no atmosphere.'

'How do you manage to deal with such people?' I asked.

'By being polite,' she said, shrugging. 'What else can one do?'

There is the story (probably apocryphal) about the man at the check-in at the airport, who berated the poor member of staff for a considerable period of time. The young woman behind the counter answered him calmly and politely and checked in his bags.

'How do you stand for this sort of thing?' asked the next passenger. 'It's disgraceful the way that man spoke to you.'

The young woman smiled. 'The gentleman is going to New York,' she replied, 'but his bags are going to Beijing.'

The Photograph

My sister, Christine, arrived for lunch one Sunday with the family photograph albums, which she had taken charge of when our parents died and which had been in her loft ever since. That afternoon, we spent a good couple of hours looking through the contents and reminiscing. In one album there was a collection of photographs of our father, taken before and during the last war, when he was a despatch rider. I had never seen the photographs before and was intrigued. There were two portraits, taken in a Cairo studio, of this striking-looking, serious-faced young man, his hair neatly parted and his beret tucked in regulation fashion under his epaulette, a couple of him standing to attention by a motorbike and sidecar, a group photograph of a squad of fourteen smiling soldiers in full uniform, sitting straight backed and cross-legged at Catterick Camp, and several of my father astride a horse.

'What's he doing on a horse?' I asked my sister. 'I never knew he could ride.'

'He was in the army equestrian team,' my sister commented casually.

'I never knew that!' I said, astounded.

It occurred to me that Sunday afternoon that I knew very little about my father's war service. He never spoke of it. For that matter, nor did my Uncle Alec, who was a warrant officer in the Royal Air Force and flew bombing missions over Germany, or my Uncle Jimmy, who served with the Irish Guards. My Uncle Ted, a sergeant in the Army Medical Corps and a Dunkirk veteran, only once told me about the panic and the horrors he had witnessed on the beaches as the British Army retreated. Perhaps these men had seen things that they wished to forget. I was very proud of them and still am and their medals are on the wall in my study.

When I was a lad, my father, a great storyteller, amused and entertained me with the exciting exploits of the Three Musketeers and Biggles, Long John Silver and Rob Roy McGregor, Huckleberry Finn and Robinson Crusoe, but he never told me anything about his time in the British Army. I guess the subject was never raised. Perhaps it was too painful for him to recall or that he just wanted to return to his home and family and get on with his life; then again, he might have considered it such an ordinary, uneventful few years of his life and therefore of not much interest to a boy keen on adventure stories.

I do remember my father's last Remembrance Sunday, when I accompanied him to the war memorial with my three young sons. He was in a thoughtful, sombre mood during the service, and stood a little apart from us. Richard, my eldest son, noticed as the Last Post was being played that his grandfather was in tears.

On that special Sunday we should all, especially the young, remember those who fought and those who died in defence of our freedom. My poem is dedicated to all those brave men and women, members of today's armed forces, who are still fighting in those 'far-off lands of blistering heat and burning sand' in defence of freedom, justice and humanity.

Remembrance Sunday

On Remembrance Sunday Grandpa cried
For his two brothers, who had died
In some forgotten far-off land
Of blistering heat and burning sand.
He touched a medal on his chest
Which sparkled brighter than the rest:
'The Africa Star,' he gently sighed,
'A badge of honour, of those who died,
A symbol of our Ted and Jack
Who never made the journey back.'
We watched old soldiers stride on by,
Straight of back and heads held high,
And we clutched our poppies of brightest red
And we wept for the brothers Jack and Ted.

A Real Hero

Like many in this country, I was appalled by the pictures in the newspapers and on the television screen of the homecoming parade of the soldiers from the 2nd battalion, The Royal Anglian Regiment, returning from serving abroad. 'Butchers of Basra!', 'Cowards!', 'Killers!', 'Extremists!', the placards proclaimed. I was deeply saddened by the sight of the grieving parents at the funeral of their son, Sapper Patrick Azimkar, murdered in Northern Ireland, a young man who pulled his friend to the ground and saved his life before he was killed. These men and women who serve in our armed forces are dedicated to help bring peace to war-torn lands and are abused and sometimes maimed and killed for trying to do so.

That same week, I was privileged to share a platform with Doug Beattie at the Manchester Literary Luncheon. One of a tiny contingent of British troops, the Royal Irish Regiment captain went to help Afghan forces recapture the town of Garmsir – known as the Taliban gateway to Helmand Province. For two brutal and bloody weeks, he and a few soldiers, who shrunk to just three men, faced a ferocious enemy in impossible conditions and with inadequate supplies. For his repeated bravery, Captain Beattie was decorated with the Military Cross.

There was a strange hush in the audience, and a good few tears, as this brave soldier told us with heartfelt honesty about his experiences and of the resilience, courage and humanity of the British soldiers who served with him. At one point, when serving in Iraq, he was responsible for forming and running the holding pen for 1,500 enemy soldiers with a small defence platoon to contain them.

'It was a tense period,' he said. 'I understood why my men's frustrations might so easily boil over: the heat, the physical exhaustion, the real danger and the imagined danger. But I was clear in my own head. We would treat the prisoners correctly and with compassion. It was what I asked of the men under my watch. The response was fantastic. Not only did they do what was requested but they often did more, giving up their own water and food so at least some of our charges could be satiated. I was, and am, extremely proud of them.'

The morning after the literary lunch, I travelled to London with a heavy case in tow. As I struggled to lift my burden off the packed luggage rack, a young soldier took it from my hands.

'OK, pop,' he said, 'I'll give you a hand.'

Doug Beattie would have been proud of him.

Someone at the Door

I have to say that I admire the sheer persistence and determination of Jehovah's Witnesses. Near where I live, their bright modern church has been built, and many a weekend I have received the attention of a couple of zealous members of the congregation wishing to debate their beliefs with me. Without exception, I have found these visitors smartly turned out, courteous and good-humoured but, sadly for them, singularly unsuccessful in converting me to their way of thinking. I was brought up to be polite to people who appear on one's doorstep so have, unlike some, I should guess, never been discourteous to these dedicated proselytisers.

However, one weekend I was not in the mood for any disturbance. I had a deadline to meet. My long-suffering wife had departed on the Friday evening for a weekend with her parents in Shipley, to give me some peace and quiet to complete a book I had been struggling to write. The final manuscript had to be on my editor's desk first thing Tuesday. So, nine o'clock Saturday morning found me on a roll in my study, rattling away happily at the keyboard, making real headway. Then the doorbell rang. I decided to ignore it. The wretched bing-bonging continued so, hair a mess, unshaven, barefooted and in my old green towelling dressing gown, I stomped down the stairs and threw open the front door. On the doorstep were two well-dressed, smiling individuals. The middle-aged man held a briefcase and his young woman companion held a clutch of papers.

'Good morning,' said the man cheerfully.

'Morning,' I grunted.

'Beautiful day, isn't it?' said his companion. 'Don't you feel glad to be alive?'

'Look . . .' I began.

'Might we interest you in what we believe?' said the man.

'No,' I replied bluntly.

They both were clearly taken aback. This was somewhat surprising to me since I should think they often receive such a response.

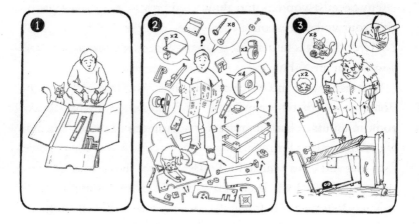

'I do not wish to appear churlish,' I told them, 'but I am exceptionally busy and have not the time, nor indeed the inclination, to debate your beliefs this morning.'

'We would welcome the opportunity of explaining our views,' said the man, undeterred by my sharpness.

'And what we stand for,' added the woman.

'I am fully aware of what you stand for,' I said. I pointed to the clutch of papers in her hand. 'I have read all about your beliefs and have debated them a number of times with your colleagues on this very doorstep and I am not interested. I shall never be converted to your way of thinking.'

'Really,' said the man, looking very interested.

'And I have to tell you,' I continued, 'that the only thing you and I have in common is God.'

The man looked at the woman, smiled weakly and then turned his attentions back to me. 'So I take it, then,' he said, 'that you won't be voting Liberal Democrat?'

Consulting the Doctor

I have been having a bit of trouble with my throat recently.

'It's because you talk too much,' said my wife. 'You want to give your voice a rest once in a while.'

My doctor was rather more sympathetic and I was sent to the hospital for an X-ray.

So much is said and written about the failings of the NHS, but I have to say that I received five-star treatment. I sat with my book in an easy chair, in a comfortable lounge area, with a cup of coffee, waiting for my name to be called. It wasn't long before a smiling and chatty nurse took me to have the X-ray.

A week later, I was back. They had discovered something.

Then followed a battery of tests, all done with cheerfulness and accompanied by an explanation of what was happening.

The specialist appeared and introduced himself, and I followed him into a room that smelt of antiseptic. Leaning over me with a long, thin piece of tube-like equipment, he explained that the bronchoscopy would be a little uncomfortable when the probe went down the back of my throat and into my lungs, but it would soon be over.

'It sounds quite fun,' I managed to murmur. I eyed the tube. 'I hope it's had a thorough wash,' I told him. 'I hazard to think what other orifices it's explored.'

He smiled, and assured me this equipment was used solely for lungs.

It was the speech therapist (a Joanna Lumley look-alike) who did the endoscopy (the tube this time went up my nose and down the back of my throat) – another fun experience. All was explained to me, and I watched in fascination as the miniature camera displayed my insides on a small screen.

'You can have a copy of the photographs if you like,' said the smiling nurse, who held my hand throughout.

'Great,' I croaked. 'I'll put them in my album next to the holiday snaps.'

'Well?' said my wife when I arrived home.

'I've got to go back for the results next week,' I told her, 'and in the meantime I have to try and rest my voice.'

She gave a hollow laugh.

The following week I was called into the specialist's office.

He sat behind his desk, half-moon spectacles perched on the end of his nose, a wodge of papers before him. He tapped the desk with his pen for a moment as if considering what to say.

I feared the worst.

He took a deep breath. 'Before I go through the test results, Mr Phinn,' he said, 'may I ask you something?'

I knew it, I thought, my heart thumping in my chest and my throat becoming dry. It's serious. He's going to ask me if I have made a will. I nodded. 'Yes, of course,' I managed to mouth.

He reached into a drawer and produced a copy of my latest Dales book, which he passed across the desk. He smiled. 'My wife is a big fan of yours,' he said. 'I wonder if I might trouble you to sign this for her?'

With trembling hand, I wrote my name.

There was something on my throat, he explained, but it was damaged cartilage which was not life-threatening. He suggested, however, that I might undergo a course of speech therapy.

'I don't think I will find that too arduous,' I said, thinking of the breathing exercises I would be doing with the Joanna Lumley look-alike.

The Best Medicine

There's the story of the man (no doubt from Yorkshire) who, coming out of a Ken Dodd show where the audience had been weeping with laughter, responded to his friend's question, 'What did you think of the comedian then?' with the observation that: 'Well, he was all right if you like laughing.'

It is a fact that some people don't like to laugh. Lord

264

Chesterfield, for example, thought it extremely vulgar to express amusement. 'There is nothing so ill-bred,' he wrote, 'as audible laughter, with its disagreeable noise and shocking distortion of the face.' He was clearly not a barrel of laughs. Queen Mary was also a bit of a killjoy, by all accounts, and instructed her family never even to smile in public.

I feel sorry for these wet blankets, because laughter not only makes you feel good, it does you good.

According to Dr Pierce J Howard, Director of Research, Center for Applied Cognitive Studies, NC, USA: 'Laughter increases our immunity to illness, improves sleep, enhances natural growth and results in tests of problem-solving ability improve when preceded by laughter.' A colleague, Michael Miller of the University of Maryland, agreed that a chortle a day can keep the doctor away and found, after extensive research, that laughter 'offsets the impact of mental stress which is harmful to the endothelium'. He further discovered that, compared with healthy people of the same age, those with heart disease were 40 per cent less likely to laugh in a variety of situations.

Laughter, of course, can come in different forms. It can be defensive, cynical, embarrassed or cruel as well as good-humoured. Sometimes we laugh to be polite or to cover up, to be part of the group or just to be sociable. And what makes one person laugh might not amuse another. I remember, as a child, gathering around the laughing policeman in the glass case on Blackpool pier. This large puppet came to life when a penny was put in the slot. Then he shook and guffawed, and his infectious laughter had those who watched doubled up with laughter. There was always one, however, who looked on with a face like a death mask, perhaps wondering why so many people found it funny.

I have to admit to having a chuckle when I read about the

hoax telephone calls to Dublin Zoo. It can't have been much fun for those receiving them.

'Good afternoon, Dublin Zoo. How may I help you?'

'I'm responding to an urgent call from Mr Rory Lion. If he's not available, Anna Conda will take the call.'

'We have not lost our sense of humour,' said the marketing manager, 'but with the calls coming in at a rate of thirteen a minute, it's no laughing matter.' In desperation, she has recorded the following welcome message on the answerphone: 'If you are wanting to speak to a Mr Rory Lion, C Lion, G Raff, Ann T Lope or E Guana, you are the victim of a hoax message.' This, of course, might cause something of a problem should Mr Don Kee or Mr Jack Rabbit be appointed to the zoo.

Believing in Miracles

Alan, a friend of mine, recently spent a time in hospital. He retired as head teacher on the Friday and on the Tuesday he had a stroke. Fortunately he is on the mend and when I visited him he was cheerful and optimistic, and spoke warmly of the care and attention he had been receiving from the doctors and nurses.

I had arrived at the hospital rather too early for visiting time, so had retired to the café for a cup of tea before seeing Alan. When I came to pay, I encountered in front of me a large, tattooed woman in fluffy bedroom slippers and shocking pink dressing gown. She was berating the poor woman at the till.

'There's not much flipping cheese in this sandwich and it's flipping expensive as well and I don't like the flipping tea either,' she complained.

Needless to say 'flipping' was not part of her vocabulary, but the other 'f' word was.

As the vision in pink shuffled off, the woman on the till sighed. 'You certainly get to see life in here,' she told me.

'Think yourself lucky,' I replied. 'You don't have to treat her. Can you imagine her as a patient?'

I was clearly mistaken for a member of the medical team, for the woman on the till nodded and said, 'You're quite right, Doctor. I don't know how you and the nurses have the patience.' Then she smiled. 'I've taken off the staff discount.'

The man in the bed next to my friend, who had also suffered a stroke, was in a considerably worse condition than Alan, and lay prone and speechless, his body stiff as a plank. On his second day in the hospital, Alan was visited by a former colleague, a devout Roman Catholic, who brought with him some holy water from Lourdes. This he sprinkled liberally on Alan's arm and leg, and said a short prayer of healing.

The visitor of the man in the next bed watched proceedings in interested silence and then asked: 'What are you doing?'

Alan's former colleague told her the story of how a young woman called Bernadette saw a vision of the Virgin Mary in 1858 and, since then, the grotto at Lourdes, where she appeared, spouts spring water that possesses healing properties.

'Can my husband have some of that?' asked the woman.

'Is he a Catholic?' she was asked.

'No.'

'Does he believe in miracles?'

'I don't suppose he's ever thought about it but he's game to try anything if it helps him get better.'

So the holy water from Lourdes was sprinkled on the prone individual who, such was his condition, really had no choice in the matter and looked somewhat bemused.

The next morning, when Alan awoke, his neighbour had gone.

Oh dear, he thought, the man has suffered another stroke. He did look very ill.

'Has the man in the next bed died?' asked Alan of a nurse.

'Oh no,' she said, 'he's having a shower. He's going home later today.'

A miracle, thought my friend. He had witnessed a miracle.

Later that day the doctor called and, after hearing Alan's account, informed my friend, with a wry smile, that the man had not, in fact, had a stroke but had suffered a particularly bad migraine.

Tricks in the Hospital

When my mother was a theatre sister, young doctors sometimes played tricks on the nurses. They were harmless enough, but my mother warned the trainees to be wary of being sent for 'a Fallopian tube' or a box of 'Bower's Capsules' or to get the doctor's 'anatomical snuff box'. One young nurse, attending her first operation, watched nervously as a formidable surgeon performed in the theatre. He was known for being humourless, rude and irascible, a man who never said 'please' and 'thank you'. When he turned to the young nurse and snapped, 'Fetch sister's coat!' the poor young woman jumped.

'P . . . p . . . pardon?' stuttered the young nurse.

'You heard me, nurse,' snapped the surgeon, speaking through his mask. 'Fetch sister's coat!'

'Is this a joke?' she asked feebly.

'A joke!' exploded the surgeon. 'Fetch sister's coat! Now!'

The young woman scurried off, returning a moment later with my mother's coat.

The surgeon sighed deeply and articulated, 'I said, "Fetch the cystescope".'

On another occasion, a bubbly, good-humoured West Indian nurse was observing the self-same surgeon.

In those days when the patient was anaesthetised, his or her arm was placed on what was called an 'arm board'.

The surgeon turned to the nurse. 'Arm bored!' he snapped.

'Pardon, Doctor?' asked the nurse.

'I said "arm board",' repeated the surgeon.

'Well I'se bored too, Doctor,' she replied pleasantly, 'but we'll soon be going home.'

The Funeral

My sister Christine taught an art class in Kinvara, a village on the west coast of Ireland where she once lived. In the group was an elderly man who found, late in life, that he had a real talent for painting, and became prolific in turning out the most beautiful and sought-after watercolours. Sadly, on his ninetieth birthday, he died. My sister, along with members of her art group, attended the funeral in a small church in rural Connemara. Prior to the requiem mass, the deceased man's daughter invited my sister to view the body, which lay in an open coffin in the front room of her small cottage. On the walls surrounding the coffin were her father's paintings. The artist himself reclined in the casket, clutching a set of paintbrushes and a palette.

One aged aunt, leaning over the coffin, stared for a moment at the corpse before remarking to the daughter: 'You know, Bridget, sure your father's never looked better.'

Death comes to all of us but people in the country can still find humour in this most serious situation. Those in rural communities see life and death at first hand every day and perhaps, therefore, have a better understanding and indeed appreciation of such things. Some of my favourite stories, which I am assured by the tellers are true, include the following.

The cortege was leaving the crematorium. It was a bitterly cold day and the ground was dangerously icy. Two elderly women, instead of using the steps, decided that they would exit via the ramp, up which the coffin had been wheeled. One of the women lost her footing, slipped and nearly fell, but, grasping the handrail, managed to right herself.

'Dear me!' she said to her companion. 'I nearly went full length.'

'Well, it's very slippery,' replied her friend. Then she added: 'I mean, you would have thought they would have put some ashes down.'

Some years ago, in a mining village in South Yorkshire, a veiled figure in the deepest black arrived at a cinema, followed by what appeared to be a funeral party. She handed the usherette a sheaf of tickets, and, noting the look of surprise on the young woman's face, said solemnly: 'Ee, lass, my Jack never did care for funeral teas and such but he did enjoy a good cowboy picture.'

The owner of a butcher's shop in North Yorkshire died. His friend, a lugubrious character called Tommy, attended the funeral tea along with the other mourners. Amongst the spread on the table, he observed some sausages on cocktail sticks.

'Come along, Tommy,' said the widow, 'will you not have a sausage?'

'No thank you,' came the reply. 'I'd soon as not.'

'Don't sausages agree with you then?' asked the widow.

'Well,' said Tommy, shaking his head, 'I've got nowt against sausages as such, but I think black pudding would have been more seemly at a funeral.'

The undertaker, having been upstairs to measure the corpse, joined the silent and sorrowful family group in a Wensleydale farmhouse. He waited for a moment before asking in a solicitous voice: 'And when would you like the funeral to take place?' There was a long pause. 'Might I suggest Saturday?'

'Aye, that'll be all right,' sighed the widow, sadly.

Another long silence ensued, then the eldest son announced: 'Nay, that'll not do.'

'May I ask why?' enquired the undertaker.

'It's t'bull sale at Hawes on Saturday,' came the reply.

A Precious Gift (a Smile)

It cannot be bought or borrowed
It cannot be stolen or sold
But this precious gift
When freely given
Is a pleasure to behold.
For it reassures the frightened,
It soothes those who are sad,
And comforts the dejected,
And makes the mournful glad.

It brightens up this weary world
And lightens up our life
Brings sunshine to the shadows
At a time of pain and strife.

Acknowledgements

With thanks to the Yorkshire Post newspaper, the Dalesman and the Countryman magazines in which publications some of these articles appeared; to my editors Rowena Webb and David Moloney for their advice, patience and encouragement, and to my long-suffering wife and children who have heard these views expressed and listened to the anecdotes so many times around the dinner table.

'See With My Ears' by Ruth Meachin. Reproduced with Ruth's kind permission.

'On a Frosty Morning' by Thomas Hood. Reproduced with Thomas' kind permission.

Richard McCann's teachings reproduced here with his kind permission.

'When I Was a Young Lad'. A traditional Yorkshire folksong.